The Prewrath Rapture

Answering the Critics

The Prewrath Rapture: Answering the Critics

Published in the United States of America

ISBN-13: 978-1466304994

Cover Design by Christopher Perdue

Table of Contents

Part I
The Prewrath Rapture

Chapter 1: Introduction

When is the rapture of the church in relation to end time events? That is one of the most debated questions in the church, today. Opinions range from pre-tribulationism to post-tribulationism to one within the seven year Tribulation, among others. Some even try to set dates, ignoring scriptures which say we cannot know the day nor hour (Matthew 24:36).

Some even deny the rapture of the church. But if we take Scripture in its literal sense, it cannot be reasonably denied. The Apostle Paul explained it to the Corinthians (1Cor. 15:52) and to the Thessalonians (1Thess. 4:13-18). Jesus Himself promised to come back for His church (John 14:1-3). Admittedly, the word *rapture* is not found in the Bible. This term comes from the Latin word *rapere*, translated as *caught up* in 1Thessalonians 4:17. The Greek word is *harpazo*. This word means *to snatch up quickly or forcefully*.

The most popular rapture theory, at least in free countries, is pre-tribulationism. Understandably so, as it guarantees the removal of the church prior to the all of the events of the final seven years of this age. Also, most adherents believe those who previously rejected Christ will receive a second chance at salvation after the rapture. This is not to say that all, or even most, believe pre-trib for these emotional reasons. However, it certainly adds much to its allure, as seen by the emphasis some pre-trib books place on them.

Post-tribulationism also has a sizable following. In fact, many of the great Bible teachers of the past held to some form of post-trib, or else a historicist view. Among these greats are John Calvin, Martin Luther, Charles Spurgeon, Robert Gundry, William Erdman, Matthew Henry, and many others.

Adherents of each of these are able to point out logical and

Scriptural flaws with the competing views, some of which are impossible to explain away. Then when you add mid-tribulationism, the partial rapture, a-millennialism, post-millennialism, and the pre-wrath view, you end up with a large number of theories to consider. This has led to much confusion among some in the church.

Many resolve this confusion by simply picking the one they like best, or the one they were taught in their church. Often times they are not even aware other theories exist, as was once the case with me. Some give up deciding on a position all together. Their slogan is, "I am a pan-millennialist. It will all pan out in the end!"

It has been said as much as one-third of Scripture concerns predictive prophecy. A significant number of these concern the end of this age and Christ's second coming. Herman Hoyt noted that

> In comparing the proportion of emphasis given to the two comings of Christ, it is interesting to note that for every prophecy concerning Christ's first coming, there are eight for His second.[1]

He counts over 300 New Testament references alone concerning the second coming. Obviously the issue is of some importance to God else He would have devoted less of His Word to the topic.

Some see no purpose in the study of eschatology, believing it is of little practical value. On the contrary, the study of last things is eminently practical. First, Christians should desire to know the whole counsel of God. If God and His chosen vessels considered it important enough to write frequently about it, it must be important enough to look into it. Second, many prophetic passages have built in applications. For example, 2Peter 3:11-18 assures us that God's coming judgment is great motivation for living in holiness. He further promises a new heaven and earth where the righteous will dwell for eternity.

---

[1] The End Times: Moody Press of Chicago, 1969, p.11

Also, if the church is to enter the Tribulation, as many believe, we should desire to know everything we can about this time. This will encourage and strengthen us to stand for Christ come what may. It will also help us mentally prepare for the things we may have to face. A number of passages then become very significant (for example: Matt 10:16-42; 24:3-25, Revelation). These advise believers what to expect, and some of the things we should do (and *not* do) while enduring to the end of this age.

Significantly, Revelation is the only book in the Bible, outside of the books of Moses, which explicitly promises a blessing to those who read it and obey it (Rev 1:3; 22:16). This book is specifically addressed to the church, and concerns the second coming of Christ from start to finish. These facts make abundantly clear the practical nature of the study of eschatology.

How I Came to Believe Pre-Wrath

After much prayer and research on the rapture question, I have concluded that the pre-wrath view best fits Scripture. It provides solid answers to the admitted problems with the other theories, but recognizes and supports those things in which they are strong. Just as important, it maintains a consistent method of interpretation. Allow me to explain how I came to hold this position.

Like many, I used to be a pew-warmer, going to church and trusting the pastors to have correct doctrine. As they were pre-trib, so was I, but not from any clear understanding of what Scripture says. One day God brought conviction that I should understand His Word for myself. So I began reading and studying.

As I read, occasional passages caught my attention, such as Matthew 24 and 2Thessalonians 2. They did not seem to fit the pre-trib position I had been taught. Eventually, I began to have inner doubts about it, but obstinately continued to profess belief in it because teachers I loved and respected taught it. It was a tradition! Also, I was largely unaware there were other options.

A short time after these scriptural seeds started growing and cracking my pavement of tradition, this issue came up with a minister friend one day. I was going through a difficult time and expressed my wish that Christ would come and rapture us out of here, soon. He said it was unlikely, because he thought the Antichrist must come first. He had also seen the problems with pre-trib and was conducting his own study to find answers. With this confirmation I promptly brought in the jack hammers and began tearing out the pavement of pre-trib tradition from my system of beliefs. I did not yet know what the correct answer was, but it seemed clear the road would enter the Tribulation rather than end before this time.

A few months later I was attending a Bible class. The teacher began a study on Revelation, doing his own analysis rather than just teaching from what others had written. At the beginning of his study he was a firm pre-tribulationist. I showed him the problems I had with that theory. His answers were weak and unconvincing - even to his own ears, he later admitted. Several months into the study he came to seriously doubt the pre-trib view. But neither of us had resolved the issue.

God put it together for me by placing Robert Van Kampen's book, The Sign[2], in my path. This book convinced me that the pre-wrath view was the answer. I had seen a correlation between Matthew 24 and Revelation 6 and 7, and his book agreed and thoroughly explained it. The more I meditated on Scripture and considered pre-wrath, the more certain I became.

Later, I came upon Marvin Rosenthal's[3] book on the pre-wrath rapture, and became even more certain. As I have matured in the faith and spent time in the Word, I see more and more evidence supporting this view.

---

[2] The Sign, Crossway, 1993
[3] The Pre-Wrath Rapture, Marvin Rosenthal: Thomas Nelson, 1990

Eventually, I felt led me to write this book. I have researched it carefully, reading many books on different positions because I wanted to be sure I presented the truth. I carefully considered several articles and books attempting to refute pre-wrath, and could easily answer their complaints from Scripture.

As you read this book, keep your heart and mind opened to the Holy Spirit. If the position I present is true, the ramifications for the church are vital. Be like the Bereans and search the Scriptures for yourself (Acts 17:11).

Let me be clear, I still greatly respect those who believe and teach differently on the rapture. A difference of opinion concerning the timing of the rapture is not suitable grounds for breaking fellowship with other believers. Some churches have been split, friendships destroyed, and people hurt and disillusioned because of dogmatism in non-critical doctrines such as this. That should not be! While some doctrines should be held so tenaciously, the timing of the rapture does not belong on that list.

Most importantly, we must recognize that the rapture is not about an event, but about a Person, Jesus Christ. Jesus calls Himself *the resurrection and the life.* Paul taught in Titus that Christians should be *looking for the blessed hope and glorious appearing of Jesus Christ.* As far as our focus is concerned, it does not matter whether Christ's coming is pre-trib, post-trib, or pre-wrath. We should always live as if today were our last day on earth. Always we should look unto Christ as the Author and Finisher of our faith. If we truly seek Jesus and maturity, when any fiery testings come our way we will see them as opportunities to grow in Christ and learn directly from Him. When we are living in His Kingdom, it will not matter whether we are persecuted or safe, whether we miss the Tribulation or must endure part or all of it. We will cry out with Paul: *"For me, to live is Christ, and death is gain."*

My greatest desire for this book is that it leads believers closer to Christ, exhorting them to purify their hearts in preparation for the coming of Christ.

Chapter 2: Before We Begin

Before building a house, a person must have and know the proper use of the tools he needs. Likewise, a familiarity with common end time terminology and Bible study methods helps us correctly assemble the rapture doctrine.

We must first establish the basic rules for interpreting Scripture. Different people use differing methods. For example, some believe prophecy should be interpreted allegorically, that is, as having some spiritual or secret meaning which has little to do with what it literally says. Others believe the entire Bible should be taken literally, allowing for figures of speech or hidden meaning in the parables.

The biggest danger with an allegorical method is that a person can literally make the Bible say almost anything they want (pun intentional) - making it easier for people to have wildly conflicting ideas. But sticking to a literal method, taking God's Word at face value, makes it easier to arrive at a general consensus. After all, if God wants us to understand the basic concepts of His Word, which He does, then logically He would tell us like it is.

Hank Hanegraff[4] uses the acronym **LIGHTS** to explain the basic rules of understanding Scripture. I will also use this convenient device.

The **L** stands for the literal interpretation of the Bible. Take it at face value, while still making allowances for clear metaphors and other figures of speech. Even parables have a directly literal meaning behind their picturesque story. Jesus taught us how to

---

[4] Christianity in Crises, Hank Hanegraff: Harvest House Publishers, Eugene OR, 1993 (pp. 219-225)

interpret parables in Luke 8:5-8; 11-15. We find a central theme in this parable - plant God's Word deeply in your heart. Yet each major element adds important details. This method holds true for all parables. Now the literal method does not negate the need for spiritual understanding and discernment (1Cor. 2). Even so, the spiritual understanding and application will still be tied to a literal reading of the text. This is where the next letter comes in.

The letter **I** reminds us we need the illumination of the Holy Spirit. He will guide us into all truth (John 16:13). What He reveals will not contradict the Bible when correctly divided (2Pet. 1:21; 2Tim 2:15). Many things in the Bible picture spiritual truths.

I'll briefly illustrate how the Spirit illuminates deeper truths with an example which I believe every Christian should know. In Joshua we read the account of the battle of Jericho as Israel first entered the promised land. At the merely literal level we see how God gave the Hebrew people the victory. The central spiritual lesson is that God gives us the victory when we do it His way.

At the same time, there are at least eight elements in the story significant to spiritual warfare and our spiritual walk. 1) Jericho represents our sin nature, our inclination to sin. God has promised victory over sin if we do it His way (Gal. 5:16; Josh. 6:2). 2) We must persevere in our faith and testings, just as they had to march around the city for seven days. 3) They were commanded to keep silent and focus on the Ark of the Covenant, not on Jericho. We are to take every thought captive in obedience to Christ (2Cor. 10:3), focus on God and His righteousness, not on our sin. We gain true victory when our minds are hidden in Christ. 4) The praise and worship, the trumpets, the shout - Ephesians 5 and 6 tells us we should continuously be in prayer and making melody in our hearts toward God. 5) Israel was told to destroy everything and everyone in Jericho. We must not allow anything of our sin nature to survive which might draw us back into sin. 6) There is warning about what will happen if we allow anything to survive which we have been told to destroy. One person kept a few treasures from Jericho, which resulted in the destruction of him and his family. 7) Don't

14

rebuild the stronghold of sin (Heb. 6:4-8; Josh 6:26). 8) Just as Israel had many more battles to totally conquer their promised land, so we must continue progressing in the Kingdom.

The **G** in LIGHTS is the grammatical principle, understanding the Greek and Hebrew words and sentence structure. While not absolutely necessary to understand the Bible, sometimes it can help to clear up a question or gain greater value from study. Most of us do not have time or inclination to learn the original languages. There are a number of dictionaries which can be consulted, such as Strong's and Vine's, which provide much insight into the meanings of the words used.

H is the historical context of the writer. While the Bible can be largely understood without a working knowledge of the times they were written in, some passages become much clearer with that knowledge. Commentaries and Bible dictionaries can be of much help in with this. We will see a pertinent example of this when we look at the parable of the wise and foolish virgins (Matt. 25).

T reminds us God has anointed some to be teachers of His Word (Eph 4:11). They often provide much insight into Scripture. But we must still examine what we are taught and ask God to reveal Himself to us. Even God-called teachers are imperfect and make mistakes. Also, there are many wolves in sheep's clothing, false teachers who claim to be Christians. There are also those who enter a teaching ministry without the call or gift of God to do so, who are more easily prone to error.

Finally, the **S** stands for scriptural harmony. As discussed under **I**, nothing in God's Word will contradict any other. So if it seems to conflict, then either we misunderstand something or else we do not have all the information necessary to correctly interpret the passages. Every verse must be considered in its immediate context, for it is rare that a statement stands alone. They must also be related to the whole book in which it is written, for the author often had a specific purpose and theme in his writing. Last, we must compare Scripture to Scripture, for God's Word will tend to interpret itself if we let it.

Terms and Definitions

There are a number of important terms with which we must be familiar when studying eschatology. The first is *resurrection*. There are two resurrections in Scripture, that of the righteous unto eternal life, and one for the unrighteous for eternal condemnation. The first resurrection has several phases. Jesus was first to partake of it as the final proof of His identity, and guaranteeing the raising of the saints (1Cor. 15:20-23). It seems that at that time many Old Testament saints were also raised. The New Testament saints will be raised up at the rapture (1Thess. 4). It appears that those who put faith in Christ after the rapture will be raised up after the Battle of Armageddon (Rev. 20:4), though the exact understanding of this verse is debated.

The second resurrection takes place at the Great White Throne judgment following the 1,000 year personal reign of Christ on earth. This relates to the unbelievers and ungodly who will be thrown into the Lake of Fire, which is the second death (Rev. 2:11; 20:4-6, 14; 21:8).

Some debate whether the resurrection is bodily or strictly spiritual. Paul explained the resurrection in 1Corinthians 15. A false rumor had crept in like termites denying the resurrection, weakening their faith. Apparently, some even questioned the resurrection of Christ. Paul dealt with the issue strongly to ensure the extermination of this destroying pest. First he reminded them that Christ had originally been preached as raised from the dead. He then named several witnesses and referred to 500 others who had seen the resurrected Christ, many of whom were still alive who could verify it. He then declared:

> *...now if Christ be preached that He has been raised from the dead, how do some among you say that there is no resurrection from the dead? But if there is no resurrection from the dead, then Christ is not risen. And if Christ is not risen, then our preaching to you is in vain and your faith is in vain.*

16

Yes, and we are found false witnesses of God that He raised up Christ, whom He did not raise up – if in fact the dead do not rise. For if the dead do not rise, then Christ is not risen. And if Christ is not risen, your faith is futile; you are still in your sins! Then also those who have fallen asleep [died] in Christ have perished. (15:12-18)

Paul makes it clear the gospel hinges on the resurrection of Christ.

But now Christ is risen from the dead, and has become the firstfruits of those who have fallen asleep. For since by man came death, by Man also came the resurrection from the dead. For as in Adam all die, even so in Christ all shall be made alive. But each one in his own order, Christ the firstfruits, afterward those who are Christ's at His coming. (15:20-23)

This is a serious matter! Either Christ has risen or we are still lost in sin. But what kind of resurrection did Jesus experience, physical or merely spiritual? Did the eyewitnesses see a ghost or Jesus in the flesh? Paul makes it clear the saints will undergo the same as Jesus, as does John (1John 3:2). Let's first look at the argument for purely spiritual resurrection. 1Corinthians 15:44 says:

...It is sown a natural body, it is raised a spiritual body. There is a natural body and there is a spiritual body.

Those who believe a strictly spiritual resurrection point to the word *spiritual* in this verse, putting emphasis on that adjective. But a noun is stronger than an adjective. The above verse concerns the change in nature of the same body. The natural body is subject to sin, deterioration, and death. The resurrection will raise a body which is eternal, sinless, and pure. Our current flesh cannot inherit the kingdom of God, but our new body will be able to enter into His presence because no sin nature will remain.

Second, the Bible clearly teaches the bodily resurrection of Christ, providing at least four proofs:

- When the women and disciples went to the tomb following the Sabbath, Christ's body was gone, yet his grave clothes remained. The description suggests His body was removed from the mummy-like wrappings without disturbing them.

- When Jesus appeared to His disciples He could be touched, and a ghost cannot be touched. Not only that, but He still carried the wounds of His crucifixion, showing it was the same body. (John 20:24-27).

- In fact, Jesus reassured His disciples that He was not a disembodied spirit by eating some fish in front of them (Luke 24:28-43).

- Jesus even prophesied early in His ministry that He would be raised bodily as proof that He is the Christ (John 2:18-22).

Based on this evidence, obviously Jesus rose physically, which means the saints will do the same. Romans 8:23 adds that the body will be redeemed, which qualifies it for the resurrection. Old Testament passages which proclaim bodily resurrection include Psalm 17:15, Isaiah 26:19, Job 19:26. In conclusion, the resurrected saints will be restored to their physical bodies. But these will be fully redeemed and without sin, and will be dominated by the spirit and have spiritual properties.

I frequently use the term *church age*. Some Bible teachers do not like this term, so let me explain what I mean when I use it. According to dispensational theory, God has dealt with mankind in different ways throughout history. For example, under the Old Covenant the Hebrew people were God's chosen nation and salvation was largely through the Law. When Christ died and rose again the next stage of God's plan for humanity was revealed, and we entered the times of the Gentiles (Luke 21:24 and others). The church was born as God chose to bless the Gentiles (non-Hebrew nationalities) through His Son. Israel was largely hardened in unbelief because of their rejection of their Messiah, Jesus (Rom. 11). The church became a mostly Gentile institution, thus the term *church age* in relation to the times of the Gentiles. The times of the Gentiles also refers to how long Gentiles will trample Jerusalem and Israel, or have control over parts of it.

We are in the last days and have been since the outpouring of the Spirit in Acts 3. It is called that because this is the last age before God comes to directly rule the earth in Person through His Son, Jesus, and establish an earthly Kingdom. Israel will then once again be favored of God - in much greater measure than the Old Covenant. Then, all Gentiles nations will learn about God through Israel, and be required to send representatives to Jerusalem for certain Feasts every year.

God has set aside a seven year period at the end of this age for the breaking and restoration of Israel. He will also bring judgment and wrath against the ungodly. This time is commonly called the Tribulation. This term, like rapture, has been coined to describe a real event, and is not used in Scripture for the entire seven years. I usually use a different, more scriptural, term

In Daniel 9:24-27 the prophet Daniel was given a vision of seventy weeks - which is measured in years rather than days. The first sixty-nine weeks of years began with the command to rebuild Jerusalem following Israel's captivity in Babylon, and were concluded at the start of Jesus' public ministry. The times of the Gentiles is the period between the sixty-ninth and seventieth weeks. So I use the term *the seventieth week* to describe the final seven years. Let's look at this passage, as it is important for understanding the end time.

26) *And after the sixty-two weeks [69th in context] Messiah shall be cut off, but not for Himself; and the people of the prince who is to come shall destroy the city and the sanctuary [Jerusalem and the Temple]. The end of it shall be with a flood, and until the end of the war desolations are determined.*

27) *Then he [the prince who is to come] shall confirm a covenant with many for one week; but in the middle of the week he shall bring an end to sacrifice and offering. And on the wing of abominations shall be one who makes desolate, even until the consummation, which is determined, is poured out on the desolate.*

19

The first clause of verse 26 is the crucifixion of Jesus for mankind. The rest of it refers to the fall of Jerusalem at the hands of the Roman Empire in 70 AD. The Antichrist - the prince who is to come - likely comes from the same area or root-stock of people. The Jewish people have encountered severe persecution since the fall of Jerusalem and been made desolate repeatedly, such as under Hitler and Stalin.

In verse 27 the Antichrist (the prince to come) signs or confirms a covenant with many for seven years. This is some sort of peace treaty, likely involving a number of countries. My personal belief is that this treaty sets up a mostly worldwide governmental system, known currently as the New World Order, which eventually the Antichrist is given power over for 42 months. Others believe it will only involve the European Community or an Islamic coalition. Israel will also sign the treaty, which I believe allows them to rebuild their temple. Isaiah says this is *a covenant with death, and with Sheol (the grave) are we at agreement* (Isaiah 25:15, 18).

In the middle of the week, after the Antichrist is given his power he will violate the treaty and come against Israel at the Abomination of Desolation (Matt. 24:15; Daniel 12), and bring the great tribulation upon Israel and the world.

The term *the great tribulation* in prophecy always refers to this period of time, and takes place during second half of the seventieth week. Jesus told us in Matthew 24, though, that the great tribulation will be cut short for the sake of the elect, which I explain in chapter five. It is largely to avoid confusion with this biblical term that I usually call the seven years Daniel's seventieth week rather than the Tribulation. The great tribulation is also called the time of Jacob's trouble, as Israel will face her greatest persecution in history - ultimately killing 2/3 of all Jews over all the earth.

The Antichrist is also known as *the beast* and *the man of sin* (Rev 13:1-8; 2Thess 2:3-4). Anyone who denies Jesus is the Christ come in the flesh is an antichrist (1John 2:18; 4:3; 2John 7). There is yet a man to come, however, a great deceiver, who will convince or force much of the world to worship him, much like some of the Roman Caesars and other rulers throughout history. Some also believe he will present himself as Israel's long-awaited Messiah. In the middle of the week he violates the treaty or comes against Israel for other reasons. He will bring a huge army against Israel, then set up his image or sit himself in the most holy place, in the rebuilt temple. There he will declare Himself God. His lies and power - to the calling of fire from heaven - will convince most of the unsaved world to follow him. This Abomination of Desolation will also be referred to as the revealing of Antichrist (Matt 24:15; Dan 12:11; Rev 13).

Shortly after revealing himself, the Antichrist will institute a mandatory worldwide identification system, a *mark* on the right hand or forehead (Rev 13:16-18). Only those with the mark will be permitted to buy or sell, and it will be a capital crime to refuse it. Believers living during this time must keep in mind **that those who receive this mark will abide under God's wrath**, and end up in the Lake of Fire (Rev 14:9-10). The Bible gives no indication that it will be possible to repent taking this mark, except perhaps to cut off the hand or pluck out the eye if that is where the mark is (Matt 5:30). There are apparently three different marks: the mark, the name of the beast, and the number of his name - 666.

Several possible means of this marking have been suggested. It is most probably a tiny, magnetic computer chip inserted under the skin similar to bar codes and anti-theft devices already in use. Interestingly, the work *mark* in Greek is closely related to a word which means a palisade or picket fence, which looks like a bar code. This computer chip technology is already available and in use in both animals and humans. It is called the RFID.

The 144,000 (Rev 7) are the firstfruits of Israel, to be restored during the great tribulation. We will look at them in detail later.

The Day of the Lord (DOL) is closely associated with the wrath of God. This is not a literal day, but a period of time. Many scholars believe the DOL includes not only the wrath of God, but the millennial reign of Christ, too. The timing of the DOL is one of the most important factors in determining the rapture question, and is hotly debated. Some believe it includes the entire seventieth week, some only part of the week, and some start it at the Battle of Armageddon. I will demonstrate thoroughly from Scripture that it begins with the sixth seal sometime after the Abomination of Desolation, but before the trumpet and bowl judgments.

I have already often used the term *second coming*. This is when Christ returns in glory at the end of the age (Matt 24:3, 30, et al). In the next chapter I will discuss most of the views which have been developed concerning the second coming and the rapture.

Chapter 3: Choices

In the last chapter we learned the basic tools needed to build our study on the rapture. We will now look at blueprints, examine the various layouts. Just as a house may be one story or more, modern or colonial, so has Scripture been divided and put together in various ways to produce a number of end time theories.

Before we look at these theories, we must know what qualities make solid construction. Every house needs a good foundation to make it sturdy. Every doctrine must be built on the rock of Jesus with the strong stone of God's Word to withstand the strongest storm. There is no other spiritual foundation (1Cor 3:11). Everything in God's Kingdom is centered on Christ, including the rapture. As the framework must hold the house up so must a doctrine of this complexity have a strong core. The walls and roof add strength and protection as the related supportive point make a stronger doctrine. And last, a house should be well laid out for convenient plumbing, electricity, and usage; A doctrine should be of some practical value in the life of a believer.

A number of eschatology designs are commonly found in the church today. Some believe in a pre-millennial coming of Christ and some do not. This chapter looks at each of these and reveals their key weaknesses.

The first two we will look at are poorly-built mobile homes and sit on a foundation of sand. A-millennialism and post-millennialism both rely on an allegorical, so-called *spiritual*, method of interpretation.

In deciding which method to use, literal or allegorical, the critical element is whether it does justice to all of Scripture. A simple fact, however, provides strong testimony against using the allegorical method for prophecy: When the fulfillment of non-eschatological prophecies are examined, they were typically fulfilled literally as written, though sometimes in surprising ways or over a period of time. More to the point, Christ fulfilled those prophecies concerning His first coming just as they were written. It is reasonable, logical, and consistent, therefore, to study those that concern His second coming the same way. I have learned that God is consistent in all things.

Someone might argue that the picturesque language in Revelation and Daniel makes a literal interpretation difficult, if not impossible. Seven-headed, ten-horned dragons? A beast of iron and clay? These are not meant to describe physical appearance but are metaphors revealing characteristics of their subjects. This does not mean every prophetic passage has a hidden meaning. Metaphorical passages are usually quite obvious, and Scripture should otherwise be taken literally.

A-millennialism teaches that Christ will not really rule the earth for 1,000 years in person. Rather, adherents teach this as an indefinite time span in which Christ reigns in the hearts of believers between His two advents. The Olivet Discourse (Matt 24-25) and Revelation are viewed has already fulfilled, or else spiritualized away. In the end, they believe Jesus will return and receive His saints, and then judge the wicked. The roots of this position can be traced back to Origen (184-254 AD), who was influenced in his doctrine by Greek philosophy. It was popularized by Augustine (354-430 AD), who essentially founded the Roman Catholic Church, the primary proponent of this theory.

But Revelation 20, when taken literally, clearly foretells that the saints will rule the earth with Christ while Satan is bound in the bottomless pit, unable to deceive the nations. The nations certainly are deceived and follow the enemy's lead, now. A-millennialism falls flat on this point alone.

Post-millennialism, on the other hand, teaches that mankind will bring about the millennial kingdom through spreading the gospel and fostering civic righteousness and world peace. They conclude that Christ will truly be present when this is accomplished or else that

Christ will return at the end of the period of blessing. They believe that through the efforts of man the existence of sin will be negligible. The primary scriptural support claimed for this is Luke 17:21.

Daniel Whitby (1638-1726), an English Unitarian minister, was the first to teach this view. It had some popularity during the Reformation, when the gospel spread rapidly through the world. Variations of this view are held in some liberal churches.

This view is very similar to one of the tenets of the New Age Movement (NAM). The NAM maintains that eventually mankind will bring about world peace and happiness through their *enlightened* spiritual beliefs. But these beliefs do not include faith in the real Christ. Some believe the NAM will be a major part of the religious harlot, Babylon, described in Revelation 17.

The Bible prophesies that the exact opposite will happen - that sin and lawlessness will abound more and more. Even the church, as a whole, will fall away from the true gospel (1Tim 4:1, 2; 2Tim 3:1-9, 13; 2Pet 2:1-3, 12-22). We see these fulfilled today. Post-millennialism is clearly not built on the solid rock of the Bible.

Both of these use the risky and malleable allegorical method. Furthermore, key points in both contradict clear, biblical teaching. It is best we look elsewhere for safe ground to build our position.

Pre-millennialists agree with Scripture that Christ will rule the world in person for 1,000 years after His second coming (Rev 20:6). This view was almost unanimously held by the early church until the third century, when the Alexandrians, Dionysus, Clement, and Origen introduced the allegorical method of interpretation.

> Papias (AD 155): There will be a millennium after the resurrection from the dead, when the personal reign of Christ will be established on this earth. (Fragment IV)

> Justin Martyr (AD 110-165): I and others, who are right-minded Christians on all points, are assured that there will be a resurrection of the dead, and a thousand years in Jerusalem, which will then be built, adorned, and enlarged. (Dialogue with Trypho, LXXX)

Tertullian (AD 150-225): We do confess that a kingdom is promised to us upon the earth, although before heaven, only in another state of existence; inasmuch as it will be after the resurrection for a thousand years in the divinely-built city of Jerusalem. (Against Marcion, Book III, Ch xxv)

All of the pre-millennial views claim to follow a literal method, building a foundation of good stone. However, as we will see, some adherents of various of these views are inconsistent in applying this method, leaving cracks and gaps in their foundation.

The Partial Rapture

The partial rapture theory can be traced back to 1883, and has only been held by a relatively small minority of believers. But the flaws with this theory are serious, like a bad case of termites in a house, so I will spend a little time on it.

The partial rapture is a pre-trib variation which teaches that not all Christians will be caught up in a pre-trib rapture. Adherents believe only those who are *watching and waiting* will qualify to go at this point. The remainder must suffer through part or all of the seventieth week to mature. These privileged believers are described as having achieved some degree of spiritual maturity to make them worthy to escape the Tribulation. Luke 21:36 is their key verse.

Watch therefore, and pray always that you may be counted worthy to escape all these things that will come to pass and to stand before the Son of Man.

They also use Philippians 3:20; Titus 2:13; 2Timothy 4:8; and Hebrews 9:28. We will examine each of these.

*...we shall **ALL** be changed... the dead will be raised incorruptible, and we shall be changed.*(1Cor 15:52 emphasis mine)

...For if we believe that Jesus died and rose again, even so God will bring with Him those who sleep [have died] in Jesus...The dead in Christ will rise first. Then we who are alive and remain will be caught up together with them...Comfort one another with these words. (1Thess 4:14, 16-18)

These two key rapture texts encourage all who believe. The first promises that *all* will be rapture/resurrected, while the second explains the criterion for this promise is true faith in Jesus. It would be difficult to find comfort in Christ's coming if some true believers were in danger of being left behind simply because they did not grow up fast enough or as far as they might have. Fruit is expected and required in the life of a believer (John 15; Gal 5), but no scripture defines a certain amount required to be saved. The key is to endure to the end in faith in Christ, even if it means dying for Him.

To be thorough and fair, we must also address their key passages.

(Luke 21:36) *"Watch therefore, and pray always that you may be counted worthy to escape all these things and to stand before the Son of Man."* Jesus is here advising us to make sure we are truly saved, for an active, living faith is the only thing that can make us worthy to stand before Jesus (see James 2). The rapture is also in this verse, as we will see in a later chapter – but not a partial rapture.

(Matt 24:40-42) *"Two men will be standing in the field: one will be taken, and the other left. Two women will be grinding at the mill: one will be taken, and the other left. Watch therefore..."* The problem here is that this passage, out of its context, does not clearly state who is taken and who is left behind, so the partial rapture interpretation is highly subjective; we cannot tell for absolute certain from this portion alone which of these were saved, let alone their degree of spiritual maturity.

27

Basically, there are two ways these verses are usually interpreted, each centered on a different time frame for the context. The first, held by most pre-tribs, is that the one is taken for judgment while the other remains to enter the millennial kingdom, at the end of the seventieth week. The second view, held by pre-wrath adherents and others, is that the one is taken in the rapture while the other is unsaved and remains on earth to face God's wrath. We will see later why the context better supports the latter view.

(Heb 9:28) ...*to those who eagerly wait for Him He will appear again, apart from sin, for salvation.* First, ALL believers should be eagerly awaiting the return of their Savior Jesus Christ, for it is an integral part of His gospel. We live in a wicked and sinful world, full of suffering and pain, which should cause God's children to long for and lust after the coming of Jesus to set things right. Second, this verse does not contrast with those believers who do not eagerly await the second coming. And finally, the author's point is that Jesus has already come once for the sake of deliverance from sin; when He returns, it will be to deliver us from this body of death and complete our salvation. Again, the rapture is in mind here, a complete catching up of the saints.

(Ph'p 3:11) ...*if, by any means, I may attain to the resurrection of the dead.* When quoted by itself this verse can be deceiving, seeming to emphasize the need for works. Taken in context the true meaning becomes clear. In verse 8 Paul declares that he counts all of his own works as loss when compared to knowing Christ. His real revelation here, then, is that he attained to the resurrection by faith and a personal relationship with Christ, and that he has laid aside attempting to earn it through his own good works. This is the only *means* to attain *to the resurrection.* This partial rapturist error illustrates the need to consider the context of every verse before offering an interpretation.

All other Scriptures raised up by partial rapturists can likewise be easily answered. This blueprint has serious flaws and should be tossed straight into the trash can.

Mid-tribulation Theory

Mid-tribulationism, which many prefer to call the mid-week theory, is also held by only a few. With the rising popularity of pre-wrath it has largely dropped by the wayside.

This view became prominent in 1941, when "Norman B. Harrison published *The End: Rethinking the Revelation*5, in which he said the rapture would occur in the middle of the seventieth week, prior to God's outpouring of wrath. He noted that the Apostle John called the first half of the seventieth week as "sweet," because of the presence of the church, while the second half was called "bitter," when the church is absent (Rev 10:9-10). He thus identified the second half as both the great tribulation and God's wrath."6

This view typically places the rapture at the Abomination of Desolation. Some believe that the seven seal and seven trumpet judgments of Revelation take place during the first half of the week and are not God's wrath. They identify the *last trump* at the rapture (1Cor 15:52) with the seventh trumpet, and equate the seven bowls with God's wrath. Others, such as Gleason L. Archer, believe the trumpets also take place in the second half of the seven years and place the rapture at the sixth or seventh seal. Mr. Archer suggests as a key evidence for mid-trib the frequent emphasis on the midpoint in Daniel, the Gospels, 2Thessalonians, and Revelation.7

Several points create difficulty for this theory (weakening pre-trib at the same time). In Revelation 14:9-13 the third angel warns

5 The Harrison Service, Minneapolis, MN

6 The Rapture: Pre-, Mid-, or Post-tribulational, Richard R. Reiter contrib.

7 The Rapture: Pre-, Mid-, or Post-tribulational,, Gleason L. Archer, contrib.

mankind not to receive the mark of the beast, nor to worship him. In this context John adds the following:

> *Here is the patience of the saints. Here are those who keep the commandments of God and the **faith of Jesus**. Then I heard a voice from heaven saying, "blessed are those who die in the Lord from now on...*(emphasis mine)

Revelation 13:7, 10 describes the same time frame:

> *And it was granted to [the beast] to make war with the saints and to overcome them.... Here is the patience and the faith of the saints.*

These parallel passages take place following the Abomination of Desolation. If the rapture has just taken place, then who are these saints who have been keeping the faith of Jesus, and now especially must persevere? This suggests they have been saved for some time through faith in Christ. As we will see later, 2Thessalonians 2:9-12 and Revelation 13:8 make a strong case against significant numbers turning to faith after the beast comes on the scene.

Revelation 14:14-16 describes a harvest that best fits the rapture from a heavenly viewpoint (see Matt. 13:24-30), as most mid- and post-tribs also agree. The problem arises in the context - the prior angelic warning about the mark of the beast and martyrdom and patience of the saints of Jesus. Jesus has a sickle to reap the first harvest, while another angel has the sickle for the second. The second is specifically to reap the grapes of wrath while the first has no mention of wrath. Scripture says Jesus Himself gathers the saints following a shout from an angel (1Thess 4), which fits this first harvest. These facts indicate the rapture cannot take place until sometime after the rise of Antichrist. As we study, we will see that Scripture consistently teaches this.

Understanding the Order of Revelation

The idea that the last trumpet of the rapture is the seventh trumpet judgment also has problems. Most of these I discuss in chapter 10, but a couple of points should be discussed here. First, the beast is promised a full forty-two months (1260 days) to rule (Dan 12:7; Rev. 13:5). On the other hand, Revelation 11:15-19 explicitly states Jesus begins ruling the earth at the seventh trumpet. I seriously question the validity of a position which allows the beast not only to be in power, but to prosperously and successfully rule the earth at the same time Jesus is declared King of all the nations. Yet many expositors believe the seventh trumpet sounds around the time of the Abomination of Desolation, in spite of this issue.

The first key to understanding the order of Revelation is in 10:11. This says John will prophesy *again* about many people, meaning that the vision is about to backtrack in time and approach from another angle. This does not mean, as some have supposed, that John will be one of the two witnesses which are next described - it says he will prophesy *about* many people, not to them. When you look at the whole context, it becomes clear.

Up to this point after chapter five, very little has been said concerning the players of the end time drama, excepting the great multitude and the 144,000 in a context especially significant to them at the sixth seal (Rev. 7). But following this statement John sees many important people and groups of the end time. First is the two witnesses at a significant point - the end of their three-and-a-half year ministry. Then we see the seventh trumpet, concluding the current run through the seven years.

John begins prophesying again in chapter 12. The first five verses briefly show the establishment of Israel, the various past beast empires backed by Satan trying to destroy God's people, the birth of Jesus and His death by the machinations of the devil, and Christ's victorious ascension into heaven. Verse six then jumps

31

ahead to Israel's (the woman's) flight into the wilderness to escape the beast. Verses 7-12 explain why they flee. In a great battle in heaven just before the Abomination, the Archangel Michael casts Satan and his cohort out of the heavenly dimension to earth. Satan then immediately comes against Israel and the saints of Jesus (v.11) in his great wrath. The rest of chapter 12 provides an overview of Satan's wrath during the great tribulation. After a portion of Israel successfully flees into the wilderness with God's aid, the beast comes against *the rest of her offspring* who have the testimony of Jesus - that is, the church.

Revelation 13 describes the beast and his false prophet, and again mentions the saints of Jesus. Chapter 14 brings out more about the 144,000, the three proclaiming angels, the fall of the religious Babylon to the beast, the mark of the beast, the patience of the saints of Jesus, and the Son of Man at the two harvests. The first harvest is the rapture. The second harvest, the grapes of wrath, is the trumpet judgments of the initial stage of God's wrath. This brings us back to the seventh trumpet and the end of the 1260 days.

Christ takes up His authority in the seventh trumpet and quickly pours out the wine in the seven bowls, which was harvested as sour grapes during the trumpets. These probably take place during the 30 days following the seventh trumpet (Dan. 12:11, the 1290 days). After the bowls are described, additional important people are discussed - the fall of political Babylon (the Antichrist's kingdom), the marriage supper of the Lamb, Jesus' arrival for the Battle of Armageddon, and others. Thus we see that *many people* are in the prophecies following the key passage under discussion (Rev. 10:11).

Not only are the trumpets in the last half of the seventieth week, but so are the last four seals. I will demonstrate later that the fourth seal is most likely the persecution of Israel and the church by the beast, while the fifth seal specifically concerns martyrs. The sixth seal describes certain heavenly signs and their effect on mankind, which Jesus said appear when the great tribulation is cut short *for the sake of the elect* (Matt 24:22-31). Of course, the seventh seal must follow the sixth. In the section on post-trib I prove that the trumpets must follow all of the seals, which means they cannot be sounded until well into the great tribulation. This makes a seventh trumpet, mid-trib rapture impossible.

One final problem with mid-trib is openly admitted by Mr. Archer:

"...It is confessedly difficult to pick out any certain point in the Olivet Discourse [Matt 24] as indicating the disappearance of the church during the middle of the final seven years. Perhaps it is to be found after verse 14..."8

In conclusion, mid-trib is not without difficult problems. We should look elsewhere for the answer to the rapture question.

Post-tribulation Theory

Post-trib, as a systematically developed system, appeared at about the same time as pre-trib, in the early 1800's. Also, the Early Church Fathers almost universally held to a basically post-trib stance, believing the church must face the time of the Antichrist and the great tribulation. There are several variations of post-trib.

Luther and some other reformers are sometimes quoted by pre-tribs to show belief in an imminent rapture, in an attempt to assign greater weight of age to their theory than is justified. But these men were actually historicists or preterists, variations of post-trib that believe most of Revelation and Matthew 24 were fulfilled in the past - leaving no major prophesies that must be fulfilled before Christ returns. Preterists use the allegorical method a lot, but believe in a literal return of Christ before the millennial reign. Yes, some believe Christ could return at any moment, but they are still technically post-tribs. Many of the problems with traditional

---

8 The Rapture, Gleason L. Archer, op. cit.

post-trib cause the same problems with a historicist view. Due to space limitation, I will not address historicism separately.

There are two primary versions of post-trib, classic and Gundry's modified theory. James McKeever also suggested another variation in which the end time is only three-and-a-half years rather than seven. But he otherwise mostly agreed with classic post-tribs that the church is raptured when Christ comes for Armageddon. Gundry suggests an important modification. He places the rapture at the seventh trumpet prior to the bowls of wrath and Armageddon, in recognition that Scripture promises the church exemption from the time of God's wrath. He believes it is the climax of wrath in the bowls from which we are exempt.

A frequently divisive issue among post-tribs is dispensationalism. Some believe in the future restoration of Israel, and others do not. McKeever is one who does not, believing that eschatological prophecies concerning Israel really apply to the church.9 This issue is critically important for understanding the end time, so we will look at it. One of McKeever's key passages is Romans 2:26-29.

> *Therefore, if an uncircumcised man keeps the righteous requirements of the law, will not his uncircumcision be counted as circumcision? And will not the physically uncircumcised, if he fulfills the law, judge you who, even with your written code and circumcision, are a transgressor of the law? For he is not a Jew who is one outwardly, nor is that circumcision outward in the flesh; but he is a Jew who is one inwardly, and the circumcision is that of the heart, in the Spirit...*

Other passages include Isaiah 56:6-9 and Ezekiel 47:21-23.

This passage states that true Jews have their hearts set to serve God - the rite of physical circumcision does not determine it. God commanded circumcision as a sign of separation of the Hebrew

---

9 The Coming Climax of History, James McKeever: Omega Publications, POBox 4130, Medford, OR.

race from the Gentiles. This demonstrated their faith in God and the Abrahamic covenant which made them God's chosen nation. Circumcision of the heart, on the other hand, never knew racial boundaries, and anyone may freely worship Jehovah. Paul is not saying Israel has permanently lost its part in God's plan. On the contrary, Paul stated even now salvation is for *the Jew first, and also the Gentile* (Rom 1:16; 2:9, 10).

McKeever also quotes Romans 11:13-24 as evidence that Israel is permanently cast out. Branches were broke off the cultivated olive tree so that wild olive branches could be grafted in. The olive tree represents spiritual *Israel* - all of the saved. Its original branches are the Hebrew people. The wild branches represent the Gentiles who put faith in Christ. The root and fatness, which feed the tree and are its lifeblood, picture Jesus Himself. It is true that Israel, as a nation, has been cut off for the church age, though individuals can still be saved. But McKeever takes this passage out of context. The verses before and after his snippet clearly teach this condition is only temporary.

(Rom 11:12, 25-29) *Now if their fall is riches for the world, and their failure riches for the Gentiles, how much more their fullness... I do not desire, brethren, that you should be ignorant of this mystery, lest you should be wise in your own opinion, that this hardening in part has happened to Israel until the fullness of the Gentiles has come in. And so ALL ISRAEL will be saved, as it is written: "The Deliverer will come out of Zion, and He will turn away ungodliness from Jacob; for this is My covenant with them, when I take away their sins." Concerning the gospel they are enemies for your sake, but concerning the election they are beloved for the sake of the Father. For the gifts and the calling of God are irrevocable.*

It is clear Israel's hardening is only temporary. They are only cast off for a time so God can show his love and mercy toward all men and so Israel might become jealous and repent (Rom 11:13, 30-32). There are many prophecies which promise the future restoration of Israel, so it is clear they are still part of God's plan.

35

Another compelling evidence Israel is not permanently cut off is the fact that they survived as a distinct people and culture for nearly 1900 years without a homeland until they regained control of much of Israel following WWII. This feat is unique among all the nations that have ever been so thoroughly conquered and divided.

For further biblical evidence for the restoration of Israel, see the following: Isaiah 4:2; 14:1-2; 19:18-25; 60:1ff; 63:7-19; Jeremiah 23:6; chapters 30-33; Ezekiel 16:60-63; 17:22-24; chapters 36,37; Hosea 1:10-2:1 (see Matt 21:43); 2:14-3:5; Amos 9:11ff; Obadiah 17-21; Micah 4; Zephaniah 3:8ff; Zechariah 8:1ff; 12:7-14.

The most glaring problem with post-trib is that it leaves the church on earth during God's wrath. The Bible is clear believers are not appointed to wrath, but to deliverance away from it (1Thess. 1:10; 5:9; Eph 5:6). Even Gundry falls short, for Revelation 6:17 and other passages clearly introduce God's wrath with the sixth seal. As we will see shortly, the trumpets must follow the seals, and then the bowls after that. No passage suggests it is less than *all* of God's Day-of-the-Lord wrath from which we are delivered.

Post-tribs deny an interval between the rapture and Christ's coming for Armageddon. But there are two things which must occur between. First is the judgment of believers. Jesus taught there would be a private judgment of the saints (Luke 19:15), as did Paul (1Cor 3:10-15). The purpose is to judge our works and hand out appropriate rewards. Since rewards will be given at the seventh trumpet when Jesus begins His millennial reign (Rev 11:18; 19:14, 19), the rapture must precede this.

Second is the wedding feast (Rev 19:10). The wedding supper of the Lamb takes place before Jesus returns on His white horse for Armageddon. Some think this feast actually takes place on earth afterward. As I show shortly, however, in Jewish wedding customs the bridegroom would bring the bride from her home to his for the feast. The pre-wrath rapture solves both of these problems.

36

It is understood by the other positions that the saints will ascend into heaven at the rapture. Post-tribs, on the other hand, claim that we will immediately reverse direction and descend to Mount Zion after meeting the Lord in the air. Gundry explains it this way (from 1Thess 4:16):

> Other things being equal, the word *descend* (Gr. katabaino) indicates a complete, uninterrupted descent, like that of the Spirit at Christ's baptism (Matt 3:16; Mark 1:10; Luke 3:22; John 1:32,33), and that of Christ at His first advent (John 3:13; 6:33,38,41,42,50,51,58). Where a reversal from downward to upward motion comes into view, a specific statement to the effect appears as in Acts 10:11, 16 ("a certain object coming down... and immediately the object was taken up into the sky"). In the absence of a statement indicating a halt or sudden reversal of direction, we naturally infer a complete descent to the earth, such as will take place only at the post-tribulational advent.[10]

I like how Walvoord rebutted this:

> ...Gundry is attempting to solve this problem by definition of a word, a definition quite arbitrary and slanted in the direction of his conclusion.... Gundry here again appeals to the argument from silence, which he so often disavows for the pre-tribulational view.... Gundry argues from silence that there should be mention of a change in direction if such took place, but he discounts the silence of the passage on any indication of its continued direction to the earth.[11]

Additionally, no other Greek word is translated *descend* in the New Testament. In other words, it cannot be contrasted with a word which includes the idea of a reversal of direction or an incomplete descent. Gundry's argument is broken by this simple

---

[10] The church and the Tribulation, Robert Gundry: Zondervan, 1973, p.103

[11] "Post-tribulationism Today"; Bibliotheca Sacra, Dallas Theological Seminary, Oct-Dec 1976, p. 304

observation. Furthermore, his supporting verses in Acts 10 do not help, for when the purpose of the descent was completed, the object returned to heaven. Likewise, when Jesus descends and gathers the saints He will return to heaven.

Note especially John 14:2, 3, when Jesus said He will come get us and take us to His Father's house, which is heaven. This provides explicit scriptural confirmation for a rapture to heaven. Post-tribs must continue to argue from silence.

McKeever uses a different word to make the same point:

> In 1Thessalonians 4:16-17...we saw that the Christian will *meet* the Lord in the air. The Greek word for *meet* in this passage is *apantesis*. This word... [only occurs two] other places in the New Testament.... [In Acts 28:14, 15] we see that the brethren came out to meet Paul. However, the principal actor in the drama, which was Paul in this case, kept going and the people doing the meeting did the reversing of direction, as one would expect.

> The only other place this word is used in the Scriptures is in the parable of the bridegroom and ten virgins (Matt 25:1-13). The ten virgins went out to *meet* the bridegroom. The bridegroom, who was the principal actor in this drama, kept coming, and those doing the meeting reversed course.

> If this same usage holds true in 1Thessalonians, then when we *meet* Christ in the air, He will not reverse course, we will.12

First of all, just as with Gundry, McKeever builds his case on silence. In his two "proof" texts any movement was explicit, while 1Thessalonians says nothing of further movement, only that we will be with the Lord forever.

Nor does Acts 28 illustrate what he wants. Paul was headed under guard to Rome to be imprisoned. The brethren went out to meet him on the way to encourage him. As Paul continued on his

---

12 James McKeever: Omega Publications, pp 96-97

journey the brethren naturally reversed direction to return home, for they were neither going to prison nor to Rome. They did not travel with Paul, nor Paul with them. The saints will go wherever Jesus does after that grand meeting in the air.

The parable of the ten virgins does not support McKeever, either (Matt. 25:1-13). Knowing the historical setting and cultural customs of the day can help us understand this parable. Jesus told His parable from a first century Jewish perspective, so it must be interpreted with this in mind. According to H.L. Ellison:

> At a Jewish wedding the bridegroom, surrounded by his friends, went, generally after sunset, to the home of the bride to fetch her. The bride, dressed in her best, was carried in a litter to the bridegroom's house, a procession being formed by her and the bridegroom's friends.... When the bridegroom's home was reached, the wedding supper was eaten.13 [see Psalm 45:14, 15]

The central theme of this parable is readiness to meet the Lord, as also is much of the previous context. Jesus is called the bridegroom and the church His bride in other passages (2Cor. 11:2; Matt. 9:15; John 3:28-29). Since this parable is told in an end time context, it obviously concerns the rapture. Most expositors agree from all positions, and many of them include the subsequent parable of the talents (Matt. 25:14-30). Both pre-wrath and post-trib adherents add the preceding passages (24:29-51) as the same context and topic, since no change in thought is seen.

As we learned in chapter two, the details of Jesus' parables usually hold meaning, and this one is no different. The story, in retrospect, appears to give a brief history of the church as it relates to the expectation of Christ's coming. The virgins' going out to meet the bridegroom is the founding of the church (Matt. 25:1). Since they must wait for Him, not knowing the hour of His coming (25:5; 24:36-51), the rapture is yet future from this point. During

---

13 *Matthew*, H. L. Ellison; The International Bible Commentary, ed. F. F. Bruce: Zondervan Publishing House, 1979, p.1147

the long wait (see 25:19) the virgins fell asleep - probably the nearly 1500 years during which the second coming was spiritualized away. The midnight cry warning of His coming, awakening the sleepers, is the restoration of expectation of the Lord's coming, most notably in the early 1800's. Finally, the bridegroom arrives after an additional short wait, coming from His home with His friends (read *angels*; see Matt. 24:31 and 2Thess 1:7). He gathers the five wise virgins and returns to His home for the wedding celebration as per custom (25:10). In short, when the church meets her Bridegroom, it is He who will reverse direction.

Moo raises another point recommending post-trib.14 He claims a rapture-to-heaven scenario would require the saints inhabit their heavenly mansions for only a short period, only to vacate them during the millennium while the rule the earth with Christ.

Remember that the judgment and reward of believers and the wedding supper must follow the rapture but precede Armageddon. They have the greater onus to solve this scriptural issue than we their supposedly logical problem.

Second, not every believer is going to rule the earth. Several passages make clear this honor is given to those who have matured in the faith, who are overcomers, and who manifest certain beatitudes (Matt. 5:5; Rev. 2:26). While every believer has the same opportunity to earn a position, not every one will receive one.

Third, Moo bases his case on the assumption believers will have to move out of their heavenly mansions while ruling the earth. Why should this be the case? Our new bodies will have spiritual capabilities such as the ability to move from one place to another instantly (Luke 24:31, 36). Thus no difficulties of transportation from home to work would exist. Furthermore, I doubt God will place so much work on the saints they all will need to work 24/7 just to keep up. God believes in the work ethic, but He also approves of taking time off each week for rest (Exod. 20:11), and commanded several holidays throughout the year, some lasting a week at a time.

---

[14] Op. cit., pp. 178-179

Also, if this supposed problem seems awkward, the yo-yo rapture of post-trib is even more so. In his response to Moo, Archer explains:

...We maintain that this yo-yo procedure of popping up and down presents a very great difficulty. At one moment the faithful followers of Christ are lifted up out of the revolting scene of the sin-cursed, evil-dominated world in order to meet with the Lord Jesus... in the clouds of heaven. But, this means that He will descend mounted upon His white horse, followed by the hosts of heaven. If so, He would hardly be apt to check His course for any length of time as He makes His way... to the battlefield of Armageddon. If anything, these upward-bobbing saints will only impede the momentum of His earthward charge as He rushes down to crush... the Beast and all his minions. The most that can be said of such a "Rapture" is that it is a rather secondary sideshow of minimal importance.15

The Order of the Revelation Judgments

Like pre-wrath adherents, post-tribs recognize a sixth-seal rapture in Matthew 24:29-31. Unlike pre-wraths, however, they place this at the end of the seventieth week, at Armageddon. They accomplish this feat by overlapping the seal, trumpet, and bowl judgments in creative ways. McKeever presents the first two charts as most likely in his opinion:[16]

SEALS 1 2 3 4 5   6 7

  TRUMPETS   1 2 3 4 5 6   7

          BOWLS   1 2 3 4 5 6   7

OR

---

[15] The Rapture...

[16] The Coming Climax of History, op. cit., pp. 164-165

```
SEALS  1 2 3 4 5                    6 7
   TRUMPETS  1  2  3  4  5  6      7
      BOWLS      1  2  3  4  5  6  7
```

Douglas Moo suggests the following:17

```
SEALS   1 2   3   4       5       6   7
TRUMPETS 1  2 3    4     5     6   7
   BOWLS        1 2  3 4   5   6   7
```

Post-tribs bases their overlap schemes on similarities found in the sixth seal and the seventh of each series. All four mention an earthquake, while the sevenths also describe thundering, lightning, and hail (Rev. 6:14; 8:5; 11:19; 16:18-20). They conclude from this that all are tied together at Armageddon. As for the rest of their overlap schedules, these are based solely on imagination rather than on any clear scriptural marks. *It should be noted that pre-tribs likewise cannot agree on a basic order of these judgments.*

Their method of overlap is in error. Because they place the rapture at Armageddon, they must place the immediately preceding sixth seal at that point (Matt. 24:29-31), too. And pre-tribs claim the gathering of Israel is in Matthew 24:29-31, which clearly matches the sixth seal (see next chapter), so they must likewise find a way to place the sixth seal at the end of the seventieth week.

Let us take the rapture completely out of the equation for a moment and see if Scripture orders these events aside from pre-conceived rapture doctrine. If we discover clear indicators of

---

17 The Rapture, op. cit., p. 204

timing, then any related issue such as the timing of the rapture must take this into account.

Looking at the seventh seal, we find *explicitly stated* that the angels receive their trumpets as part of this seal (Rev. 8:1-6). Thus they cannot sound the trumpets until all of the seals have been opened. Also, the 144,000 firstfruits of Israel are sealed during the sixth seal to protect them before the angels can harm the earth (Rev. 7:1-4). The first four trumpets, the four winds, specifically harm the earth, so the trumpets must follow the sixth seal.

The first bowl can be tightly linked to the seventh trumpet, as well. When the seventh trumpet sounds God's heavenly temple *is opened* and the Ark of the Covenant is seen within (Rev. 11:19). In the prelude to the bowls (Rev. 15:5-8) we see the temple *still* open. The angels come out with the bowls containing the final plagues of God's wrath. The temple then fills with smoke so that none may enter until the bowls are completed. This evidence demonstrates the seals, trumpets, and bowls will be fulfilled sequentially. They cannot overlap in the ways suggested above.

But there is an overlap, one which is different than they envision, as the following chart explains. This accounts for the similarity in the sevenths but also fits the scriptural order:

SEALS 1 2 3 4 5 6 7 ----------------------------------I
　　　TRUMPETS 1 2 3 4 5 6 7 ----------------I
　　　　　　BOWLS　　1 2 3 4 5 6 7

The trumpeting angels receive their instruments as part of the seventh seal, making them part of that seal. When Christ begins His earthly reign at the seventh trumpet the angels are given bowls of unrestrained wrath to pour out as part of His cleansing the earth of the ungodly. This ends with the Battle of Armageddon and the sheep and goat judgment (Matt. 25). This makes the bowls part of the seventh trumpet, which in turn makes them part of the seventh seal.

In support, you will notice no direct special judgment is associated with the seventh seal or seventh trumpet - only forewarning of wrath to come.   This is because the following trumpets and bowls are those judgments.   As for the earthquake, thundering, etc. of the sevenths, these are all the same, happening all at once, waiting fulfillment until the seventh bowl brings completion to seventh seal and seventh trumpet;   In the seventh seal and trumpet these almost seem to be an afterthought, while they are greatly expanded upon in the description of the seventh bowl.

The earthquake described in the sixth seal moves islands and mountains to ensure no-one misses the heavenly signs of truth announcing the Day of the Lord (Rev. 6:12, 14; Luke 21:25-26). This is only a forerunner to the even more awesome earthquake of the seventh bowl, which sinks the islands and flattens the mountains (Rev. 15:18, 20); the first says, "I'm coming," and the second says, "I'm here."   One other prophetically important earthquake destroys one-tenth of Jerusalem immediately prior to the sounding of the seventh trumpet (Rev. 11:13), when Christ splits the Mount of Olives so repentant Israel can flee to Azal (or safety, Zech. 14).

The final critical problem with post-trib is the possibility of determining to within a couple of days the timing of Christ's coming several years in advance. It would be exactly 1260 days after the Abomination of Desolation (Dan 12:11, 12; Rev 12:6; 13:5). In contrast, Jesus explicitly said we cannot know the day or hour and must watch and be ready (Matt. 24:36). While we can see the signs and know it is near (24:33) based on the signs of the times - the events described in Matthew 24 - that day cannot be precisely determined. Other passages support this (1Thess. 5:1-11).

We have seen that post-tribulationism also falls short of harmonizing all the pertinent Scriptures concerning the rapture. We must look elsewhere.

Pre-tribulation Theory

The most popular and widespread literalist theory in America and parts of Europe is pre-trib. This view states that the rapture could occur at any moment, unheralded by signs, and requiring no other prophecies *must* be fulfilled first. It also insists that the rapture precedes or starts off the seventieth week. On several issues it is somewhat difficult to nail down exactly what they believe, as they vary widely in opinion on almost every sub-topic.

I will only briefly discuss pre-trib in this chapter as I show its *many problems* through the rest of this book. But for each of their arguments here I tell in which chapter I discuss it.

The key to this theory, as presented by many teachers, is the dispensational doctrine. They insist there can be no overlapping of ages because God has a different plan for each. Supposedly the seventieth week will focus on Israel and restore the Mosaic covenant of the Law which existed for the first 69 weeks. This, they say, excludes the presence of the church during this time. In *Things to Come*, Pentecost repeatedly uses this doctrine as a battering ram against mid- and post-trib, and some have used it against pre-wrath in more recent times. The truth is, dispensational theory does absolutely no harm to pre-wrath when correctly understood. I discuss this in chapter 10.

Second, pre-tribs often state unequivocally that a literal hermeneutic supports only their theory. For example, Pentecost says:

> Thus we can see that our doctrine of the pre-millennial return of Christ to institute a literal kingdom is the outcome of the literal method of interpretation of the Old Testament promises and prophecies [this is a true statement]. It is only natural therefore, that the same basic method of interpretation must be employed in our interpretation of the rapture question.... It can easily be seen that the literal method of interpretation *demands*

a pre-tribulational rapture of the church.18

It must not be so *easily seen*, or else there would be no conflicting ideas except among those who use a non-literal method. When I read the Bible for myself I certainly could not see evidence of the pre-trib rapture I had been told about and would have preferred. Instead, I saw frequent evidence the church would enter the Tribulation Period.

Also, all the pre-millennial systems claim to use the literal method. Claiming this does not necessarily prove they consistently use it. Even some pre-tribs have been known to allegorize an occasional passage or define a word arbitrarily in defense of their view, as we will see. Those who do this cannot be said to rely upon a literal hermeneutic, regardless of whether their ultimate conclusions are true.

Other frequent arguments raised by pre-tribs include the theory of imminency (chapter 10), the belief that the Holy Spirit's influence through the church must be removed prior to the seventieth week (chapter 7), and the fact the church is not named in Revelation's account of the seventieth week (chapter 8). I present my case against these and all other accounts as I present the pre-wrath position.

The Pre-wrath View

As a systematically developed theory, pre-wrath is the most recent of these. When compared to nearly 2000 years of church history, though, all are of recent origin. Even modern pre-trib and post-trib can only be traced back to the early 1800's. As we will see in chapter 10, however, the earliest and most reliable church fathers universally taught that Christians would face the Antichrist. While this does not prove the point, since doctrine must be based

---

18 Things To Come, J. Dwight Pentecost: Dunham Publishing Company, Grand Rapids, MI, 1958, p. 194, emphasis mine

on Scripture, this still lends some ancient weight to pre-wrath and post-trib, and none to pre-trib or mid-trib.

Simply put, pre-wrath teaches that the church will enter the great tribulation only to be rescued from the midst of it at the sixth seal. We will be snatched out just before God pours out His wrath on the whole world. We see the rapture addressed in 1Corinthians 15:52; 1Thessalonians 4:13-17; Matthew 24:29-31 (see Mark 13 and Luke 21); and Revelation 6:12-7:17. This will take place at the sixth seal as the Day of the Lord is introduced. Pre-wrath is the term we coined to identify our basic system to differentiate it from the other views. Sadly, some inconsiderate writers have jumped on this name and used it to teach one of the other positions because of its growing popularity. What I teach is true, "classic" pre-wrath.

I urge you to approach this study with a mind and heart open to the Holy Spirit, for He is the one who teaches truth. I believe you will find that when everything is put together the pre-wrath view will be like a well-built house, solid and practical for our use.

May God richly bless you. Amen.

Chapter 4: A Strong Foundation

Like building a house, developing a doctrine as involved as the rapture must start with a good foundation. We will begin by looking at the undisputed rapture passages. These we will compare with those usually placed by other theories at Armageddon. 1Thessalonians 4:13-17 and 1Corinthians 15:51-52 are the key rapture passages. Post-trib and pre-wrath includes Matthew 24:29-31 to this list, but with differing timing. Edward Hindson, a pre-trib, divides the key passages like this:[19]

Rapture Coming

John 14:1-3   Rom. 8:19   1Cor. 1:7-8; 15:51-53; 16:22

Ph'p 3:20, 21   Col. 3:4   1Thess. 1:10; 2:19; 4:13-18; 5:9, 23

2Thess 2:1   1Tim 6:14   2Tim 4:1   Titus 2:13

Heb. 9:28   Jam 5:7-9   1Pet 1:7, 13   1John 2:28-3:2

Jude 21   Rev. 2:25; 3:10

Armageddon (Second Coming)

Dan 2:44-45; 7:9-14; 12:1-3   Zech 14:1-15

Matt 13:41; 24:15-31; 26:64   Mark 13:14-27; 14:62

Luke 21:25-28   Acts 1:9-11; 3:19-21   1Thess 3:13

2Thess 1:6-10; 2:8   2Pet 3:1-14   Jude 14, 15

Rev 1:7; 19:11-20:6; 22:7, 12, 20

---

[19] <u>When the Trumpet Sounds</u>, contrib. Edward Hindson

When comparing these same passages, post-tribs conclude the numerous similarities between many of them prove they all describe the same event. Pre-wrath adherents are more cautious, noticing that while many share in important details a few really are quite different. This leads us to the conclusion that the rapture is within the great tribulation but before Armageddon. John Feinberg states the significance of the issue:

> If post-tribs are right that the similarity between the two types of passages is so great as to render them identical, then the battle is lost before the discussion ever can turn to the theological implications of the positions. What pre-tribs must do is squarely face those passages and see whether there is enough dissimilarity between rapture and Second Advent passages to warrant the possibility that the two events could occur at significantly separate times.... Both pre-tribs and mid-tribs should *begin* at this point.

We will begin by comparing those which pre-wraths tie together at the sixth-seal rapture. Afterward, we will look at Armageddon and see that it is clearly separate.

> (Matt 24:29-31) *Immediately after the tribulation of those days the sun will be darkened, and the moon will not give its light; the stars will fall from heaven, and the powers of the heavens will be shaken. Then the sign of the Son of Man will appear in heaven, and then all of the tribes of the earth will mourn, and they will see the Son of Man coming on the clouds of heaven with power and great glory. And He will send His angels with a great sound of a trumpet, and they will gather together His elect from the four winds, from one end of heaven to the other.*

> (Mark 13:27) *...and then He will send His angels, and gather together His elect from the four winds, from the farthest part of earth to the farthest part of heaven.*

> (Luke 21:21-28, 36) *And there will be signs in the sun, the moon, and in the stars; and on earth the distress of nations,*

50

with perplexity, the sea and waves roaring; men's hearts failing them from fear and the expectation of those things which are coming on the earth, for the powers of heaven will be shaken. Then they will see the Son of Man coming in a cloud, with power and great glory. Now when these things begin to happen, look up and lift your heads, because your redemption draws near... Watch therefore, and pray always that you may be counted worthy to escape all these things that will come to pass, and to stand before the Son of Man.

(Acts 1:11, when Jesus has just ascended onto the clouds of heaven. Then the angel tells the disciples) *"Men of Galilee, why do you stand gazing up into heaven? This same Jesus, who was taken up from you into heaven, will so come in like manner as you saw Him go into heaven."*

(1Cor 15:51b-52)...We shall not all sleep, but we shall all be changed – in a moment, in the twinkling of an eye. For the trumpet will sound, and the dead will be raised incorruptible, and we shall be changed.

(1Thess 4:16, 17) *For the Lord Himself will descend from heaven with a shout, with the voice of an archangel, and with the trumpet of God. And the dead in Christ will rise first. And then we who are alive and remain will be caught up together with them in the clouds to meet the Lord in the air.*

(2Thess 1:6-8) *It is a righteous thing with God to repay with tribulation [or, affliction] those who trouble you, and to give you who are troubled rest when the Lord is revealed from heaven with His mighty angels in flaming fire taking vengeance...*

(2Thess 2:1,2) *...Concerning the coming of the Lord and our gathering together to Him, we ask you not to be soon shaken in mind or troubled...as though the day of Christ [or day of the Lord] had come.*

(Rev 1:7) *Behold, He is coming with clouds, and every eye shall see Him, and they also who pierced Him. And all of the tribes of the earth will mourn because of Him.*

51

(Rev 6:12-16) *...He opened the sixth seal, and behold, there was a great earthquake; and the sun became black as sackcloth of hair, and the moon became like blood. And the stars of heaven fell to earth...then the sky receded as a scroll... and every mountain and island was moved out of its place. And [everyone on earth] hid themselves in the caves and the rocks, and said... "Fall on us and hide us from the face of Him who sits on the throne and from the wrath of the Lamb."*

(Rev 7:9, 14 still context of sixth seal) *After these things I looked, and behold, a great multitude which no one could number, of all nations, tribes, peoples, and tongues, standing before the throne and before the Lamb.... These are the ones who come out of the great tribulation...*

(Rev 14:14-16) *...Behold a white cloud, and on the cloud sat one like the Son of Man... and another angel ... cried with a loud voice, "Thrust in Your sickle and reap... for the harvest of the earth is ripe."*

To begin, over half these describe Jesus in heavenly clouds, with visibility often explicitly stated. Several add that He is descending from heaven at the time. All three are in the gospel passages and in Revelation 1:7 - which Hindson's chart places at Armageddon. We also find exact correlation in two important rapture texts: 1 Thessalonians 4:17 pictures the saints caught up in the *clouds* to meet the Lord *descending* from heaven; And in Revelation 14:14-16 Jesus sits in a cloud at the time of harvest, just before the harvest of wrath in the next three verses. Additionally, Acts 1:11 says the disciples would see Jesus descend in clouds just as they saw Him ascend into heaven. Thus both clear rapture passages and some claimed for Armageddon share in details the appearance and movement of the Lord.

Non-post-trib teachers understand that Jesus will not descend all the way to earth's surface at the rapture, but will for Armageddon. Significantly, the gospel accounts also say nothing of Christ landing on earth or of any earthly activity except gathering the *elect.* In fact, this account resembles 1Thessalonians when Jesus descends for the catching up of the saints.

In Matthew 24 a trumpet signals the gathering of the elect. In the key rapture texts a trumpet sounds at the gathering of the saints, too (1Cor 15:52; 1Thess 4:16-17). (Note, in a later chapter we will see the *elect* are Christians.) It's a match.

The fifth unifying point is angels. In Matthew the angels are sent to gather the elect. In 2Thessalonians 1:6-8 God gives us rest when Jesus is revealed from heaven with His angels. This *rest* refers to the resurrection - when God's saints bodily enter eternity as pictured in the promised land (Heb. 4:1-10). The *vengeance* is God's wrath under which unbelievers will remain. I will grant these angels are not said to gather, but their presence is a match to consider. The parable of the wheat and tares also show angels gathering at the rapture (Matt 13:24-30, 36-40). And don't forget the friends who come with the bridegroom to collect the virgins (Matt 25) discussed in the last chapter.

Next compare the gospel accounts to the sixth seal (Rev. 6:12-7:17). The gospels vividly describe the same fantastic, terrifying signs in the heavens as found at the opening of the sixth seal. They also describe man mourning and fleeing God's coming, implacable wrath (Luke 21:26). In the last chapter I demonstrated that the trumpets and bowls must follow the sixth seal, so it is easy to see why Matthew 24:29-31 cannot be Armageddon as most other theories claim. At Armageddon they are gathered to fight Christ, while here they flee to hide from God's wrath. Revelation 1:7 also says mankind, particularly the Jews, mourn when Jesus appears in the clouds, clinching it even tighter.

Revelation 6:16 even suggests Christ's visibility (*hide us from the face...*). In the context of the sixth seal, in Revelation 7, saints from all the earth washed by the Blood of the Lamb appear in heaven standing before Jesus - an apt description of the rapture.

The seventh similarity is *the four winds*. These represent the first four trumpet judgments. We learn in Revelation 7 that the

53

four winds are held in check until the 144,000 are sealed. The four winds will harm the earth and sea, and the first four trumpets do exactly that. Then in the second half of this chapter we see the saints in heaven in the same time frame. When we look at the Matthew and Mark, we see that the elect are *gathered away from the four winds*. The church is promised deliverance away from God's wrath, which begins in the trumpets.

Then there is the gathering in these texts, the gathering of the elect (Matt. 24:29-31), and the appearance of the saints in heaven (Rev. 7:9-17). The vision of these saints is between the sixth and seventh seals because it is tied to the sixth seal and the gathering of the elect *from the farthest part of earth* **to the farthest part of heaven** (Mark 13). Furthermore, these saints in Revelation who came out of the great tribulation are said to be standing before Jesus. You may recall that Luke 21 said, *"Pray always, that you might be counted worthy to escape from all these things which are coming on the earth, and to stand before the Son of Man."* This was in the context of the sixth seal as described in Luke.

1Thessalonians 4:16 says an archangel gives a shout or cry of command at the rapture. In Revelation 14:14-16 an angel tells the Son of Man (Jesus) to reap the first harvest. This is followed by *another* angel announcing the harvest of wrath. Also, Jesus is described here in clouds, further tying it all together. Scripture says exactly the same thing wherever we turn.

Only one of the cited passages remains to be tied in, 2Thessalonians 2:1, 2. This clearly places the rapture (*our gathering together to Him*) with Christ's second coming (*coming of the Lord*) on *the Day of the Lord*. This is part of the previous context of Jesus giving us rest when He appears with His angels to introduce wrath. If you read a little further, the apostasy and revealing of Antichrist must precede this day, which matches the order found in Matthew 24. I discuss this in detail in a later chapter.

We have seen that many *second coming* passages share in virtually every detail with key rapture texts, with clear ties to the sixth seal. We have reasonable grounds to conclude these are the same event. Paul Feinberg rebutted a similar, less detailed comparison made by post-trib Douglas Moo.

> ...Let me repeat that in contrast to these few similarities [Moo provided about four], there are many significant differences. Matthew says that the angels gather the elect; 1Thessalonians says that the Lord Himself does it. Matthew uses the great trumpet to call the elect from the four winds; 1Thessalonians teaches that it announces the descent of our Lord. Matthew makes no mention of either a resurrection or a translation of the saints. These are important points in the Rapture passage. In Matthew the gathering appears to be on earth (24:31-32), while it is in the air in 1Thessalonians. First Thessalonians 4 makes no mention of the effects of the sun, moon, and stars, yet this is an important part of Matthew 24. First Thessalonians gives the order of ascent; it is not clear there is any ascent in Matthew 24:31.[20]

Just a little careful searching will show the critical flaws in his reasoning. First, we must understand that not every single passage is going to include every single detail concerning Christ's coming. It would be tedious if they all included every detail. Also, each writer had a specific purpose and approach in their lessons, so logically the primary details each included would be those related to their purpose. Let's look at the specifics.

First is the lack of angels in 1Thessalonians. But remember that 2Thessalonians 1 describes angels when Jesus comes to give us rest - though I admit this does not say they gather anybody. But their presence is food for thought. Feinberg rightly argues that Christ Himself will gather the church, for He is the Resurrection and the Life. Mark 13:27 agrees, for *He will send His angels, and gather together His elect.* However, Feinberg's logic that this means the angels cannot gather is faulty. Consider this: You go to the grocery store to gather some items, taking your children with

---

[20] The Rapture, op. cit., p231

you. You are in a hurry, so you send them to collect the items. Now tell me, who is gathering the items? You, of course - the children are just helping under your direction. So Jesus tells the angels to go bring Charlie, Beth, and John, and they do. No problem.

Next, Feinberg claims the trumpet in Matthew 24 signals the gathering of the elect, while the one at the rapture in 1Thessalonians 4 announces the descent of the Lord. But this reads meaning into Paul's account, for it only says the trumpet sounds as He descends. The possibility of a rapture signal is not excluded. On the other hand, 1Corinthians 15:52 explicitly states the trumpet announces the rapture, for *the trumpet will sound, and the dead will be raised... and we will be changed.* We must look at all the related scriptures, and this verse is universally agreed to be a rapture text.

Why doesn't Jesus mention the resurrection or give an order of ascent in the Olivet Discourse? Because this was not his purpose - but to give signs pointing to the end of the age in reply to the disciples' question (24:3). However, the words He used easily fit a concise description of the rapture. Feinberg states this gathering of elect is on earth. Mark says they are gathered *from the farthest part of earth to [Greek, as far as] the farthest part of heaven.*

Feinberg's final complaint is that the heavenly signs and their effect on mankind are not found in 1Thessalonians 4. Paul was comforting and encouraging the Thessalonians that their saved, dead friends and family would not be excluded from the rapture, but actually would immediately precede them. It was not Paul's purpose to describe worldly events or heavenly signs that would announce Christ's coming, but the rapture itself. The primary purpose of the signs is to announce God's wrath to the world (Acts 2:20; Rev. 6:12-17). These have nothing to do with the saints other than signal us to lift our heads *for our redemption draws near.*

Mid-trib Gleason Archer also protests Moo's comparisons21, noting that the Old Testament appearances of Christ [Theophanies] share in some of the same details (Ex. 20, trumpet; Is 6, angels; cloud pillar during Israel's wanderings). He argues that these elements are common whenever the Lord appears. He adds that the moods of the rapture passages consistently differ with those of the second coming (Matt 24).

He case is easily answered. The OT theophanies shared details with second coming texts in only about three points, with Scripture only recording one or maybe two at the same time. But the Olivet Discourse and the accepted rapture texts share in at least four, simultaneous points (clouds, Jesus descending, a trumpet, a gathering to heaven). Then when you add the other related texts, no less than twelve points are found (see Chart A).

As for the difference in moods, it is again due to the purpose of the instructor. 1 Thessalonians concerns the promise of rapture, so the mood is joyful and comforting. Matthew 24, on the other hand, includes the much greater scope of the world and the end of the age, thus the mourning and fear of mankind. Luke 21:25-28 puts both moods together - wicked fearfully fleeing while saints lift their heads in anticipation of Christ.

Post-tribs then include Christ's coming at Armageddon, claiming there are sufficient similarities to tie this in, too. But is there enough to move the rapture to the end of the seventieth week? Read Revelation 19, which describes the great Battle:

> (Rev 19:11, 14, 15, 19-20) *Then I saw heaven opened, and behold, a white horse. And He who sat on him was called Faithful and True... and His name is called the Word of God. And the armies in heaven, clothed in fine linen... followed Him on white horses. Now out of His mouth goes a sharp sword, that He should strike the nations.... And I saw the beast, the kings of the earth, and their armies gather together to make war against Him who sat on the horse and His army...*

---

[21] The Rapture, op. cit., p. 217

First compare this to Matthew 24:29-31, which pre- and post-tribs both relegate to Armageddon. Well, Jesus is present in both, though Matthew describes Him descending in clouds with glory while Revelation says He descends on a white war horse, being mutually exclusive. Also, Revelation describes the calling of the birds to feast on the dead (Rev. 19:17), which they compare favorably to the mention of vultures in the context of Matthew.

But if you look at the grammar, Jesus is using a simile to explain the gathering of the saints, not referring to the prophetic gathering of birds (we examine this later). The armies of heaven are probably angels, another similarity to the gospels - but this tie is uncertain as many believe these are the returning saints (Jude 14, 15; Rev 19:8). Furthermore, the angels in Matthew gather *the elect* from around the globe, a term used only for the righteous in Scripture. The armies at Armageddon only gather the beast and the false prophet, however, merely slaying the wicked. So we find only two or three vague, uncertain similarities.

In contrast, many differences are apparent which they cannot reconcile logically or by comparing scriptures. Where are the spectacular heavenly signs in the Armageddon account? They are not here because they were fulfilled at the sixth seal, which we saw must precede the trumpets and bowls, thus before Armageddon. Where are the fearfully fleeing men described in the gospels? Here they have desperately gathered to fight in a last ditch attempt to keep Christ out. Why isn't a clear gathering of God's elect found anywhere in the Armageddon context? Because there is none; even the wicked armies are merely slain.

Why is no mention made of the defeat of the beast and his armies, or at least a hint of this Battle, in either Matthew 24 or in *any* of the other cited passages claimed to describe Christ's coming at Armageddon? The general tone of the Olivet Discourse would make this a logical place to allude to these, yet they are conspicuously absent. Why is Jesus riding clouds in Matthew but a horse in Revelation if these are the same account? Because His coming in clouds identifies Him to the Jews as the one who led them in the wilderness by a cloud pillar, and to the saints who look for Him to return even as He left (Acts 1:11). His coming on the white war horse, though, signifies His authority as King of kings as He finally brings earth under His complete authority. During His first advent He rode a young donkey into Jerusalem just before His crucifixion in humility as the Messiah; At Armageddon He will come on a war horse in victory!

In conclusion, the clear rapture passages share in every detail with most of those claimed to be Christ's second coming at Armageddon, apart from the actual account of that Battle. Additionally, they all line up with the sixth seal, which is opened after the rise of Antichrist but before God's wrath. A strong foundation is laid. As we begin building on this foundation, we will see that the pre-wrath position is like a well-planned home, and every passage slips easily and snugly into its place.

Rapture Coming

Matt 24:29-31; 26:64	Ph'p 3:20-21	Tit 2:13
Mark 13:24-27; 14:62	Col 3:4	Heb 9:28
Luke 17	1Thess 1:10	Jam 5:7-9
Luke 21:25-28	1Thess 2:19	1Pet 1:7, 13
John 14:1-3	1Thess 4:13-18	1John 2:28-3:2
Acts 1:9-11	1Thess 5:9, 23	Jude 21
Acts 3:19-21	2Thess 1:6-10	Rev 1:7
Rom 8:19	2Thess 2:1-3	Rev 2:25
1Cor 1:7-8	1Tim 6:14	Rev 3:10
1Cor 15:51-52	2Tim 4:1	Rev 22:7, 12, 20
1Cor 16:22		

Armageddon Coming

Dan 2:44, 45	2Thess 2:8 (both are in mind)
Dan 7:9-14	2Pet 3:1-14
Dan 12:1-3	Jude 14-15
Zech 14:1-15	Rev 19:11-20:6

Chapter 5: Introduction to Matthew 24

Understanding Matthew 24 plays a crucial role in answering the rapture question. Most other views maintain that the entire seventieth week is covered and that verses 29-31 occur at Armageddon. Pre-tribs believe the rapture precedes the events of this chapter. Post-tribs believe this gathering of elect is the rapture at the end of the seven years. Pre-wraths agree this is a sixth seal rapture, but prior to the trumpets and bowls of wrath. Thus it will occur sometime before the end of the week. The sheep and goat judgment in Matthew 25 follows the seventieth week and God's wrath.

> (Matt 24:1-3) *Then Jesus went out and departed from the temple, and His disciples came to show Him the buildings of the temple. And Jesus said to them, "Do you not see all these things? Assuredly, I say to you, not one stone shall be left here upon another, that shall not be thrown down." Now as He sat on the Mount of Olives, the disciples came to Him privately, saying, "Tell us when will these things be? And what will be the sign of Your coming, and of the end of the age?"*

Jesus prophesied the fall of Jerusalem and the temple. This spurred the disciples to ask about the timing of His second coming and the end of the age - surely such an event would signal the end of the world!

Matthew did not record the answer to the first question, when the temple would be destroyed; but Luke did.[22] Some believe Luke 21:7ff directly parallels Matthew 24, much like Mark 13. But a close look at the details reveals a different focus, and even a different location for the discourse. We will look at Luke 21 first.

---

[22] <u>The Bible Knowledge Commentary</u>, John F. Walvoord and Roy B. Zuck: S. P. Publications, Inc., Wheaton, IL, 1983, p.76

Luke 21

Luke's account takes place while Jesus was still teaching at the temple, immediately after He prophesied its destruction. Later, when they had gone to the Mount of Olives to their camp, the disciples asked Jesus to expound on what He had said. This was recorded in Matthew and Mark.

Most of the things He spoke at the temple concerned the fall of Jerusalem in 70 A.D. This is made clear in the questions the disciples asked: *"When will these things be? And what will sign will there be when these things are about to take place?"* (Luke 21:7) Jesus had just told them the temple would be torn down, and they wanted to know when. Jesus relates it to the end of the age and His coming, which spurred the disciples to further questions that night.

It's because Jesus begins and ends both discourses similarly that some believe they are parallel. But Luke's account has a lengthy middle section which is different. He starts both passages off warning of false christs, wars, famines, and earthquakes. In Luke, however, He breaks off by saying, *"But before all these things..."* (21:12). Here Jesus tells of the fall of Jerusalem under Titus Vespasian. While this section bears superficial resemblance to the Olivet Discourse, close examination reveals they are different.

Verses twelve through nineteen were to prepare early Christians for persecution by the Jews and the Roman government. They were delivered up to Jewish synagogues and brought before kings for the name of Christ, as Jesus had previously warned (Matt 10:16-26). Even friends and family betrayed believers to the authorities out of zeal for the Jewish or Roman faiths, or out of fear of being counted guilty by proximity. Many were imprisoned and martyred. *But not a hair of [their] heads shall be lost*, for the saints shall all be resurrected at the end of the age.

Luke 21:20-24 describes the fall of Jerusalem under Titus. Israel *fell by the sword, and was led away captive into all nations. And Jerusalem will continue to be trampled by Gentiles until the times of the Gentiles be fulfilled.* While the Jews have regained control of part of their homeland, we are still in the times of the Gentiles (Rom 11:24, the hardening of Israel in unbelief). Some parts of Jerusalem still remain under Muslim control, including the temple mount, and Israel has not accepted Jesus as their Messiah. According to Scripture, at the sixth seal the 144,000 firstfruits of Israel are sealed at the same time the church is caught away, as the Day of the Lord comes upon the earth. In fact, that is precisely where Jesus finishes the discourse in Luke.

He finishes by switching back to the seventieth week, describing the same heavenly signs that He mentioned in Matthew 24. Luke gives greater detail on the earthquake and the effects these signs have on mankind. Then Jesus appears in clouds in glory. We are encouraged that *when we see these things begin to happen, look up and lift up our heads, for our redemption* [Strong's #629, deliverance] *draws near* (21:28). After warnings to take heed to our conduct, Jesus promises that the prepared saints will escape from the midst of all these things to stand before Jesus (21:36; see Rev 7:9-17). The certain expectation of our Lord's return strengthens those who must endure tribulations and persecutions, especially in the end time. The chapter concludes by informing us Jesus taught in the temple by day and camped on the Mount of Olives by night, which is where we find ourselves in Matthew 24.

Matthew 24

The Olivet Discourse concentrates on the events of the second coming (Matt 24; Mark 13). Before we look at this, we must first understand to whom this prophecy was intended, Israel or the church. Pre-tribs mostly believe that Matthew 24 is intended for Jewish instruction, and perhaps a group of Gentiles who supposedly get saved after the rapture. Post-tribs and pre-wraths, on the other hand, maintain this entire teaching is for the church as it enters the seventieth week.

The disciples came to Jesus PRIVATELY, saying, "Tell us when will these things be? And what will be the SIGN OF YOUR COMING AND OF THE END OF THE AGE? (24:3, emphasis mine)

Jesus gave this privately to the disciples. This suggests the knowledge is for the church, not Israel. The frequent use of the second person pronoun, *you*, to the disciples supports this. He briefly singles out those specifically living in Judea with the third person pronoun, but otherwise uses the second person. In Matthew 13:10, after openly telling the parable of the sower and the seed, Jesus later explained it privately to His disciples, adding, "*...it has been given to you to know the mysteries of the Kingdom...*" In other words, Jesus explained some of His parables privately to the disciples that they might pass it on to the church which they would start. Likewise, He addressed the Olivet Discourse privately to the disciples following a partial discourse of His coming at the temple. Based on these facts, it is reasonable to conclude Matthew 24 is for the church.

The disciples' second question concerned the sign of Christ' coming at the end of the age. Of which age are they enquiring - the Jewish age under the Law or the church age? He had mentioned the times of the Gentiles earlier that day, and alluded to the church several times in previous teachings. In Matthew 28:20 Jesus told the disciples to teach everything He had commanded to the church, so logically the things they wrote were for believers. It is the church that is *built on the foundation of the apostles* (Eph 2:20), not Israel. Thus logically this also was written for the church.

The Parousia

Most pre-tribs believe in a dual *parousia* [Greek for *coming* or *visitation*]. They generally believe Christ's coming at the rapture is essentially unrelated to His second coming, necessitating a second and third coming.

The disciples asked Jesus for signs pointing to His *parousia*. The problem with pre-trib is that Jesus made no mention of a *parousia* prior to Matthew 24:27-31, following the Abomination of Desolation. Why would Jesus answer their question by telling of an Armageddon coming (according to pre-tribs) which would neither affect them nor the church they would found, yet fail to instruct them of a prior visitation which would affect them? They were asking for practical information, not something to pass on to unbelieving Jews to signal His second coming. Pre-tribs insist Jesus totally ignored this and chose to instruct them privately concerning Israel, instead. This does not add up.

Some try to answer this by affirming the disciples would not have understood instructions for two, separate comings. It supposedly would have confused them. That never stopped Jesus before, for many things He taught they did not understand until later (John 12:16). Also, the disciples had already received some instruction concerning the second coming (Luke 21, earlier that day), for they knew enough to ask about it when the Jews believed there would only be one coming. In fact, if a dual *parousia* was a part of God's plan, this would have been the ideal time to explain it. Being omniscient, God would have known of the confusion that would result if it was true by not even suggesting another coming. Furthermore, the lack of ANY single text describing or suggesting two comings strongly argues against the dual *parousia*. There are literally dozens of passages concerning Christ's second coming, and not one tells of two of them.

The truth is: absolutely no scriptural evidence supports a dual *parousia*. In fact, the word *parousia* is never used in undisputed relationship Armageddon. Robert Van Kampen neatly summarizes the significance:

> When the Greek word parousia is used in association with the return of Christ in the last days, Scripture speaks of only one coming of Christ which is initiated by the rapture of the church. The Scripture makes no mention of a dual parousia....Both Jesus and Paul make it clear that Christ's

second coming – which includes the rapture of His saints and His immediately following Day-of-the-Lord judgment – follows the revealing of the Antichrist. This occurs...sometime during the second half of the seventieth week. Therefore...the possibility of an extra, pre-seventieth week parousia is clearly ruled out on exegetical grounds.23

But is his conclusion sound? I carefully studied the seven Greek words translated as *coming, appearing,* and *revealing* in reference to Christ's second coming and the rapture and found it correct. In the next section I carefully define each of these Greek words. Then I look at how each is used to portray Christ's coming.

The Coming of Christ in Scripture

Parousia, the key word under discussion, is a noun which carries the idea of presence. Often it is extended to include the idea of becoming present by one's arrival (Strong's #3952). It is usually translated as *coming*, such as in Matthew 24:3, 27, but would be more accurately understood translated as *presence* or *visitation.* It is the advent. This word refers not only to His arrival, but to everything associated with His visitation - from the rapture to the Day of the Lord to Armageddon. Notably, this word never appears in the plural in relation to the second coming.

Heko (Strong's # 2240) is a verb, also usually translated *coming.* The basic meaning is *to come, to be present.* Parousia is the entire visit while heko is the actual arrival of the visitor.

The verb *erchomai* (Strong's 2064) has no corresponding noun. It contrasts with heko in that it describes movement between two points rather than the arrival. It is also translated *coming.* Here is a sentence designed to explain these three words: My friend is coming (erchomai), and when he arrives (heko) for his visitation (parousia) we will have a grand time.

---

23 The Sign, Robert Van Kampen, p. 463

Next is *epiphaneia* (Strong's # 2015). This is a manifestation, particularly the advent of Christ, and is closely related to the Greek word for light. This word always implies visibility or something memorable (examples Acts 27:20; 2Tim 1:10; Titus 2:11).

Phaino (Strong's # 5316) is also related to the Greek for light, and is usually rendered *appear* or *shine*.

Phaneroō (Strong's #5319) is a stronger version of phaino. It means to reveal or make clear. It is the act of becoming openly, shiningly visible.

Finally, we come to *apokalupsis* – the apocalypse. This verb, usually translated *revealing* or *revelation*, also carries the idea of visibility, with the further meaning of uncovering something previously hidden.

The first use of parousia in relation to the end times is Matthew 24:3 when the disciples asked Jesus about the end of the age and His coming. Jesus replies by describing various disasters which will come first (Matt 24:6), that the end is not yet. The final phase of the age is introduced by the Abomination of Desolation and the great tribulation (24:15-26). Jesus compares His parousia to the brightly visible flash of lightning. He then explains that when the great tribulation is cut short for the elect the heavenly lights will darken in obeisance at His coming in glory (24:27-31). This is the only visitation mentioned, which Mark 13 and Luke 21 confirm.

Two key rapture texts also use the word *parousia* (1Cor 15:23; 1Thess 4:15). In 1Corinthians Paul states that *each one will be resurrected in his own order ... those who are Christ's at His parousia.* In 1Thessalonians he says the ones still living at Christ's parousia will not precede those who sleep, but that the dead in Christ will rise first and the living immediately after. Nothing in these texts suggest they are separate from other parousia passages or give a hint of the timing in relation to end time events.

2Thessalonians 2:1-4 associates the rapture and parousia directly with the Day of the Lord [we will look at this in another chapter]. Interestingly, this is plainly stated to follow the revealing of

Antichrist, exactly the same order found in Matthew 24. Parousia is also used in several other passages, most telling believers to wait expectantly for their Lord (1Thess 2:19; 3:13; 5:23; Jam 5:7-8; 2Pet 3:4, 12).

Nothing in these verses can be reasonably construed to allow a pre-trib parousia. Pre-tribs almost always separate the rapture from the second coming, relegating the latter to Armageddon. Yet these passages tell us to wait for the parousia, not for the resurrection. The resurrection is a promise, but Jesus is our resurrection. So we look for Him. The fact we are told to wait expectantly for Him does not necessarily mean He could come at any moment. They mean exactly what they say - expect it, for He IS coming again.

Erchomai is the most commonly used word of this group. Many warn that Jesus is coming as a thief so we must watch. Pre-tribs ask how He could approach unexpectedly if His coming were heralded by signs, or by fulfillment of prophetic events such as the Abomination of Desolation. Surely the only way this criterion could be met is if Jesus gathers believers prior to the seventieth week. They miss the fact that these very same passages strongly imply those who watch should not be caught off guard. If we are living as we should and paying attention, we can know when His coming is near.

More significantly, His coming as a thief in context **always, without exception**, is to institute the Day-of-the-Lord wrath on the unsaved. The passages do not say, "Be ready to go." They warn, "Be ready when I come, or you won't go." In many cases, these warnings are given in the context of Christ's coming after the Abomination. The following passages use erchomai

- Jesus is coming like a thief, suddenly, unexpectedly, so watch (Matt 24:43, 44; 25:13; Mark 13:25, 36; Luke 12:40; 1Thess 5:2; Rev 3:11; 16:15; 22:7, 12, 22)
- Jesus is coming in clouds, descending from heaven in glory (Matt 16:27; 24:30; 25:31; 26:64; Mark 13:26; 14:62; Luke 21:27; Acts 1:11; Rev 1:7)

- The next passages are associated with the rapture or second coming with various subtopics, such as judgment, works, and time (Matt 24:48; 25:27, 31; Luke 18:8; 1Cor 4:5; Rev 14:15)
- Hebrews 10:37 says *"He who is coming [erchomai], will come [heko, arrive]"* in relation to the promise of rest at His second coming.
- And finally, 2Thessalonians 2:3 says, *"...that day* [the parousia and the gathering of the saints, and the day of Christ (v.1)] *will not come [erchomai] unless the falling away come first, and the lawless one be revealed..."* this last passage clearly and explicitly states that the parousia and rapture will not erchomai [approach] until after the revealing of Antichrist. This is consistent with Matthew 24:15-31, and by itself virtually disproves the pre-trib position.

The only passages using erchomai which have sufficient data to deduce a time frame consistently place it after the revealing of the beast.

This brings us to heko, the arrival of our Lord. We have already seen this word in Hebrews 10:37b for the rapture. In Revelation 2:25 Jesus tells the few faithful saints in Thyatira to hold fast their faith until Jesus arrives. The remaining verses all declare that Jesus and the Day of the Lord will arrive like a thief upon those who do not watch (Matt 24:50; 2Pet 3:10; Rev 3:3ab). So, not only will that Day's approach (erchomai) be undetected, but it's actual arrival will catch those not watching by surprise. Again, the context strongly implies those who are watching will be aware of its approach.

Epiphaneia is a conspicuous appearing. According to 2Timothy 4:8 those who have loved Christ's epiphany will receive the crown of righteousness, for the sure knowledge of His coming is a catalyst for holy living. 1Timothy insists we *"keep this commandment... until our Lord's... appearing."* Also, we are encouraged to look for *"that blessed hope and glorious epiphany of our great God and Savior, Jesus Christ,"* (Titus 2:13).

The earliest Jesus can be demonstrated in prophecy as conspicuously appearing is at the sixth seal (Matt 24:29-31; Rev 6:12-17). This is what we should be looking for, not some secret, pre-trib coming. No passage clearly depicts Him noticeably appearing at an earlier time, which leaves a bit of a problem for pre-tribs.

2Timothy 4:1 says Jesus will judge the living and the dead by His epiphany and His Kingdom. At the epiphany the spiritually living saints are demonstrated as such by their rapture, while those left behind are judged and found wanting by that fact. His Kingdom comes at the seventh trumpet, in which the judgment of the unrighteous is announced and the saints receive their rewards following their Bema seat judgment.

Apokalupsis is the uncovering of something previously hidden. Several passages urge believers to wait for Christ's apocalypse and promise one day it will arrive (1Cor 1:7, 8; 1Pet 1:13, 4:13). Christians who have successfully endured the testing of their faith, being strengthened by the test, will have a faith that glorifies and honors Jesus when He is revealed (1Pet 1:7).

2Thessalonians 1 is very significant. It says God will give the saints rest from their earthly trials and persecutions when Jesus is uncovered (apokalupsis) from heaven with His angels to take vengeance.

Additionally, this word is used in Revelation 1:1 to describe the purpose and title of the book. The first hint of Jesus being revealed from heaven is at the sixth seal, when the people cry out to be hidden from *the face of Him who sits on the throne and from the wrath of the Lamb* (Rev 6:12-17), which ties to Matthew 24:29-31. The last place apokalupsis is used is Luke 17:28-30 which promises the rapture of the saints just before God pours out His wrath, when He is revealed from heaven.

At last we come to phaino and the related phaneroō, which both mean to shine forth. In Matthew 24:27, 30 Jesus says the sign of His parousia will shine forth in the heavens like lightning. 1John

70

1:28 says we should abide in Christ that when He appears [shines] we may have confidence before Him at His parousia. 1Peter 5:4 promises that, after Jesus' shining appearance, believers will receive the crown of glory. And finally, Colossians 3:4 declares that when Christ appears [shines] His saints will appear [shine] with Him.

We have seen no evidence for a pre-trib rapture in these passages. Any time enough information is provided to deduce a location, they consistently place a single parousia following the Abomination and with the sixth seal. As Edward Hindson admits:

> These terms are often used interchangeably to refer to the rapture or the return of Christ. One cannot build a convincing case for the distinction between the two events merely on the basis of the terms themselves.24

I can hear someone complaining that pre-wrath adherents disallow the multiple parousias of pre-tribs while maintaining a multi-staged second coming for their own position. This seeming double standard must be cleared up before the point is settled.

This is not the contradiction it seems. The dual parousia theory has two separate comings with virtually nothing in relationship to each other. Most pre-tribs are very careful to make a clear distinction that the second coming is at Armageddon, and the rapture is separate.

The pre-wrath position maintains that everything from the rapture to Armageddon, and even beyond, is part of a single parousia. There are three stages, but each builds upon the last on every point.

The first stage concerns the removal of the saints before God's wrath. It includes the sealing of the firstfruits of Israel (Rev 7). Also, the sudden appearance of Christ, bringing wrath, will curtail some of the beast's power - though most will still follow him in the end as their only chance to defeat Christ, as they see it.

---

24 When the Trumpet Sounds, contrib. Edward E. Hindson, p154

At the second stage, the seventh trumpet, the saints receive their rewards as Christ officially takes over the kingdoms of the earth. Also, surviving Israel has largely repented and put faith in Christ as their Messiah, so are removed to Azal (safety) while God's wrath in the bowls is completed (Zech 14).

Christ comes for the Battle of Armageddon at the third stage. Here He will destroy the beast and his armies - frantically gathered to try to stop Christ from taking over, the initial shock of the first stage having faded. The third stage also concludes God's wrath. It is followed by Israel's return to her homeland on the Highway of Holiness, and the sheep and goat judgment of the nations (Matt 25).

Each stage is closely related to the next and they follow a logical progression. Every stage directly concerns the resurrected saints, God's wrath, the restoration of Israel to true faith, the humiliation and defeat of the Antichrist, and the introduction of Christ's millennial kingdom. All are part of on parousia, one visitation.

Allow me to illustrate. Consider an evangelistic revival meeting held at a church for three days, one service each evening. At each a somewhat different message is preached, yet all concern sin, repentance, and salvation. While each gathering is on a separate day, it can be considered one revival. Christ's single parousia will be much the same, fully developed in three stages.

Matthew Wrote for the Church

A few pre-tribs who hold an extreme dispensational view believe the entire book of Matthew contains teaching intended for Israel under the Old Covenant rather than instructions for the church. A key point for their case is that Matthew frequently refers to O.T. passages, and wrote with Israel carefully kept in mind. Also, if specific portions are for Israel, such as the Olivet Discourse, then logically so is the rest of the teachings. These teachers often even claim that messages such as the Sermon on the Mount (Matt 5-7) were for Jews living under the legal dispensation and have little to do with the church.

The truth is that Matthew wrote his history of Jesus as an instruction manual for the church, particularly to converts from Judaism.25 Also, Mark was just as clearly written for a Greek, or Gentile, audience in mind, and has many of the same lessons minus the O.T. references. Especially note that Mark 13 and Matthew 24 are nearly identical.

Many pre-tribs also exclude the possibility that the church is the elect gathered in Matthew 24 because the church age did not begin until Pentecost several weeks later (Acts 2). Because the rapture was supposedly not alluded to in the O.T. for this same reason, so Jesus could not have taught it either. He lived under the legal dispensation and would only have taught in that context.

Several obvious problems arise with this argumentation. First, Jesus mentioned the church several times prior to the Olivet Discourse (Matt 16:18). He even gave instructions for church discipline (Matt 18:15-20). Second, Jesus told the Apostles (Matt 28:19, 20) to make disciples and teach them to observe His commandments some time prior to Pentecost. It is logical that the gospel writers, in keeping with the Great Commission, would write the things the church needed to know. And third, the disciples knew enough to ask about the second coming at a time when Israel believed there was only one coming. This opens the possibility of previous instruction concerning the rapture. Thus the idea that the rapture could not be taught in Matthew 24 due to ignorance is completely invalidated.

Interestingly, there are at least two gospel passages most pre-tribs agree refer to the rapture, one of several important issues in which they contradict themselves. John 14:1-3 is universally agreed to be the rapture, and Jesus gave this promise a mere two days after the Olivet Discourse. Even more significantly, many

---

[25] "Matthew", H.L. Ellison; The International Bible Commentary, ed. F. F. Bruce: Zondervan, 1979, p1121

say Luke 21:36 refers to the rapture, which is in the portion of the Temple Prelude which concerns the coming associated with the sixth seal. We will see even more in the next chapter.

Chapter 6: The End of the Age

Matthew 24 divides into three major sections. First is the beginning of sorrows (24:4-8) or birth pangs (Mark 13:8). Most Bible teachers, including pre-wraths, believe this is the first half of Daniel's seventieth week because it appears to parallel the first four seal judgments (Rev 6). Some believe it is actually an extended period before the seventieth week, and that the end of the age is really 3 1/2 years rather than seven.

The great tribulation follows (Matt 24:9-26), like the heavy labor stage of birth (1Thess 5:2, 3; Is 13:6-8). As we will see, this time will be characterized by increased open hatred for and persecution of Jews and true Christians - even in those countries which have relative freedom of religion today.

The second coming and rapture comprises the third section (24:27-51). First Christ's coming is described, then we are warned to be ready for it. Continuing the biblical imagery of childbirth, just as the head of the baby appears first, so will Jesus appear and seal the firstfruits of Israel following the rapture, as the millennial age begins to emerge (Rev 7). The seven trumpets bring in the millennium, fully birthed at the seventh trumpet when Jesus is declared King of the earth (Rev 11:15-19). At this point Israel has repented and is taken to Azal (safety, Zech 14).

Just as there is one more stage in birth, the afterbirth of the placenta, so there is a final burst of unrestrained wrath. This represents the bowls of wrath (Rev 16) and Armageddon (Rev 19), removing the beast and his minions from the earth. This takes 30 days following the seventh trumpet (Dan 12:11; the 1260 days granted to Antichrist to rule plus 30 days to reach the 1290 days).

The bathing of the newborn relates to the sheep and goat judgment (Matt 25:31ff), cleansing the earth of any remaining rebellious God-haters who survived the wrath, like the fluids clinging to the baby's skin when it is born. The Jews return to Israel on the Highway of Holiness during this period, too. This fills up the forty-five days following Armageddon (Dan 12:12); Blessed are those who come to the 1335 days, for they are allowed entry into the millennial kingdom.

The Birth Pangs

The first three seals are the early birth pains of the millennial age. The first seal describes a rider on a white horse carrying a bow. We know this is not the coming of Christ because when He comes on his white horse He will fight the beast and his armies with a sword from His mouth. The bow is a weapon of deception, used by assassins to kill from a distance without being seen. Therefore, many believe this is the rise of the antichrist, one-world government, when the prince signs a *covenant with many for one week* (Dan 9:27). This is before the ten kings give him authority in the middle of the week (Rev 13, Dan 12). Like an assassins bow, his true motive - the destruction of Israel and the church - will still be hidden.

This seal also likely relates to a sudden upsurge in false christs and prophets as a sign of the approaching end of the age (Matt 24:5). When the seventieth week begins, many of the false teachers already in the church will begin the final preparations to get people ready to receive the mark of the beast.

In Matthew 24:6-8 Jesus mentions wars and rumors of wars, famines, pestilence, and earthquakes in many places. The second seal is war (Rev 6:3, 4, peace taken from earth). The third is widespread famine (Rev 6:5, 6), which often follows after wars and natural disasters such as earthquakes and pestilence.

The next few verses describe increasing persecution against God's people in all nations. In 24:15 Jesus says, "Therefore, when you see..." The word *therefore* tells us He is expounding on what

He just said, and He had just described the persecution which would arise - and then the end of the age will come (the question He is answering). The Abomination of Desolation is thus the means by which the persecution comes into full force. This persecution is specifically against those who put faith in Christ (*hated for My name's sake*) and is addressed to the disciples (*you*) as representatives of the church.

According to Revelation 12 the Antichrist first comes against Israel (the woman), as the Olivet Discourse agrees when it singles out those living in Judea. But Revelation tells us some will flee to the wilderness to successfully hide. Then the beast will turn against *the rest of her offspring, who have the testimony of Jesus* (the church).

If you count all the Jews and *professing* Christians from all denominations and sects, the number would be about 25% of the earth's population. The fourth seal gives power to Death and Hades over one-fourth of the earth to slay with the sword, with hunger, and with death, *and by the beasts of the earth*. The beasts are the Antichrist and the false prophet (Rev 13). Those who do not take the mark of the beast will be unable to buy or sell, so even those who hide will face hunger and starvation. Sword is a symbol of war, and Revelation says the beast will war against the saints of Jesus and overcome them. Many will be executed because they refuse the mark. That is Death. Hades follows with him.

Matthew 24 says many will betray Christ and betray other believers, caving in to the demands of Antichrist rather than suffer and die for their faith. Revelation is clear those who do so will go to Hades, and ultimately the Lake of Fire. The fourth seal is a choice between suffering and physical death at the hands of the beasts, or spiritual death by choosing to follow the beasts. Jesus said those who seek to keep their life will lose it, but those who lose their life for His sake will gain it (Matt 16:25). The fourth seal will make this very real and immediate. Thus we see Death with Hades following for those who choose wrong, and find the fourth seal described in Matthew 24:9-12.

I will prove in chapter nine that these seals are not God's wrath, though they are part of His plan. The first five seals are clearly the works of man's wickedness and some natural disasters which have commonly occurred throughout history, but on an increased scale. Jesus tells us these are not yet the end of the age; *This gospel of the kingdom* must be preached worldwide, *and then the end will come* (Matt 24:6, 14).

The obvious question is: What is the significance of *the end of the age?* Those pre-tribs who agree these signs line up with the seals in the first half of the week usually believe it is the end of the legal age. They claim the Old Covenant will be restored by God for the seventieth week to more directly tie to the first sixty-nine, noting that Daniel speaks of restored animal sacrifices in the temple - a key part of the covenant.

But Jesus did away with that system of approaching God 2000 years ago by fulfilling the sacrificial system through His death on the cross. God's plan is not to restore the imperfect system but to get the Jews to receive Christ as their true Messiah. Scripture says when those who pierced Jesus see Him they will mourn (Rev 1:7), and in the end finally accept Him. When the Jews are gathered after Armageddon, it is the dawn of the next age, not the end of this one.

Nor can *the end* refer to the age following the church age, for the next on God's calendar is the millennial reign of Christ.

So, this end yet to come *must be* something that would be significant to the disciples or those following them, it *must* conclude with Christ coming and a gathering of *elect*, and it must bring the *end* of an age. The only possibility that meets all these is the church age, the times of the Gentiles.

S. Maxwell Coder explains the next attempt to keep the church out of Matthew 24:

> One of the most misunderstood verses... is the statement: "This gospel of the kingdom shall be preached in all the world for a witness unto all nations; and then the end shall come."

The gospel of the kingdom must be distinguished from the good news of the grace of God (Acts 20:24), called the "gospel of Christ" a dozen times in the epistles (2Cor 4:3-6). The gospel of Christ is defined as the good news of Christ's death, burial, and resurrection on our behalf (1Cor 15:1-4). The gospel of the kingdom is the message that Christ and the disciples proclaimed when the kingdom was being offered to the people of Israel... (Matt 4:17; see also 4:23; 10:7). No evangelist...in the present age would preach this message, for the kingdom is not now being offered as it was during Christ's earthly ministry.26

To this, Walvoord and Zuck add:

The message preached today in the church age and the message proclaimed in the Tribulational period calls for turning to the Savior for salvation. However, in the Tribulation the message will stress the coming kingdom, and those who then turn to the Savior for salvation will be allowed entrance into the [millennial] kingdom.27

I'm sorry pre-tribs, but you must have missed a few verses in your study. Peter preached the kingdom shortly after Pentecost, resulting in many converts to Christianity (Acts 3:11-16). Since dispensationalists agree the church age began at Pentecost, it is inconsistent to say the kingdom was still being offered to Israel at this point. More to the point, in the same context of Mr. Coder's reference (Acts 20:25) we learn that Paul preached *the gospel of the kingdom*, as he still did in Acts 28:23, 31. By this time Paul was the apostle to the Gentiles, so he certainly was not still offering the kingdom to Israel. Furthermore, the coming kingdom is an important facet of the gospel of Christ (Eph 5:5; 2Tim 4:1, 18; Heb 12:25-28).

---

26 The Final Chapter, S. Maxwell Coder: Tyndale House Publishers, inc., Wheaton, IL, 1984, p. 70
27 The Bible Knowledge Commentary, op. cit., p77

Many people misunderstand the significance of the word *kingdom* in the original Greek. The modern meaning is simply a country ruled by a king. But the Greek word *basileia* is not primarily a reference to the nation, but to the sovereignty of the king. The central focus of this word is not on the people but on their king. To better understand this verse, it would be better translated: *This gospel of the sovereignty of God shall be preached in all nations as a witness.* This is the good news that God is in control even in the midst of tribulations. His plan is being fulfilled. Part of the plan includes the gospel of salvation, and part includes His wrath on the ungodly. Part also concerns the coming Kingdom.

This gospel is not merely preached verbally, but through the lives of those who take a stand for Christ even in the midst of the persecution of the fourth and fifth seals. During this period many of the merely religious will be offended and fall away (see also, 2Thess 2:3). Great hatred will be manifested against true Christians who stand for righteousness and believe the whole Bible. Many will be imprisoned and killed for their faith. False prophets and teachers of the religious Babylon will abound, deceiving many. Lawlessness will run unchecked as genuine love for Christ and man grows cold, replaced by a counterfeit which defends evil. Those who stand firm for Christ will preach this gospel with their very lives, while those who give in and betray Christ will face Hades.

The world system is poised on the brink, ready to collapse. I believe it is this collapse which convinces the world they need to be unified under a single leadership to fix things, and sets it up for the Antichrist. And there are those who believe many of these things are happening on purpose by the schemes of the New World Order to produce such a system (as do I).

As the seals are opened, mankind will be released to even greater evil than we see today. Through it all faithful Christians will continue to preach and live the gospel of the kingdom to the world regardless of the opposition, *and then the end will come* (Matt

24:14). Notice again that nowhere has Jesus even hinted at a prior removal of the church.

The Great Tribulation Amputated

Matthew 24:15 begins: *Therefore when you see the Abomination of Desolation... standing in the holy place...* This will alert us the fourth and fifth seals are about to unfold. This verse is addressed to the church as a whole (*you*), while the following few verses concern specifically those living in Judea - who must flee immediately because that is where it will start. We know that a portion of Israel successfully flees into the wilderness to Egypt and Assyria where they are protected by God for three-and-a-half years (Rev 12:13-16; Is 27:13; Dan 12:1). I believe the unbelieving Jews are alerted in part by the arrival of the two witnesses (Rev 11) who appear at this time, and are slain just before the seventh trumpet.

For then will come the great tribulation. After the woman flees the depredations of the Antichrist, he will turn against the church (Rev 12:17). But have no fear, for Jesus has not abandoned His people. He promises (Matt 24:22) that the great tribulation will be cut short for the sake of the elect, else all flesh on earth will be destroyed by the rabid beast. Pre-wrath adherents believe the elect to be the church, and this cutting short is the rapture.

Arnold Fruchtenbaum explains the usual pre-trib view:

> The period of Jewish persecution ... will be suddenly cut short in the sense that it will not be allowed to continue even one day beyond its allotted time. God will allow the Antichrist to persecute Jews for exactly 1260 days, and not one second beyond that. Once the last second comes, it will be suddenly cut short for the sake of Jewish survival. In fact, Mark's Greek tense (13:20) speaks of this shortening as already having taken

81

place: as an accomplished fact....28

The Greek word *koloboō,* translated *shortened,* Strong defines *to curtail, amputate.* While the word can mean what Fruchtenbaum explained, it often means an amputation. Thus it implies that your right arm is amputated at the elbow, not cuts short at the fingertips. The past tense only means that this is certain, not necessarily that it is limited or cut short to exactly 1260 days.

Also, I agree that the Antichrist will persecute the Jews for the full 1260 days, for Scripture makes this clear (Dan 9:26-27; 12:7; Rev 12 and 13). It is amputated only insofar as it concerns the elect, which we will shortly discover is the church. Also, the beast will pursue Israel and the church with such hatred that all of humanity is at risk. The Jewish persecution will be greatly curtailed by the coming of Christ at the sixth seal, though.

Coder offers a different argument from this Greek word, one which recognizes its root idea of amputation. In Amos 8:9, it says the sun will go down at noon, bringing darkness. He then adds Revelation 8:12 where the sun, moon, and stars are smitten so *as a third part of them was darkened, and the day shone for not a third part of it, and the night likewise.* From this he concludes the days are literally shortened because earth's rotation has speeded up.29 It is supposedly for Israel's sake that this takes place.

While this is the best pre-trib explanation I have seen, it still has problems. First, Revelation says the heavenly lights are darkened or blocked, not that the cycle was shortened. A much more consistent explanation would be some supernatural or natural event obscuring one-third of the sky. In fact, the first three trumpets appear to be severe meteor activity which could produce the very effect of the fourth trumpet. God will not *cheat* by literally shortening the days to reduce the actual time the beast reigns.

---

28 A Review of "The Pre-Wrath Rapture of the Church" by Marvin Rosenthal, by Dr. Arnold G. Fruchtenbaum: Ariel Ministries, PO Box 3723, Tustin, CA 92681, nd, p.12
29 The Final Chapter, op. cit., pp 72-73

Second, the heavenly signs in Matthew 24 produce mourning in mankind. Amos 8 suitably fits the pre-wrath schedule; The sixth seal ends the worldwide preaching of the gospel by means of the rapture, bringing spiritual famine on the earth with people unable to find the Word of God preached anywhere (Amos 8:9-13). Just when the world thinks it is winning against those bigoted, trouble-causing Jews and Christians, their sun will be darkened and they will mourn. The true light of Christianity will be removed from the earth just as the heavenly lights are darkened. The Day of the Lord arrives, and this tells of both spiritual and physical famine during the terrible time of God's wrath.

The Elect

Who are these *elect*? Up till now I have mostly assumed for argument's sake they are the church. But most pre-tribs believe they are either Israel or those taken to judgment and not allowed entry to the millennial kingdom. This point is critical to the rapture question and must be carefully considered.

Pre-tribs provide numerous reasons for their claims. Most often cited is that Israel was the elect under the Old Covenant and that Jesus lived and taught strictly in that context. We saw some of the problems with such dispensational extensions in the previous chapter. Christ brought the New Covenant with Him and several times mentioned the church in His teachings. Also, He told the disciples to teach the church what He said, so on this point there is no reason the elect cannot be believers.

Also, the New Testament almost exclusively reserves this term for the church. (Rom 11:7, 28 for Jewish converts to Christ; Rom 8:33 and 11:5 for all Christians; also see 1Thess 1:4; Tit 1:1; 1Pet 1:2; 5:13; Pet 1:10; 2John 1, 13). In 2Peter 2:9 Christians are called *a chosen generation*, the word chosen being the same Greek word as *elect* (Strong's #1588). This adds to our list (John 15:16; Rom 16:13; Eph 1:4; 1Pet 2:4).

83

Let's take a quick look at N.T. references which call Israel *elect*. Don't blink! 2Tim 2:10. Yep, that's it. Besides this, it is used once for angels (1Tim 5:21), once for Jesus (1Pet 2:6), and once for believers in general, Old or New Testament (Luke 18:7). *It is never used for the unsaved.*

Dake, in his popular reference Bible, offers a long list of reasons why he believes Israel is the elect.[30] Almost all employ circular reasoning and straw man arguments.

For one, he states the warnings against false christs and prophets (vv. 5, 11, 23-26) primarily concern Israel. I beg to differ. These warning are very timely for the church today, and will be even more so in the end time. We have many false teachers introducing cults based on the Bible, but denying critical doctrines such as the deity of Christ or the need for holiness. Many times professing Christians fall for their subtly deceiving lies. Take Transcendental Meditation (TM) for example. This is based on Buddhist beliefs, and has been adopted by the New Age Movement (NAM), which is largely based on Hindu and Buddhist beliefs. They, in turn, infiltrate the church and teach *christianized* versions under pseudonyms, such as stress management and relaxation techniques, visualization, the power of positive thinking, etc.

One method of TM is to blank the mind and repeat a word or sound to enter a hypnotic state of mind. A while back I heard about a so-called Christian movement which uses the same method. They are not actively praying or praising, but just blank the mind while repeating a "prayer word" over and over again, such as the name of Jesus. Sounds dangerously similar to me! Biblical meditation is to think on good, pure, holy, and just things (Ph'p 4), and on God's Word and person - not to blank the mind and repeat vain babblings. We are to love God with our minds. I could give other examples.

---

[30] Dake's Annotated Reference Bible, Finis Jennings Dake: Dake Bible Sales, inc. Lawrenceville, CA. 1991, notes on Matthew 24:22

False teaching abounds in the church. From the very beginning of church history believers have had to beware of and contend with false teachers. Paul frequently warned churches not to be deceived by the wolves in sheep's clothing, but rather remember the simplicity of the gospel of Christ (1Cor 11:3; Gal 1:6-9; Col 2:4; et al). The other N.T. writers also felt compelled to issue warnings (2Pet 2:18ff; 1John 2:18-27). Obviously, the warning against false christs and prophets in Matthew 24 can concern the church.

Dake also insists Matthew 24:9 describes anti-Semitism and Jewish persecution. This is circular reasoning based on the assumption that the church has already been raptured. Thus this must be persecution of Jews, which makes them the elect in the later verses. But if the church is still present on earth, as this study demonstrates, then the elect can indeed be the church. These are specifically persecuted for *His name's sake*.

Dake also associates *the beginning of birth pangs* with the travail of Israel (Dan 12:1). First, no specific people are named in the gospels. Moreover, contextual clues strongly suggest these birth pangs fall on much of the earth rather than a specific ethnic group such as the Jews, for the wars, famines, diseases, and earthquakes happen *in diverse places. These are the beginning of sorrows.* Second, Daniel 12:1 is the great tribulation associated with the Abomination of Desolation (Dan 11:31), which means it cannot be part of the earlier birth pangs. This is the heavy labor stage.

Dake also notes that Matthew 24:15-21 is directed specifically at those in Judea. He believes references to the Jewish temple, the Sabbath, and fleeing Judea all serve to prove Israel to be the elect. I noted earlier that the key is in the pronouns used. Most of the passages are addressed to the disciples as representatives of the church, while a few verses single out those living specifically in Israel using the third person.

Dake also maintains that the great tribulation is directed only against Israel. I'll concede Daniel 12:1 seems to imply this. On the other hand, the church was still a hidden entity when he prophesied, so that would be consistent. Revelation 12, though, teaches that after the woman [Israel] who had given birth to the manchild [Jesus] flees to safety the beast attacks the rest of her offspring who have the testimony of Jesus.

He also insists that the gathering of elect in Matthew 24 can only be Israel, basing his case on this being at Armageddon. We saw in an earlier chapter why this cannot take place at the end of the seven years. Remember, Mark's account says they are gathered from the farthest parts of earth to the farthest part of heaven, not to Israel or Jerusalem as would be the case if this was the gathering of Israel. Also, whereas Matthew says angels do the gathering, neither Dake's reference (Zech 14) nor any other O.T. prophecy say angels gather Israel on the Highway of Holiness. Pre-tribs deny this as a rapture gathering because of the lack of angels in their accepted rapture passages while making the same argument with the gathering of Israel - with the same problem.

Dake's last argument relates the gathering of vultures mentioned in Matthew 24:28 to Ezekiel 39:17-22, which directly ties to Armageddon. A closer look reveals Jesus uses a simile describing the suddenness of Christ's return, as pre-trib Stanley Horton explains:

> But the time will come when Jesus will return. It will be sudden event, like a lightning flash [v.27]. Like the lightning also, we shall see it as we look up. Jesus compared it to the sudden appearance of eagles or vultures when an animal dies in the desert. There may be nothing in sight for miles around, but suddenly, out of the sky, the vultures swoop down.31

None of Dake's arguments offer any real case for identifying the elect as Israel rather than the church. We will continue following Matthew's account.

---

31 Welcome Back, Jesus, Stanley Horton: Gospel Publishing House, Springfield, MO, 1967, p. 32

The Sixth Seal

Switching back to the second person and addressing the whole church, Jesus once again warns against false christs and prophets, some of whom can even work miracles, as also the Antichrist will do (2Thess 2). Because of severe persecution many believers, longing for Christ's return (Luke 17), will be open to possible deception. Some may be led astray to follow rumors and follow false teachers. *Jesus would not have warned us if it were impossible.* Since Jesus essentially repeats a warning given moments earlier, we know this is critically important for us.

Then in 24:25 Jesus states, *"See, I have told you beforehand..."* This emphasizes His warning so we might be prepared. You cannot use the excuse that you did not know better if you find yourself falling into one of these traps - ***He told you!***

And as if this were not enough, He continues His warning in verse 26. We are not to listen to false rumors of a secret coming as if Jesus were some underground resistance leader calling us to go meet Him. The next verse tells us how to recognize the real thing: *As the lightning comes from the east and flashes to the west so also will the coming of the Son of Man be.* Verse 28 continues this train of thought with the sudden appearance of vultures over a carcass.

In Matthew 24:29-31 Jesus describes certain, unmistakable signs in the heavens which accompany His parousia. The sixth seal will produce a darkening of the sun, moon, and stars (Rev 6:12-17), and a great earthquake. The sign of the Son of Man will shine forth like lightning in the preternatural darkness, and mankind will mourn and flee what is coming (Luke 21:26). You will not have to be told when He comes, for there's nothing like the *real thing*, brothers and sisters!

Now if the Olivet Discourse describes Christ's coming for Armageddon, as other theories suppose, why are men just now getting worked up? The trumpets and bowls of wrath which must precede Armageddon bring plainly told, yet unimaginable suffering and terrors upon the earth, killing over one-third of all mankind (Rev 9:15). Why would the world, everyone having lost numerous friends and families in the great disappearance [rapture] and endured the wrathful judgments just now, at Armageddon, begin to flee what is coming on the earth? Hello, anybody home?!?

The sixth seal provides exactly the information we need to understand this passage. After describing the same heavenly signs John notes that people from all walks of life, from the mighty king to the lowly slave, flee to hide *from the face of Him who sits on the throne, and from the wrath of the Lamb. For His wrath has come and who will be able to stand.* (Rev 6:12-17) This also agrees with Luke 21. We saw earlier why this seal must precede the trumpets and bowls.

Next, Jesus will send His angels with the sound of a trumpet to gather the elect (Matt 24:31). We have already seen much evidence against this as the gathering of Israel, but a couple more arguments must still be addressed. Many pre-tribs associate this verse with Isaiah 27:12, 13 and Deuteronomy 30:1-5. Robert Van Kampen refutes this:

> But that Isaiah passage refers to the Lord's gathering the remnant of Israel from Assyria and Egypt and bringing them back on the Highway of Holiness. A trumpet is blown, as in Matthew 24:31, but there is no mention of angels. That in-gathering is specifically limited to Israel and to those two countries just mentioned, whereas the gathering of Matthew 24:31 is just as specifically worldwide and is not limited to any national or racial group, referring only to "His elect…"

> But this Deuteronomy passage… pertains to unbelieving Israel, gathered before the seventieth week commences, as described in the vision of the dry bones in Ezekiel 37. On the other hand, the account in Matthew 24:31 is the in-gathering of God's elect and occurs after the great tribulation is cut short. In addition, the Deuteronomy passage depicts God Himself doing the gathering, not His angels – as is clearly depicted in

Matthew 24:31 and as taught by Christ when the wheat is harvested into God's heavenly barn (Matt13:30) by His angelic reapers (v.39).32

He concludes that this leaves no scripture with which to back the pre-trib opinion that Matthew 24:31 is the gathering of Israel.

Another problem is that the elect are gathered away from the four winds. You will recall that in chapter 4 I compared this with the only other N.T. mention of the four winds, also in relation to the sixth seal (Rev 7:1-8). Here the angels temporarily withhold the winds from harming the earth while the firstfruits of Israel are sealed. A few verses later a great multitude appears in heaven from all nations (the farthest parts of earth), standing before the throne. The first four trumpets harm the earth, as the four winds. The last three trumpets are the three woes (Rev 8:13). In one context the elect are gathered from the four winds while in the other a great host other than Israel appears standing before Jesus (see Luke 21:36) while the four winds are held in check. When all the evidence is added up, it equals that the gathering of elect in Matthew 24 is the rapture of the church.

This is exactly what the early church believed. In the second century, for example, *The Teachings of the Twelve Apostles* twice quotes Matthew 24:31 substituting the word *church* for *elect* (chapter IX and X). The defense rests.

Jesus tells the disciples (Matt 24:32-36) that when we see all these things, know that the time is near. Everything in the Olivet Discourse up to this point is part of the sign of His coming and the end of the age. Only when we see the Abomination of Desolation should we consider His coming as any-moment, for we must see *all these things* to know it is at the very door. Concerning the sixth seal, Jesus added in the temple prelude (Luke 21:28) that when these things begin to happen we should look up and lift up our heads for our deliverance is at hand. Only then will it be time to search the darkened skies to find the Lord coming brightly in the

---

[32] The Sign, p. 505

clouds in glory. We cannot know the exact hour or day, but when these last few signs appear the church shall be caught up into glory!

Luke 21:34-36 adds some important information to Christ's coming. First, Jesus warns us to *take heed to* ourselves lest that day catch us unawares. We must be striving to live a life pleasing to God to avoid blindness to the early signs of Christ's coming, for it will come as a snare on those who do not watch. *Watch therefore, and pray always, that you may be counted worthy to escape all these things that shall come to pass, and to stand before the Son of Man.* (Luke 21:36)

At first glance this verse almost seems to promise a pre-trib rapture, and some pre-tribs say this is the first clear reference to the rapture in Scripture. I agree this refers to the rapture, but not pre-trib. The word *escape* is the Greek word *ekpheugo*, which is *to flee out of a place*.33 It is used of prisoners escaping from prison (Acts 16:27) and of Paul's escape from Damascus (2Cor 11:33). Thus the idea in Luke is escape from the midst of these things, specifically the sixth seal as described in Luke 21:25-28 (Matt 24:29-31). The elect will be gathered away from *those things which are coming on the earth*, God's wrath (see Rev 6:15-17). I will prove in chapter nine that these heavenly signs signal the start of God's wrath.

Also notice that the worthy will *stand in front of the Son of Man.* The great multitude stands in front of the throne at the sixth seal (Rev 7). There is an old saying that the devil is in the details. I don't really like that phrase, so I will change it. God's truth is found in the details!

---

[33] The Expanded Vine's Expository Dictionary of New Testament Words: Bethany House Publishers, 1984, p. 370

Taken

In Matthew 24:37-39 Jesus compares the time of His coming to when God delivered Noah from the great flood. The next three verses describe some who are taken while others are left behind. Most pre-tribs today believe the individuals who are taken are the unrighteous taken to judgment while those who remain enter the millennial age. The example of Noah they claim expresses the same idea - Noah's family representing those who enter the millennium while the flood takes the rest to judgment.

Again, the Greek suggests otherwise. Two different words are used for *take away* in these two examples. Verse 39 uses *airo*, which simply means to remove or separate (Strong's #142). John the Baptist used this when He declared Jesus as the Lamb of God who takes away the sin of the world (John 1:29). Thus in our context the unrighteous were taken away by the flood of God's wrath while Noah was placed safely in the ark.

On the other hand, the word used for those individual taken in the second example, leaving behind companions, is *paralambano*, which means *to take to oneself* (Strong's #3880). Jesus used this word in only one other context, one most agree is the rapture. In John 14:3 He promises that He is going to prepare a place for believers, and will come again to *receive you to myself [paralambano]*. The immediate context here is His coming in 24:29-31 and the personal gathering of the elect to heaven. First, Noah and family is gathered into the ark while the flood takes away those not delivered. Then here Jesus takes some to Himself while others are left behind. A warning follows, to watch and be ready or Christ's coming will catch us by surprise like a thief. Many pre-tribs freely quote this last part for the rapture, ignoring the context in which it is given.

So we see Jesus had consistency in teaching through Matthew 24. He did not wander from instructions to unbelieving Israel until Armageddon to a discussion of who would enter the millennium to an obscure warning of a pre-trib rapture, then back to again to the sheep and goat judgment which follows Armageddon. Instead He answered the disciples' question concerning His coming and the end of the age in a straightforward manner. He told them things which must precede His coming, and that they would be gathered when He appeared at the sixth seal. He also warned of the need for readiness, so that when He appears we are not left behind or else ashamed before Him at His coming.

Pre-tribs often turn to the dragnet parable (Matt 13:47-50) to support that the individuals are actually taken to judgment rather than raptured by quoting the last two verses. Let's look at the whole parable:

> 47. Again, the kingdom of heaven is like a dragnet that was cast into the sea and gathered some of every kind, 48. which, when it was full, they drew to shore; and they sat down and gathered the good into vessels, but threw the bad away. 49. So it will be at the end of the age. The angels will come forth, separate the wicked from among the just, 50. and cast them into the fire.

They take the last two verses, which would seem to support their concept, but notice verse 48. This clearly says they first gathered the good fish into vessels, and then threw away the bad. Similarly, in the parable of the minas (Luke 19:12-17) Jesus taught He would come to judge and reward the saints, and then destroy His enemies. The parable of the wheat and tares agrees perfectly (Matt 13:30; see also Matt 3:12), where the tares are bundled and laid to the side while the wheat is put in the barn (raptured), and then the tares are finally burned. (We will look at these again, later.) As Robert Van Kampen notes, there is no prophetic passage in either Testament supporting the idea that God takes or receives the ungodly directly for judgment when He comes.

Actually, some pre-tribs have also recognized the example of Noah best fits the rapture. For example, Jerry Vines summarizes:

> When the great flood occurred, only the people in the ark escaped the devastation. When the rapture occurs, only the

born-again people of God will be taken away to safety.34

While I agree, pre-tribs who believe this is the rapture must ignore the context in which it was given the gathering of elect when the tribulation is cut short. There is no suggestion of an earlier coming even suggested. Also, nothing in what Jesus said even implies God's wrath until the sixth seal gathering of the elect, and the flood is obviously equated to God's wrath.

Yet many say the great tribulation is God's wrath. Jesus claimed that the great tribulation would be more severe than any that had gone before (Matt 24:21), as did Daniel (12:1). So the great tribulation will be more severe than the ancient, worldwide flood? Something doesn't quite compute, here. On the one side, some survive the great tribulation and wrath to enter the millennial kingdom; on the other side of their equation, God brought a great flood which destroyed all human and non-aquatic animal life except those previously placed on the ark. Again, on the first side some, perhaps many, wicked survive through the great tribulation to be slain at Armageddon and the sheep and goat judgment (Matt 25). But on the second side all the wicked are killed within days after God's rain of wrath begins, none surviving.

This equation does not balance, so it is in error. The great flood was certainly more severe in nature than the great tribulation or God's end-time wrath. The flood lasted for one year and killed all the ungodly, while the Tribulation lasts three-and-a-half and still leaves some wicked to face judgment as goats. God's wrath and the great tribulation cannot be synonymous. The great tribulation is actually Satan's wrath (Rev 12). It is comparable to previous beast empires which came against Israel. God's wrath, as we will see in a later chapter, must be separated from the great tribulation.

---

34 "I Shall Return"...Jesus, Jerry Vine: First Baptist church, Jacksonville, FL, 1977 [orig. published by Victor Books, Wheaton, IL]

Noah and Lot

In Luke 17:22-36 Jesus gave further instruction about the world system at His second coming. He used the same historical example of Noah, and included Lot as a parallel. Notice Jesus again privately discusses this with the disciples.

In the first three verses Jesus warns that the time will come when believers will desperately long for and lust after (Strong's # 1937) the return of Jesus, but will not see it yet. Much of the church today does not feel such desperation of Christ's return. Many live in countries where they can practice their faith in relative safety. While they may somewhat wish for Christ's return, they are not really consumed with the desire. In fact, many really desire His continued delay so they can keep enjoying life in this world. Once the terrible persecutions of the fourth seal come, those who stand for Christ will begin to truly desire His speedy return.

In verse 23 Jesus warns against false christs, as He did repeatedly in Matthew 24. When Christians so desperately long for Christ, those who are not alert or properly taught may be deceived into following rumors of a secret coming. Jesus repeatedly warns that ***He will not come in secret!*** His true coming will be unmistakable with a darkening of heavenly lights and a worldwide earthquake. Then His sign shall appear like lightning, and He will appear in the sky in glory with His angels. I know I repeat myself, but I want everyone to know the truth, just as Jesus did when He put so much emphasis on it!

Then Jesus uses the most frequently cited historical example, that of Noah:

> (Luke 17:26, 27) *And as it was in the days of Noah, so it will be also in the day of the Son of Man: they ate, they drank, they married wives, they were given in marriage, until the day that Noah entered the ark, and the flood came and destroyed them all.*

Pre-tribs misinterpret these verses in three primary ways. Dake says this relates to Armageddon:

> *Destroyed them all* (Luke 17:27), that is, the ones that needed to be destroyed and saved Noah and family, so Christ will destroy some at His coming and leave some to replenish the earth in the millennium.35

He misses the entire point. Jesus clearly stated Noah was put in the ark *before* the rest were destroyed. Dake insists some were destroyed by God's wrath while others were kept safe through it to replenish the earth. The second example, Lot's deliverance from Sodom, confirms that His point is physical separation of the elect before wrath. Unless following a post-trib understanding of prophecy, nowhere does the Bible describe protection through God's wrath (except the 144,000; Rev 7:1-7) for some to enter the millennial kingdom, and Dake is pre-trib. His view is untenable.

The second pre-trib case is to include Enoch in the historical example. Enoch was translated to heaven before the flood (Gen 5:24). They say that he represents the rapture of the church while Noah pictures the remnant of Israel and/or a great multitude saved within the seventieth week. Just as Enoch was translated before the flood, so will the church before the seven years; And just as Noah was protected through the flood, so will those who pass through the Tribulation to enter the millennial kingdom.

The most glaring problem is that Enoch is never mentioned as an example for the gathering of the church - anywhere. Second, Enoch was translated at least *669 years before* the flood, for that is how long Methuselah lived following his disappearance - an awfully long gap to demonstrate their point. Third, the example of Lot contains no parallel to support the point. Lastly, this interpretation assumes Matthew 24:29-31 is Armageddon, a position impossible to defend as we have already seen.

---

[35] Dake's, op. cit., Note on Matthew 24:39

The third common misinterpretation is explained by McLean:

> After Noah's family and the animals entered the ark, the flood waters did not begin for seven days (Gen 7:7, 10).36

This allows them to place the rapture of the church at the beginning of the seven years. This demonstrates their recognition that these examples best fit the rapture before God's wrath, with which pre-wraths agree. Thus it at least partly recognizes the truth.

However, a number of serious problems arise. First is the context of Matthew 24, where the only coming of Jesus is with the sixth seal. Further, this pre-trib view means the flood *must* equate with Armageddon so it can be seven years after the rapture, and the coming in Matthew cannot be at Armageddon.

The second problem is even greater. Jesus stated unequivocally that the floods came on the *same day* that Noah entered the ark. He said the same in the example of Lot. Both describe the righteous removed to safety on the same day wrath came. To be completely fair we should look at the account in Genesis to determine who correctly understood it, Jesus or these pre-tribs.

> (Gen 7:1, 2, 4) *Then the Lord said to Noah, "Come into the ark, you and all your household, because I have seen that you are righteous before me in this generation. You shall take with you seven each of every clean animal, a male and his female: two each of animals that are unclean, a male and his female...for after seven more days I will cause it to rain on the earth for forty days and forty nights, and I will destroy from the face of the earth all living things that I have made.*

They take *after seven more days* to mean that Noah was shut up in the ark seven days before the rain began. And if you stopped reading in verse 10 this could be a reasonable deduction. But considering Jesus' clear explanation, it should be obvious some fact is missing:

---

[36] "Another Look at Rosenthal's Pre-Wrath Rapture", John Mclean; <u>Bibliotheca Sacra</u>, Oct-Dec 1991, p394

(Gen 7:11-13) *In the six hundredth year of Noah's life, in the second month, the seventeenth day of the month, on that day all of the fountains of the great deep were broken up, and the windows of heaven were opened up. And the rain was on the earth forty days and forty nights. ON THE VERY SAME DAY NOAH AND NOAH'S SONS...ENTERED THE ARK.*

In other words, Noah and family were shut up in the ark the very same day the floods began. How clear is that? In fact, the portion I emphasized seems to have been stressed by God Himself in the very wording of the passage, as if to prevent the exact error we are discussing. Thus we find a unified teaching in Scripture that the church will be raptured on the same day Jesus is revealed from heaven on *the day of the Son of Man*, escaping His wrath. In chapter nine we will see that God's wrath is tied to the sixth seal.

But what about the seven days? This is how long it took Noah and his family - only eight people, remember - to load all the animals and remaining supplies into the ark. Creation scientists estimate around 35,000 animals entered the ark, the average size likely about that of a sheep. [The vast majority of species could survive the flood, including most insects, some amphibians, and all full-time water-dwelling creatures. Only a relatively small number of kinds of animal needed saving.] The ark was as large as a WWII aircraft carrier, easily capable of carrying the animals, food, and water, with room to spare. 37 It would have taken some time to make the final preparations when the time came for Noah to enter the ark.

There *may* be a symbology in the seven days, though. Noah was shut in the ark on the seventh day, the same day as the flood. This would support either a pre-wrath or a post-trib rapture, but none of the other views. A close look gives the edge for this interpretation to pre-wrath. If we equate the seven days to the seven years of the

---

[37] Acts and Facts; *Act #273: A Resource for Answering Critics of Noah's Ark*, John Woodmorappe: Institute for Creation Research, El Cajon, CA (www.icr.org)

seventieth week, then in the seventh year the rapture takes place. A couple of Old Testament passages suggest God's wrath is a year of recompense (see chapter nine). Then we look at Genesis and realize the flood lasted about a year (Gen 7:11 and 8:13). The church is exempt from DOL wrath, so we would be removed at the start of that Day.

Many teachers ignore or minimize the example of Lot (Luke 17:28-30) and focus nearly all their attention on Noah. This is probably because it contains none of the extraneous details as above that they can twist to make it fit their theories. They either miss it blindly or figure they can fast-talk their way past this example. But Jesus included it to help insure the correct understanding. Lot and His family were completely removed from the scene of God's wrath before it fell on Sodom and Gomorrah. Therefore, just as Lot was delivered before God's wrath, so was Noah, and so it will be for the righteous saints when Jesus returns. Jesus left no other options.

> (Luke 17:28-30) *Likewise as it was also in the days of Lot: they ate, they drank, they bought, they sold, they planted, they built; but on the day that Lot went out of Sodom it rained fire and brimstone from heaven and destroyed them all. Even so will it be in the day the Son of Man is revealed* [*apokalupsis,* unveiled].

First note the word *likewise*, indicating both examples teach the same truth. Second, it was business as usual until the day Lot left Sodom, at which point wrath fell. And lastly, this pattern will be repeated when Jesus returns.

Let's briefly review the original account (Gen 19). Two angels, appearing as men, came to Sodom to determine whether a sufficient number of righteous people lived there to forestall God's destruction of the region, in accordance with Abraham's deal with God (Gen 18:17-33). Lot invited them to stay at his house. A group of men saw them and came to try to homosexually rape them. Lot tried to turn them away from their purpose by offering his two virgin daughters - the law of hospitality in that culture and

98

time requiring the host to protect his guests at all costs to avoid wars. But the Sodomites would have none of it. They forced their way in, tired of the judgment of his righteousness (v. 9). Even when the angels struck them blind, they kept coming.

Then the angels gathered Lot's family and hurriedly led them out of the region marked for destruction. As soon as they were clear fire and brimstone began falling. It was still the same day. McLean argues:

> Genesis 19:15-19 suggests that a period of time may have elapsed between Lot's escape from Sodom to the small town of Zoar and God's outpouring of judgment on the wicked in Sodom and Gomorrah. Lot's escape began at dawn (v.15) and brimstone and fire did not fall on the twin cities till Lot reached Zoar and "the sun had risen over the earth."[38]

He compares this to the seven day period in the flood account to demonstrate a gap between deliverance and wrath. But this says it was the same day, as even McLean admitted. Jesus also said it was the same day. A gap of a couple of hours does nothing to support the pre-trib case, but fits in fine with pre-wrath.

Jesus' comparison of the last days with the days of Lot seems increasingly apt when you look at today's society. The homosexual lifestyle is becoming more and more acceptable in much of the world. They are even taking away the rights of those who believe it is sin so they can practice it without rebuke.

In fact, part of their agenda is to force or influence acceptance of their lifestyle by the church, or else takes away our freedom of speech. This is seen in the way some denominations have accepted practicing homosexuals into the pulpit and defend it as acceptable to God. This is prefigured prophetically by the example of Lot. Lot's household represents the church, to be delivered when God's wrath begins. The homosexuals have inserted themselves into the

---

[38] "Another Look at Rosenthal's Pre-Wrath Rapture"; Bibliotheca Sacra, p 394

church. Those who partake in this abomination, like those in the example of Lot, have been struck spiritually blind. They will likely be left behind when the church is rescued.

And lest it seem I am picking on homosexuals, many other evils prevailed in Sodom, just as in Noah's day. God's judgment came because of evil minds in general, not for a specific sin. We live in evil days when violence, hatred, and acceptance of sin abound. It has even infiltrated the professing church. Scripture says this would typify the last days.

In another attempt to discredit pre-wrath, Arnold Fruchtenbaum argues:

> When Rosenthal cites Luke 17:30, he even misses the point of his own analogy! Jesus is describing what will be the "days" of the Son of Man, using a plural, not a singular (Luke 17:22). The question pertains to: what will the world society be like, and be doing when the climactic changes take place? Jesus answers that society will be eating and drinking, marrying and given in marriage. This was true in "the *days* of Noah" (Luke 17:25-27) and in the "*days* of Lot" (Luke 17:28-29). In verse 30, when the phrase is used *after the same manner*, it is *not* a reference to judgment coming immediately after deliverance, but it is a reference to the practice of eating and drinking, marrying and giving in marriage. That is the real point of the analogy in its own context, and not what Rosenthal wishes to teach: judgment immediately follows rescue.39

This is an example of taking half the context and calling it a whole. I agree these relate to society in the last days. But both examples say this continues until the *day* the righteous were delivered, and then God's wrath fell on the same day.

---

39 A Review of "The Pre-Wrath Rapture of the Church" by Marvin Rosenthal, Dr. Arnold G. Fruchtenbaum: Ariel Ministries, PO Box 3723, Tustin, CA, p. 19

Additionally, verse 31 warns us not to go collect our things *in that day*, suggesting something will happen almost immediately. This does not parallel the similar warning at the flight from Judea (Matt 24:15-20) for two reasons. First, those in Matthew are told to flee from the Abomination, while those in Luke 17 are not told to flee.

Second, and more importantly, the immediately following verses describe the individuals taken or left behind, which Matthew 24 relates to the gathering of elect at the sixth seal. ***Remember Lot's wife*** (Luke 17:32), who looked back on Sodom and the things she was leaving behind! Don't worry about the things you are leaving behind, but look forward to the things you are going to gain when Christ comes to catch away his church to heaven. Looking back reveals the real treasure of your heart.

And finally, why would Jesus have bothered to specify God's deliverance of the righteous before God's wrath fell unless it was part of the message? All the usual business merely leads up to *the day of the Son of Man*. Fruchtenbaum accuses Rosenthal of ignoring the context while focusing his entire argument on a single word. You decide who is true to the context.

There are even more problems. These verses say it will be business as usual until *the day the Son of Man is revealed*. Mankind will be oblivious to the approaching wrath until it punches them in the nose. If the rapture were to occur any significant time before this day, it could hardly catch the world by surprise. The sudden disappearance of 500,000,000 people or more (half the professed Christians, five wise and foolish virgins) would alert the whole world the Bible is true. When the favorite pre-trib thriller stories of unpiloted planes and missing loved ones took place, it could not help but fill all the news channels. Dwight Pentecost claims that this translation of believers apparently has little effect on those left behind. He thinks they will be totally indifferent to the significance of the great disappearance.[40]

---

[40] Prophecy for Today, J. Dwight Pentecost: Discovery House

That is totally illogical. On the contrary, there would be mass panic. Christians will have preached the gospel to all nations (Matt 28:19; Act 1:8), so every land would have witnesses to the truth. Those who had heard but not really believed would be left behind to remember and tell others what happened. Furthermore, pre-trib practically requires that the rapture have considerable effect on society, for a great multitude from all nations appears in heaven out of the great tribulation, having put faith in Christ (Rev 7:9ff).

Perhaps someone will point out how the plagues God brought upon Egypt did not convince the Pharaoh to let Israel go, thus the rapture wouldn't necessarily frighten the world. Don't forget, however, that when the last plague brought death to the firstborn, their loved ones, the Pharaoh immediately told Israel to leave. The loss of loved ones was a plague they could not ignore. Likewise, the sudden disappearance of loved ones at the pre-trib rapture would have an effect. Furthermore, just because Pharaoh refused to listen does not mean the entire populace was in agreement.

There is an even more significant problem with equating this day with His coming at Armageddon. Supposedly, it will be business as usual until the day He is revealed (apokalupsis). All literal views agree Armageddon follows the trumpet and bowl judgments - Scripture is clear on this. Have you ever read what will happen during these judgments (Rev 8, 9, 16)? Have you ever considered such a claim in the light these? If not, then do so now. Go ahead and read these three chapters - I'll wait for you.......

To summarize, God's wrath includes demons tormenting those who take the mark of the beast, at least one-third of mankind killed by a great (possibly demonic) army, fire mixed with blood destroying one-third of earth's vegetation, water turning to blood, scorching heat, and world-spanning earthquakes. The list goes on and on. We don't even know what the seven thunders might produce (Rev 10:3, 4).

Publisher, Grand Rapids, MI, 1989, pp 29-30

Could it be that, while all these horrifying and deadly judgments are falling, it will be business as usual? While God's furious wrath produces disaster after disaster on a global scale the like of which has not been seen since the flood over the space of perhaps a couple of years? *Reality check*!

Matthew 24:37-51 warns that Christ's coming will be like a thief, with the only coming described in context in 24:29-31. If this coming is Armageddon, then mankind would have to ignore judgments that make the Egyptian plagues of frogs and flies seem like a day at the park on a warm summer's day to have business as usual up until the apocalypse of Christ. This point alone **destroys *any* position** which claims Matthew 24:29-31 is Armageddon.

So what is the proper interpretation of these examples in their context? (Luke 17, Matt 24:29-51; Mark 13:24-37; Luke 21:25-28, 36; 1Thess 4:13-5:11; 2Thess 1:6-2:12; and Rev 6:12-8:7). These passages naturally combine, showing specific heavenly signs announcing God's wrath surprising the world, and the gathering of the elect to heaven at the rapture. Thus they meet all the requirements of prophecy - rapture before wrath and Christ coming like a thief on the world. No glaring problems arise.

Scripture uniformly teaches that it will be business as usual in the world even after the Antichrist comes on the scene, because they will be blind to his true identity. When the great tribulation is amputated the elect are gathered away from the trumpets of wrath at the sixth seal. The saints of Jesus will be removed to a safe place, like Noah, escorted by angels, like Lot. Jesus' parables in Matthew 13 confirm this. The wheat and tares are allowed to grow together. At the harvest at the end of the age the tares are bundled and laid to the side until the wheat is gathered into the barn, then the tares are burned, following customs of the day.41 When Jesus appears in the sky, mankind will know they are in deep trouble.

As we continue to study, we will see this is the consistent teaching of Scripture.

---

[41] The Pre-Wrath Rapture of the Church, p. 225

Chapter 7: 2Thessalonians

We saw strong evidence in Matthew 24 that the church will enter the great tribulation. Some argue, though, that Paul taught a pre-trib rapture. In truth, Paul's teaching fully agrees with what we have already seen.

> (2Thess2:1-4) *Now brethren, concerning the coming [parousia] of the Lord and our gathering together to Him, we ask you not to be soon shaken in mind or troubled...as though the Day of Christ has come. Let no-one deceive you by any means, for that day will not come unless the falling away come first, and the man of sin is revealed, the son of perdition, who...exalts himself above all that is called God...so that he sits in the temple of God....*

First notice the topic is both the rapture (*our gathering to Him*) and Christ's parousia. Paul places both events under one heading, the Day of Christ - or as many translations read, the Day of the Lord. Regarding this variant, most of the earliest manuscripts read *Day of the Lord*, but some say *Christ*.

Oliver B. Greene will serve to represent the typical pre-trib understanding of this passage:

> These false teachers [that Paul is refuting] had declared that the tribulation was already upon them [undermining their faith]; but the Apostle Paul, through the inspiration of the Holy Spirit, assured them that they had nothing to worry about because they were not in the great tribulation – nor would they be, because believers are to be taken out of the world before the Man of Sin shall be revealed.42

I agree that they misunderstood the timing of the rapture. The verb *has come* is the Greek word *enesteiken*, which can mean either something already happening or something which is impending (see 1Cor 7:26). If the latter was intended, then Paul

---

42 The Second Coming of Jesus, Oliver B. Greene: The gospel Hour, inc., Greenville, SC 29602, 1971, pp. 224-225

was rebuking the belief in an any moment rapture. Context supports this. In Paul's first letter he taught them that the church would be removed **before** God's DOL wrath (1Thess 1:10; 5:1-11). This church was undergoing severe persecution, causing some to think Christ's coming was impending already. This thinking was in accordance with the Lord's teaching in Matthew 24 of persecution before the sixth seal gathering. Some had even stopped working in anticipation (2Thess 3:6-12).

This required Paul to correct their eschatology and to rebuke them for ceasing their employment. He pointed out two events which must precede this Day - an apostasy and the revealing of Antichrist, when he sits in the holy place at the Abomination of Desolation. I believe the following paraphrase accurately explains what Paul said:

> Now brothers, concerning the second coming and the rapture: don't worry and don't believe rumors to the contrary, for this Day is not imminent. In fact - and don't heed anything contradictory or you will be deceived - that day will not come until after the falling away, and until after the beast Antichrist is revealed.

The Apostasy

What is this *falling away* which must precede the rapture and the DOL? Some pre-tribs mistakenly translate this Greek word as *the departure* in an attempt to make it the departure of the church. This conveniently makes the rapture precede the coming of Antichrist - or so they would have you believe. Mark Cambion explains their reasoning:

> The King James Version was the first translation to render the word *apostasia* as meaning *falling away*. The early translations, such as the Wycliffe and the Tyndale, translated it *departure*. We believe that departure is a better rendition of the word apostasia, for in the light of the context it fits in

106

perfectly, showing the departure of the church must take place before the Antichrist is revealed.43

Three facts destroy this. First, he decided the correct translation based on his pre-trib doctrine rather than by the normal usage of the word when it was written. With a little research he would soon have discovered the word *apostasia* typically has negative connotations. This is regretfully but honestly admitted by pre-trib Herbert Vander Lugt.44 This word is used in Acts 21:21 by unbelieving Jews accusing Paul of telling them to *forsake* Moses' teaching on circumcision, and in Joshua 22:22 to describe rebellion against God. The neuter form of the word, *apostasion*, is used in Matthew 5:31 and 19:7 as a bill of divorce. Some pre-tribs, then, try to turn a negative word into a positive.

Second, the early translators would not have understood the term *departure* that way. Prior to the 1800's most scholars held an amillennial eschatology. Those who did not, such as Luther, were usually historicists. They believed the Antichrist had already come in the form of the papal throne, and that the apostasy was associated with this.

The third problem is that it does NOT *fit in perfectly, in the light of the context.* Quite the contrary, such a view creates an irreconcilable paradox. I again paraphrase, substituting the word *rapture* for the apostasia:

> Now brothers, concerning the coming of the Lord and the rapture...this day cannot happen unless the rapture come first and the Antichrist be revealed.

Remember the second coming and rapture are associated by Paul together as the Day of the Lord. Thus this would say that the rapture must precede the rapture. Hunh?

---

43 Come Lord Jesus, Mark Cambion: Zondervan Publishing House, Grand Rapids, MI, 1959, pp 8-9
44 There's a New Day Coming, Herbert Vander Lugt: Radio Bible Class, 1983, p19

Let's allow Scripture to interpret Scripture. In Matthew 24:10 it says many will be offended because of the rising persecution. The Greek word is *skandalon*, from which we get our word *scandalized*. It implies they fall away because of offense (Strong's # 4624 and 4625). The Amplified Bible makes this clearer:

(Matt 24:10) *And then many will be offended and repelled and will begin to distrust and desert [Him whom they ought to trust and obey] and will stumble and fall away and betray one another and pursue one another with hatred.*

Notice the skandalon begins prior to, or in relation to, the Abomination. This is consistent with 2Thessalonians.

This apostasy consists of professing Christians, for in order to be offended and fall away there must first be something from which to fall away. This word is used for rebellion against God, so it involves leaving the true gospel of Christ. Several passages prophesy this for the last days (1Tim 4:1-3; 2Tim 3:1-9; 2Pet 3:1ff). Daniel 11:31-35 warns that some who claim to know God, but don't, fall away due to the great tribulation (12:1). Also, some who do know God will fall temporarily [probably carnal believers and, perhaps, dogmatic pre-tribs [grin]], so their hearts be purified before Christ's coming. Some of those who stumble will receive help, but Daniel warns that many will join with them by intrigue [fakeness, slipperiness], pretending to help only to betray them. Jesus also warns of betrayers (Matt 24:10).

If we examine the church today, we can see there has truly been a falling away from God's ways and commandments, rebellion against sound doctrine. But this is only the prelude to the coming apostasy. Many professing believers have never faced serious persecution, and many churches teach an escape mentality - that we will be raptured out before it gets really bad. Many in the church are not ready to pay the potential cost of their faith (Luke 14:23-33). As persecution gradually increases during the first half of the seventieth week, some will turn away. Then as the church enters the great tribulation under the not-so-tolerant care of the Antichrist, the falling away shall only increase.

This will not merely be the moral apostasy we see today, but outright rejection of Christ. The fourth seal threatens Death to God's people, with Hades following to claim those who choose Antichrist. It is for this reason the great tribulation is called the hour of testing (Rev 3:10). It is a time of winnowing, when the chaff and tares are separated from the wheat (Matt 13:12-43), proving who has genuine faith. When Jesus returns, will He find true faith remaining on earth (Luke 18:8)?

Many pre-tribs are not prepared for severe persecution because they are taught a *great escape* mentality. This view is most popular in the United States and parts of Europe, where Christians have had considerable freedom to practice their faith for generations. When they suddenly find themselves facing the great tribulation, many will quickly fall away because they were not prepared to endure to the end. Scripture frequently exhorts believers to be ready to endure tribulations and persecutions which test the genuineness of our faith. But all too often pre-tribs do not address this possibility.

> Reasons can be found why God will send a time of distress to both the Jews ad the Gentiles, but there are no reasons why the final generation of Christians should be subject to divine wrath ....No-one has been able to explain how the sufferings of Christians during the final seven years before the second coming of Christ could benefit them or the body of Christ.[45]

Actually, Scripture provides explicit reasons why it is possible. Let me first make it clear we will NOT face God's wrath, for we are promised deliverance away from wrath. But we are subject to discipline, and this will in part be a time of chastisement (Rev 2:5; 3:3) and disciplinary judgment (Rev 2:16). Revelation 3:10 calls this a time of testing. The Greek word *peirasmos* conveys they idea of proving or purifying as gold is tested by fire. Let me re-emphasize that the great tribulation is not God's wrath.

---

[45] The Final Chapter, Maxwell S. Coder, op. cit., p. 152

Judgment begins with the house of the Lord (1Pet 4:16-17). Jesus is coming for a bride that is blameless, without spot or wrinkle, who has purified herself (Eph 5:27; 2Pet 3:14; Rev 19:7), *that when He appears, we may have confidence and not be ashamed before Him at His coming* (1John 2:28). Hebrews 12 says one more time God is going to shake the heavens and the earth so that everything which can be shaken loose will be, so that what remains cannot be shaken by anything. Much of the church today is wishy-washy and self-indulgent, and needs a good shaking up. Believers will be purified by the testing and proving of their faith, that *the genuineness of our faith, being much more precious than gold that perishes, though it is tested* (peirasmos) *by fire, may be found to praise, honor, and glory at the apocalypse of Jesus Christ* (1Pet 1:6-7).

We should not expect to avoid tribulations, but to count it all joy when they come as they produce perseverance, godly character, and hope (Rom 5:3-5). 2Thessalonians 1:4-8 declares there is even some cause for boasting when we endure tribulations and persecutions with perseverance and faith; These things show that God's judgment of the world is righteous and just (see Ph'p 1:28).

This is exactly how the early church felt. For example, Iranaeus said:

> 4. And therefore throughout all time, man, having been molded at the beginning by the hands of God, that is, of the Son and of the Spirit, is made after the image and likeness of God: the chaff, indeed, which is the apostasy, being cast away; but the wheat, that is, those who bring forth fruit to God in faith, being gathered into the barn. And for this cause tribulation is necessary for those who are saved, that having been after a manner broken up, and rendered fine, and sprinkled over by the patience of the Word of God, and set on fire [for purification], they may be fitted for the royal banquet. As a certain man of ours said, when he was condemned to the wild beasts because of his testimony with respect to God: "I am the wheat of Christ, and am ground by the teeth of the wild beasts, that I may be found the pure bread of God." (Against Heresies, V, 28)

The Restrainer

2Thessalonians 2:5-12 proclaims God's sovereign control over all that happens in the great tribulation.

> (2:6-8) *And now you know what is restraining, the he [the man of sin] may be revealed in his own time. For the mystery of lawlessness is already at work; only he who now restrains will do so until he is taken out of the way. And then the lawless one will be revealed...*

Several possibilities have been suggested for the identity of this restrainer, such as human government, the visible church, the Holy Spirit, and the Archangel Michael. We will look at each of these.

> Many biblical commentators from Tertullian (c.AD200) on have identified the restrainer as the Roman Empire. The neuter participle [*what withholds*] would refer to the state, the masculine [*he*], to the emperor... But the Roman Empire has long since faded away, and the lawless one has not yet been revealed. Thus it seems probable that the restraining influence refers to the principle of human government manifest in the Roman state.46

Dwight Pentecost offers this simple refutation:

> Explanations as to the person of this restrainer such as human government, law, or the visible church will not suffice, for they will all continue in a measure after the manifestation of this lawless one....47

Government and law will not be removed by Antichrist, but subject to his rule.

---

46 The Wycliffe Bible Commentary: Moody Bible Institute of Chicago, 1962, p. 1364
47 Things To Come, op. cit., p. 205

The next view, popular among pre-tribs, identifies him as the Holy Spirit. Most believe the restrainer is the Spirit as He holds back the forces of iniquity through His indwelling presence in believers.48 Pentecost concludes that while debatable, it seems to him the only one capable of doing such a restraining ministry would be the Holy Spirit. His conclusion seems somewhat tentative, as if he recognizes he has no scriptural support.

Henry Thiessen musters up one verse in support (Gen 6:3) where God's Spirit is represented as striving against wicked mankind in the days of Noah, and that He *shall not strive with man forever*:

> When He ceased opposing the wickedness of man, the judgments of God burst forth on the world. It would seem that He is the restrainer also in the end time, when the days of Noah are to be repeated. He does the restraining of evil, often through the church; ...when the church will be caught up, the salt and light will be withdrawn. For a brief time after the rapture, until individuals turn to the Lord, there will be no saved people on the earth. Evidently, the Spirit will withdraw His special ministry of restraining evil.... Then iniquity will abound, and the man of lawlessness will be revealed.49

There are several problems with this view. The first is experiential. The fact that Christians are constrained to live righteously has never had more than a minimal effect on how unbelievers choose to live. Also, 2Peter 2 and 3 suggests the world will gradually get worse and worse as the end time approaches, whereas the restrainer seems to be removed all at once.

Second, the restrainer is not said to move out of the way at the start of the seventieth week. Paul clearly associates his removal with the revealing of the man of sin as he sits in the temple of God demanding worship. This takes place at the Abomination in the middle of the week, thus cannot be a pre-trib removal of the church.

---

48 There's a New Day Coming, op. cit., p. 19
49 Lectures in Systematic Theology, Henry Thiessen: Wm. B. Eerdman's Publishing Co., Grand Rapids, MI, 1979, pp 353-354

Thiessen maintained that the Spirit was restraining evil in Genesis 6:3.   Actually, He was not so much restraining wickedness as He was calling on man to repent.   In John 16:8-11 Jesus taught that His ministry to unbelievers is to convict them of their sin so they might turn to righteousness and not be judged alongside the devil.   It does not say He restrains the evil inclinations of man.

Furthermore, it is not lawlessness in general which is being restrained, but *the mystery of lawlessness*. It is the spiritual forces behind the Antichrist being restrained. In 1Timothy 3:16 we learn that the *mystery of godliness* is God manifested in the flesh - Jesus Himself. The anti-thesis to Christ is Antichrist, the man of sin and mystery of iniquity, who will be possessed by Satan. Thus it is the devil being restrained from bringing his full weight on the world through the beast, not wickedness in general. Revelation 12:12 says Satan will attack without restraint when he is cast out of heaven.

Most pre-tribs teach there will be a great, worldwide revival following the rapture, because a great multitude from every tongue comes out of the great tribulation trusting in Christ (Rev 7:9-17). The Holy Spirit is inextractibly tied to the salvation process (John 16:8-11), indwells every believer in Christ (1Cor 6:19), and will continue to do so even until the Day of the Lord arrives with the sixth seal (Joel 2:28-31). Thus with this supposed revival He would once again quickly exert this restraining influence on the world. So even if it is the Holy Spirit who hinders the mystery of iniquity, it cannot be His influence through the church which restrains. Paul Feinberg admits this:

> ...This text is compatible with either post-tribulation or pre-tribulation views of the Rapture.   The passage nowhere requires that the restrainer be removed from the world, only that he ceases his restraining ministry so that evil can run its course. That is possible on any Rapture position.50

---

50 The Rapture: Pre-,..., op. cit., p. 229

If the restrainer is not the church, human government, or the Holy Spirit, then who is he? I believe Scripture clearly reveals this with a little digging, by comparing Daniel 12:1 with Revelation 12. Let's look at Daniel.

At that time [the Archangel] Michael shall **stand up***, the great prince who stands watch over the sons of your people [Israel]; and there shall be a time of trouble, such as never was since there was a nation, even to that time.*

The Hebrew word *'amad* is translated *stand up* in most English translations here (Strong's #5975). But this Hebrew can also mean *stand still* or *cease*, and is often so translated in the Old Testament: *stand here awhile* (1Sam 9:27); *stood still* (2Sam 2:28); *ceased* (2Kings 4:6); and others. If a man is reclining or seated and is said to *'amad*, he will stand up. If a man is standing up and active, then he will stand still. Daniel 10:13, 21 describes the Archangel Michael as actively defending Israel already. Thus when he is said to *'amad*, he stands still or ceases his defense on their behalf.

Let's look closer at Daniel 10:21, which is part of the same vision as 12:1. The angel says *"There is none who holds with me and strengthens himself against these [hostile spiritual forces - the prince of Persia] except Michael, your prince [national guardian angel]"* (Amplified Version). The phrase *holds with... strengthens* can also be translated *restrains* (Strong's # 2388), and clearly pictures a restraining ministry for Michael.

Why would Israel's defender *stand up* only to allow the beast, backed by the same hostile spiritual forces as the prince of Persia, to bring the greatest persecution ever against those he is supposed to defend (Matt 24:21)? Or conversely, if he is restraining those evil forces now, how could he arise at the start of the great tribulation? Or do we believe, in the light of the Holocaust of WWII and other desolations of Jews, that the devil is not trying with all his might to annihilate them. The timing of Daniel 12:1 easily relates to that in 2Thessalonians 2.

114

Revelation 12 briefly describes the continuing war between God and Satan. It also describes Michael's restraining ministry until the beast is cast out of heaven just before the midpoint of the seventieth week. The first six verses discuss the establishment of Israel (12:1, see Gen 37:9), the promise and birth of Messiah (12:2), Satan's original rebellion and his attempt to kill Jesus at His birth (12:3, 4, see Matt 2:12-18), the ascension of Christ with a promise of His millennial kingdom (12:5), then briefly mentions Israel's flight into the wilderness at the Abomination of Desolation.

The rest of chapter twelve describe the dragon's attack against the woman Israel after being cast from heaven, and her flight into the wilderness for three-and-a-half years. No matter what the beast does in his attempt to utterly destroy them, God will thwart him. Enraged, the beast will then turn against *the rest of her offspring who have the testimony of Jesus*, the church. God is not restraining the devil here, but preserving a remnant. Aside from this, Satan is given free reign to rule the earth through his beast. He will be so cruel that Jesus promised those days would be amputated for the sake of the elect; else *no flesh* would survive (Matt 24).

In summary, it is the spiritual forces behind the man of sin which are being restrained in 2Thessalonians 2. The beast immediately comes against Israel in his wrath when the restraint is lifted, for he knows his time is short (Rev 12). In Daniel 12 Michael ceases restraining, allowing the greatest persecution ever (Matt 24:15-22), ultimately killing 2/3 of all Jews (Zech 13:7-9). All these clearly fit together, giving us a clear picture of the identity of the restrainer and the result when he is taken out of the way.

End Time Revival?

Pre-tribs insist there will be a great revival after the translation of the church to heaven. Some argue that it will be before, and some after, the Abomination of Desolation. The *only* scriptural basis for this revival is that they must somehow explain the innumerably great multitude coming out of the great tribulation, having been washed by the blood of the Lamb (Rev 7:9ff). For example, Vander Lugt explains:

> ...multiplied thousands of men and women will turn in faith to Jesus Christ and be saved during the second half of Daniel's Seventieth week... for a... multitude will believe on Christ.[51]

He goes on to say that Christians can take comfort that many of their loved ones who did not receive Christ will have a second chance to believe on Him during this time. Supposedly the atmosphere after the rapture will be conducive to drawing many to Christ. There are several scriptural problems with this. The first is found in our passage:

> (2Thess 2:9-12) *The coming of the lawless one is ... with all power, signs, and lying wonders, and with all unrighteous deception among those who perish, because they did not receive the love of the truth, that they might be saved. And for this reason GOD WILL SEND THEM STRONG DELUSION, that they should believe the lie, that they all be condemned who did not believe the truth but had pleasure in unrighteousness.* (Emphasis Mine)

Pay heed, it is specifically God who sends this delusion. This does not violate God's gift of the freedom to choose, for those affected have already had opportunity to receive salvation, but rejected it instead. The gospel has been preached world wide by this point. God will not always strive with men (Gen 6:3 - remember the days of the flood were like the day in which Jesus will return (Luke 17), see also Rom 1:24-32).

Vander Lugt counters that this delusion is only on those who have delight in wickedness, and not everyone who rejects the gospel can be classified as delighting in wickedness. But the context includes *those who are perishing (going to perdition) because they did not welcome the truth but refused to love it that*

---

[51] There's a New Day Coming, op. cit., p. 69

they might be saved (2:10 Amp). It is *for this reason* God sends the delusion. By rejecting the gospel they have, in essence, chosen wickedness, for true righteousness comes only through faith.

Again, this delusion does not violate God's gift of free will, for God is always sovereign. It is He who gave the choice between faith and unbelief, so to those who decide not to receive the love of the truth He is under no obligation to keep that choice open. He can send the delusion that they continue to believe the lie simply because He rules and can choose to take away the choice. Consider the child who refuses to eat his dinner. The parents may save the food for him to eat later, provide him with something he will eat, or just let him go without dinner - it is their decision which action to take and when, not the child's. Likewise, God now offers salvation. But He is perfectly justified to take the offer away from those who reject it - today, tomorrow, or during the seventieth week. Man's only say in the matter is to receive the love of the truth while the choice is available. (John 1:12, 13; Heb 3:7-10; 2Cor 6:2 and others)

Revelation 13:8 parallels this:

> *All who dwell on the earth will worship [the beast], whose names have not been written in the Book of Life of the Lamb slain from the foundation of the world.*

John reveals that those who are not saved prior to the rise of Antichrist will choose to worship him, either because they believe him or because they fear him. Paul said those who willfully rejected Christ will be deluded by God to believe the beast. This certainly leaves very little room for new conversions to Christ following the Abomination. The only second chance alluded for the end time in Scripture is the sheep and goat judgment (Matt 25:31ff). This chance is based, in large part, on the treatment of Jews and Christians during the great tribulation. They also likely obey the proclaiming angels who warn mankind to fear God and refuse the mark of the beast (Rev 14).

117

It is clear there cannot be a great, world-wide revival during the seventieth week. The only large-scale group which seems to be allowed repentance at this time is Israel. Dispensational theory teaches that the seventieth week is primarily for the final restoration of Israel, so this is consistent. First we see the 144,000 sealed by God at the sixth seal (Rev 6:12-7:8), at the same time the church is removed. Then at the seventh trumpet the rest of Israel has repented.

Look again at the historical examples of Noah and Lot (Luke 17:26-30). In neither case was a second chance provided; once the righteous were delivered and wrath came it was too late to repent. Thus even if the rapture happens to be pre-trib there could be no second chance for those who had heard the gospel. And since Revelation describes an innumerable host of saved Gentiles from the whole earth washed by the blood appearing in heaven from the great tribulation, we are left with the inescapable conclusion that the church cannot be raptured pre-tribulationally.

Another problem with this great revival is that nowhere does Scripture describe such an event. Instead it warns of a great apostasy, a scandalized falling away.

The great multitude of Revelation 7 is said to be so vast that *no-one can number them*. First, consider that John roughly estimated the number of angels before God's throne to be well over 100,000,000 (Rev 5:11). But he refused to even attempt numbering the great multitude, suggesting that it is many more.

For a moment let's assume a revival takes place, for argument's sake. That means perhaps 250,000,000 repent and trust in Jesus after the rapture (double the angels he saw), a mere 5% of the assumed post-rapture population of the earth. Surely such a large scale revival would receive greater attention than these few, ambiguous verses. Instead, Scripture describes apostasy and rebellion, and announces that mankind still refuses to repent even when they see God's wrath poured out (Rev 9:20).

On the other hand, the description of this great multitude fits perfectly the rapture and resurrection of the saints. The numbers who have trusted Christ throughout this age certainly numbers in the hundreds of millions, perhaps even billions. Nothing in the text requires that they all live during the great tribulation. All that is required is that they be removed from earth to stand before Jesus' heavenly throne from the midst of it. According to 1Thessalonians 4 we will meet the Lord in the air of the earthly realm after the resurrection, and then transfer to the heavenly realm. Thus we come out of the time of the great tribulation to stand before Jesus' throne (remember Luke 21:36). This great multitude is discussed in the context of the sixth seal, so can easily be related to the gathering of elect in Matthew 24 and Mark 13, which describes the same seal. Everything still fits together perfectly.

A final problem with the pre-trib claim of a post-rapture revival is the dispensational doctrine. Many pre-tribs insist that this doctrine is the ultimate proof for their position, some using very strong words to this effect. In Things to Come, Pentecost uses this doctrine as a battering ram against all the other theories, and it is the primary support for pre-trib raised up by Brainard, whose work I critique at the end of this book. Basically, they believe that the church must be removed as a primarily Gentile institution because God is focusing on the restoration of Israel during the seventieth week. But then, because of Revelation 7, they must claim that God will have a sort of bankruptcy plan for the Gentiles, for the great multitude comes from all nations. This violates their whole argument for using dispensationalism to prove the pre-trib rapture. Is God going to remove the predominantly Gentile institution of the church so Israel can be His focus, only to allow a great Gentile revival that will have an innumerable number of Gentiles saved? Sorry, the pieces don't fit, not even close. The dispensational theory will be fully discussed in chapter 10.

Based on what we have seen here, there is no legitimate support for a seventieth week revival. Rather, Scripture uniformly warns that their will be a great falling away, and that new conversions will be rare.

Chapter 8: The Church and Revelation

The purpose of the letters to the seven churches in Revelation 2 and 3 is another issue debated by the various theories. One verse in particular is hotly argued over. Before we look at this verse we must determine the reason these letters were written.

Pre-tribs propose two primary interpretations for these letters. First is that Jesus was addressing recurring problems which would rise up throughout the church age.

> The seven churches addressed in chapters 2 and 3 were actual churches of John's day. But they also represent types of churches in all generations. This idea is supported by the fact that only seven were selected out of the many that existed and flourished in John's time and by the statement at the close of each letter that the Spirit was speaking to the churches (vv7, 11, etc.). 52

It is true that these churches exhibited the points addressed in the letters.   However, his reasoning that they primarily represent recurring problems throughout the age lacks substance. While this may be partly true, we will see shortly that there was a deeper purpose.

The second pre-trib explanation is that they illustrate seven stages of church history. The following is one suggested outline for these stages:

Ephesus: The Apostolic church (AD30-100)

Smyrna: The persecuted church (100-313)

Pergamos: The state church (313-590)

---

52 <u>Ryrie Study Bible</u>, Charles C. Ryrie: Moody Press, Chicago, 1978, p. 1243

Thyatira: The Papal church (590-1517)

Sardis: The reformed church (1517-1790)

Philadelphia: The missionary church (1790-1900)

Laodicea: The apostate church (1900-present)

Rosenthal offers a three-fold rebuttal.[53] First, he notes nothing in the text offers any clues that this is the intent of the letters. Second, he asks how we are to determine the correct division of these supposed stages, as church history has never been that clear cut and historians differ on how to divide it. Third, these designated church ages do not conform to everything contained in the letters; If these were intended to primarily describe church stages then each would be required to match its prophecy on every detail to be true (Deut 18:20-22).

Add to these the fact that such a position creates irresolvable conflict with the theory of imminency so important to many pre-tribs. In its simplest form this theory states Christ could come for the church at any moment, with no prophecy requiring fulfillment beforehand. For this theory to be scripturally true, it **must have been true** from the very beginning of the church. Most pre-tribs believe exactly that, even claiming Jesus taught an any-moment coming to His disciples.

By suggesting these letters represent stages of church history they contradict not only themselves, but also make Jesus contradict his own supposed predictions of imminency. How could the early church have held to an any-moment rapture if Revelation taught seven complete church periods?

So, what was the purpose for these letters? Actually, they have a dual purpose. The first was to address issues with some of the churches in John's day. In tandem they give warnings to the church throughout this age by which we all should examine ourselves.

---

[53] The Pre-Wrath Rapture of the church, op. cit., pp 286-292

But the larger purpose was instruction to the end time church. Out of all the first century churches, Jesus selected these seven for this prophecy for two reasons. First, the number seven often signifies completion in Scripture. This suggests that the entire church is represented. Second, these illustrate the major groupings of churches entering the seventieth week. The shared problems and strengths provided an excellent frame of reference to instruct the church at the end of the age. This is the only view consistent with the stated purpose of Revelation - to describe in considerable detail the events surrounding the apocalypse of Jesus Christ from heaven (Rev 1:1).

Furthermore, Revelation is addressed to the church (Rev 1:1-4), and promises a blessing to those who read and obey the things written in it, for *the time is near* for these things to be fulfilled. Pre-tribs object, insisting only the first five chapters are relevant for the church, while the remainder is instructions for those left behind after the rapture. Revelation 22:16 confirms, however, that the **entire** book is *to testify to you these things in the churches.* As post-trib Douglas Moo observes:

> ...it simply appears improbable that the event described at greatest length in Revelation (the Tribulation) would have no *direct* relevance for those to whom the book is addressed.54

If this is true, then we should see evidence within the letters supporting this. It also would provide strong testimony for the church entering the seventieth week. This is why pre-tribs must seek out other explanations for the inclusion of these letters in a prophetic book specifically concerning the second coming. But they always fall short in some manner, negating God's warnings and instructions for the end time church.

Pre-tribs desperately and unconvincingly try to explain away the obvious, literal meaning of these, as they do other prophetic passages. For example, if pre-trib scholars did not explain that Matthew 24 is written primarily to the Jews rather than the church,

---

54 The Rapture..., op. cit., p. 203, emphasis his

the majority of Christians would naturally assume it was intended to instruct believers. That is precisely the first problem with pre-trib I found.

With Revelation they generally take a different tack - "It doesn't mean that. It means..." Instead of taking it to mean exactly what it says, they find some *spiritual* or allegorical interpretation so they can keep the church out of the seventieth week.

Jesus tells several churches He is coming soon. He warned Ephesus to repent lest He come quickly and remove their lampstand from its place (those who really are saved be raptured). He advised Pergamos that if they did not repent He would come quickly and fight against them with the sword of His mouth (2:16; see 19:15; those who are compromising enter judgment). To the few in Thyatira who had not fallen into spiritual adultery He encourages to hold fast *until He comes* (2:24, 25). And again, to Philadelphia the faithful church, Jesus encourages to keep persevering and promises that He comes quickly (3:10, 11).

Outside of these letters, every single time Scripture says He is coming quickly, it is either a reference to the rapture or the Day of the Lord. It is logical and consistent with the purpose of Revelation to deduct the same in these letters. If these represent primarily church ages then the Lord lied when He told them He is coming quickly, for each has long since passed. Now there are patterns often revealed in Scripture, so it is possible they also represent a general pattern for the history of the church. Also, certainly various individual churches have had similar issues. I do not mean to exclude these wider applications completely. But clearly the primary purpose is instructions for the end time church.

Thyatira was also given another warning which illustrates this more strongly. Jesus, eyes burning with anger, declares that those who committed spiritual adultery under the Jezebel teaching will be thrown into the great tribulation (2:22). Every other time the term *great tribulation* appears in Scripture it refers to the time of Antichrist (Matt 24:21; Mark 13:19; Rev 7:14). Revelation spends more space teaching about the last half of the seventieth

124

week than any other topic. Therefore, it is reasonable to conclude that this refers to the great tribulation rather than just a severe, general tribulation. Remember, it is in this context that the few faithful were promised Christ's quick return. While all believers will experience difficulties during the great tribulation, those of the Thyatiran type church are especially going to suffer, for God is going to throw them into it.

Every time the Bible says Jesus is coming as a thief it refers to the Day of the Lord beginning with the sixth seal. Jesus warned Sardis that if they do not get their act together, He will come upon them as a thief (Rev 3:1-6). Jesus previously gave this warning to those not watching and waiting for His second coming in the Olivet Discourse (Matt 24:32-51). Paul similarly admonished the Thessalonians; True believers are not in darkness that this Day should overtake them like a thief. We are of the day and are not appointed unto wrath, but unto deliverance (1Thess 5:1-11). But do not spiritually sleep, for those who do will be overtaken or surprised by the Day of the Lord. The dead church of Sardis, then, is warned to wake up and repent or else they will be overtaken by Christ's coming and the DOL.

Finally, each church is promised rewards for those who *overcome*. These promises are available to all believers who overcome, regardless of which church type. This is seen in that these promises are specifically given by the Spirit to the church*es*, not just to the church addressed in each letter. Rosenthal explains:

> To overcome is to vanquish the enemy, to be triumphant over difficulty. The entire context of the seven churches is set in the arena of the seventieth week and the activity of Satan and the Antichrist. Of those who are truly triumphant John wrote, "And they overcame him by the blood of the Lamb, and by the word of their testimony, and they loved not their lives unto the death [see Matt 10:38, 39]" (Rev 12:11); that is, they were willing to be martyrs, if being an overcomer required it.

In 1John 5:1-5 we learn that the one who overcomes the world is he who truly believes Jesus Christ is the Son of God, demonstrated by seeking to keep His commandments. This is how we overcome *by the blood of the Lamb and by the word of our testimony*. Also, we must endure to the end even if the end is death (Matt 10:21-24; 24:10, 13). In this way we checkmate the enemies of God. We can certainly be overcomers outside of the great tribulation and obtain these promises of God. But in Revelation 12:11 we see overcomers in the context of the great tribulation. This lends support to the eschatological significance of these letters.

In conclusion, these letters establish compelling testimony that the church will enter the great tribulation. While the intent of the letters is not to prove this, many allusions in them do prove it. We will see later that the early church also believed this to be true.

The Hour of Trial

Many pre-tribs raise up Revelation 3:10 as "proof" for their rapture position. This is the hotly debated verse I mentioned earlier. The first time a pre-trib presented this verse to me, shortly before I came across the pre-wrath position, I was unable to immediately answer his point. So I decided to do a word study using Strong's Concordance and Dictionary, and promptly realized this verse actually promises protection within the great tribulation, not avoidance of the seventieth week. Later, further research and reading confirmed the point and provided additional evidence.

> *"Because you have kept My command to persevere, I will also keep you from the hour of trial which shall come upon the whole earth to test those who dwell on the earth."*

First we must determine the identity of this *hour of trial*. Most pre-millennial scholars agree this pertains to the great tribulation, though many equate it to the entire seventieth week. Pre-tribs use the latter to defend their theory. For example, Paul Feinberg said,

> ...the hour of trial here seems to be universal as opposed to a local persecution (Rev 2:10). Thus, if the wrath is falling

126

everywhere, it is difficult to see how preservation could be by any other means than the Rapture, or removal. Furthermore, the purpose of the trial is to test earth-dwellers. The Greek word "to test" is used in both secular and biblical Greek of a test to reveal the true character of someone. There is generally a negative intent in the word, "to break down" or "to demonstrate failure." One of the purposes of this period then is to demonstrate the complete failure of unregenerate men before God. The Tribulation period is thus the final condemning evidence against the wicked.55

I agree a large part of the purpose of this time is to fully demonstrate the failure of the unsaved over the whole earth. But I believe it relates only to the great tribulation, not the entire week. In Revelation 17:12 the ten kings give power to the beast and reign with him for *one hour*, the hour of trial. Also, this testing is not merely God's DOL wrath, from which the church will be delivered, but also includes the wrath of Satan which God uses to test the hearts of men (Rev 12:12). This is not a literal hour but an unspecified, relatively short period of time. This term fits very well that the great tribulation will be cut short for the elect at an unknown day and hour (Matt 24:22).

The hour of trial is a time of testing, a putting to the proof (*peirasmos*, Strong's # 3986). It's a time of proving the world deserves God's fast approaching wrath. I agree with Feinberg this far. But the Greek word means testing by fire as gold is tested and purified, not just proving failure. Paul explains that the persecution of believers by the world proves God's judgment on them is just (2Thess 1:4-8). But at the same time this trial is testing earth dwellers (the unsaved), it is also testing believers.

> (1Pet 4:7, 12, 13 AMP) *The end of all things is at hand.... Beloved, do not be amazed and bewildered at the fiery ordeal which is taking place to test your quality, as though something strange (unusual and alien to you and your position) were*

---

55 The Rapture..., p. 70

befalling you. But insofar as you are sharing Christ's sufferings, rejoice, so that when His glory [full of radiance and splendor] is revealed, you may also rejoice with triumph [exultantly].

This will also be a time of peirasmos for the church, a fiery ordeal to judge and purify believers before He comes. Though this verse applies to any time believers suffer for their faith, in context Peter relates it to the end of the age and the appearing of the Lord in glory. This testing proves the earth dwellers deserve God's wrath. But it also tests the church to find out if their faith is genuine (1Pet 1:7). Believers must choose - Christ or Antichrist. This testing separates the wheat from the tares, the good fish from the bad (Matt 13). Many false believers will fall away in scandalized offense when this severe persecution comes. With the fourth seal many will face death by hunger or sword at the hands of the beasts of the earth, or choose the Antichrist and betray Christ and other believers.

The Philadelphian church is promised to be kept because they have already demonstrated faithfulness and perseverance, for which Christ commends them. They have been faithful and obedient to Christ and had no negatives Jesus needed to correct, so are promised an extra measure of protection and spiritual strength during the hour of trial. As it pertains to the church this hour is to weed the garden, and the church of brotherly love does not need this weeding. This does not mean its members are perfect, but only that as a group there are no major issues. Matthew Henry, commenting on this, said:

> Those who keep the gospel in a time of peace shall be kept by Christ in an hour of temptation. By keeping the gospel they are prepared for the trial; and the same divine grace that has made them fruitful in times of peace will make them faithful in times of persecution. (Matthew Henry Complete Commentary)

Strong defines the Greek for persevere (#5281) as cheerful or hopeful endurance and constancy. It also implies remaining behind or going through. This same word is found in Revelation

13:10 and 14:12. The context of each of these is the Abomination and great tribulation, with the latter specifically the refusal of his evil mark even though it may mean death. **Here** *is the patience of the saints* implies that another passage predicted a time where perseverance was especially required. The facts that several churches are told to hold fast till he comes, that Philadelphia is promised some kind of protection because of their perseverance, and that Smyrna needs perseverance to endure when the devil sends them to prison in his wrath (Rev 2:10) fits that. And a couple of times Revelation calls the saints in the great tribulation saints of Jesus.

This brings us to the key phrase of this verse - *keep...from*. What does it mean to be kept from the hour of trial?

The word *keep* is the Greek *tereo*, which means to watch or set a guard over to protect from loss or injury. By extension it means to withhold for personal ends, and figuratively means to keep unmarried. It is usually translated to hold fast, keep, preserve, or watch (Strong's #5083). In other words, it denotes protection by watching over rather than removal, like a father protects his child at a playground by watching and guiding him. The same Greek word was used earlier in the same verse for keeping Christ's command to persevere - clearly watching to observe, not isolation or removal. If Jesus had intended to convey the idea of removal or avoidance of the hour of trial, *phulasso* (Strong's #5442) carries that connotation and would have been a better choice. *Airo* (#142), to take, would have been better still. The word *tereo* seems to signify protection through the period, then, not removal away from it.

The word *from* supports this. The Greek word *ek* usually means *out from within,* unlike apo or napa, which mean *away from.* Jeffrey Townsend argues there is sufficient extra-biblical evidence this preposition may also denote an outside position with no thought of prior existence within or emergence from the object.56

---

56 The Bib Sac Reader; "The Rapture in Revelation 3:10", Jeffrey

While this may be true, it is ultimately the context and predominant scriptural usage which we must consider. We have already seen that its linkage to tereo suggests protection within rather than removal away from the hour of trial.

Pre-tribs accuse later rapture positions of trying to weaken in every possible way the sufferings of the saints in the Tribulation by claiming most fall into this protected category. While some post-tribs do seem to promote this opinion, others recognize only a small percentage fall under this promise. The church of Smyrna, for example, has also been faithful and obedient with some measure of strength, yet will suffer at the hands of the beast (Rev 2:8-10). Even the protected remnant will not find life easy, for they will be in hiding and struggling to provide food and shelter to survive. But because they have been in the practice of listening to the Spirit and living for God, they will be more open to guidance from Him to meet these needs.

You may wonder why God would protect some of the faithful and not others. You may as well ask why He allows the church in places like India and China to suffer persecution while in America we have, for the moment, freedom of worship. God is sovereign and has a divine plan which we will fully understand only in heaven. Whatever His plan, there is a glory for those who suffer for His Name's sake and a crown only faithful martyrs may wear.

Two additional passages prove interesting when we realize the word *ek* means *from the midst*. Robert Van Kampen explains:

> In addition, when using this primary interpretation of *tereo ek*, several critical passages in support of the pre-wrath position take on special significance. In reply to John's question about the identity of the great multitude (Rev 7:9)... one of the elders explained, "these are the ones that come out of [ek, *out from within*] the great tribulation, and they have washed their robes and made them white in the blood of the Lamb" (7:14). Peter declares that "the Lord knows how to

Townsend, 1983, p. 171

rescue the godly from [ek, *out from within*] temptation [peirasmos, *testing*; same as in Rev 3:10 *hour of trial*], and to keep the unrighteous under punishment for the Day of Judgment" (2Pet 2:9).57

Pay attention to that last reference. In context, Peter was discussing Noah's and Lot's deliverance while the ungodly remained to suffer God's wrath. Remember, Jesus used these same examples to picture the rapture (Luke 17; Matt 24). The idea here is clearly the same - saints removed from the midst of the time of testing while the unrighteous remain behind to suffer wrath. Everywhere we turn Scripture says the same thing!

In conclusion, I amplify Revelation 3:10 based on this:

Because you have kept, observed, and held fast My command to persevere in daily life and under affliction, I also will keep a watchful eye on you to preserve and protect you from within the hour of testing and putting to the proof which shall come upon the whole earth to test [Strong's #3985, examine] those who dwell on the earth.

This verse obviously does not promise a pre-trib rapture. We have repeatedly seen that the church must face the great tribulation.

Revelation 4

We must consider two addition faulty pre-trib claims for the rapture in Revelation. First is Revelation 4:1.

After these things I looked, and behold a door standing open in heaven. And the first voice which I heard was like a trumpet speaking with me, saying, "Come up here and I will show you things which must take place after this."

---

57 The Sign, p. 469

They offer two explanations why this is the rapture. First, they say the voice like a trumpet telling them to *come up here* is the rapture trumpet (1Cor 15:52; 1Thess 4:16). Since this precedes the seal judgments, supposedly it makes the rapture pre-trib.

This conclusion is tantamount to using an allegorical method of interpretation, something pre-tribs profess to deplore. This is clearly a call to John on the island of Patmos to come up to heaven and see what God shows in the rest of the vision. Since pre-tribs insist they use a literal method, those who use this as much as admit their theory is weak, and that they must get creative to keep their view viable. Pre-trib John Walvoord agrees that there is no authority to connect this expression to the rapture.58

The second argument on this verse is raised by Dake.

> Gr. *Meta touta*, after these things. This Gr. Phrase is used at the beginning and at the end of this verse, thus: "After these things (after writing the things concerning the churches) I looked… and the first voice…said, 'Come up hither, and I will show thee things which must be after these things,'" that is, after the churches. This confirms and settles the question as to the time of the fulfillment of all the events of Rev 4-22. They MUST BE *after these things* of the churches, or after the rapture of the church.59

Actually, the second occurrence of meta touta does not necessarily mean after the things of the churches are completed. This phrase can also simply mean *in the future*, with no specific preceding sequence. It is so used in Revelation 1:19, where John is told to write, *the things which you have seen*, the preceding portion of this vision, *the things which are*, we must remember that these were actual churches in John's day, *and the things which will take place after this* [meta touta], that is, in the future. Furthermore, the preponderance of scriptural evidence confirms

---

58 The Revelation of Jesus Christ, John Walvoord: Moody Press, Chicago, 1966, p. 103
59 Dake's..., op. cit., note on Rev. 4:1, emph. his

and settles that the church will enter the seventieth week, as we have seen.

The second issue in Revelation is the identity of the twenty-four elders seen in Revelation 4 and 5. Some pre-tribs identify these as representing the church and Israel (12 apostles and 12 tribes). They also point out that these elders are sitting on thrones just as the church will sit with Jesus on His throne, and that they wear crowns which they associate with the rewards given the saints. They are seen in heaven with Jesus when He opens the seals (Rev 5:5), and therefore cannot be on earth during the seventieth week. Salem Kirban is a proponent of this view.

> Their number, 24, leads me to conclude that these represent the redeemed of both the Old Testament and New Testament dispensations.... Rev 21:12-14 seems to confirm this interpretation. They, furthermore, are "sitting" (they are in heaven resting from their earthly labors); they are clothed in "white raiment" (justified from their sins by a garment of righteousness provided by God); and they are wearing "crowns of gold" (stephanos – victor's crowns of leaves; hence these are in a glorified and rewarded state having been crowned as OVERCOMERS through Christ's blood in the struggle upon the earth; Rev 2:11)."[60]

The problem is that the saints do not receive their rewards until the seventh trumpet, and thrones and crowns are some of the rewards. Thus it is impossible for these to be the raptured church. On the other hand, the great multitude in Revelation 7, at the sixth seal, are not said to have crowns or thrones. The multitude is the raptured saints according to pre-wrath, and this further justifies our claim. Another explanation for these elders must be sought.

There is no complete consensus even among pre-tribs concerning the identity of the twenty-four elders. For example, some believe they are angelic beings associated with God's

---

[60] Salem Kirban Reference Bible; "Revelation Visualized": AMG Publishers, Chattanooga, TN 37422, 1979, p. 88

heavenly government. These pre-trib interpretations have little or no scriptural support. While we will probably never know who they are for certain this side of eternity, Marvin Rosenthal suggests the following:

> The significance of the fact that there were twenty-four elders is clarified in the Old Testament. The priesthood of ancient Israel, made up of the house of Aaron, was divided into twenty-four courses or groups of priests (1Chron 24). Each group served for two weeks each year on a rotation basis.... Each group of priests had one priest that represented it. When these... met together, they represented the entire priesthood and, at the same time, the whole nation of Israel. (See Walvoord, <u>The Revelation of Jesus Christ,</u> p.106)
>
> These elders were specifically said by John to be "sitting" (Rev 4:4; 11:16). To any Jewish contemporary of John, that would have been an amazing statement. They knew that the Levitical priests... work was never done because the sacrifice of animals... could never take away sin – they could only cover sin for a year.... These were seated on thrones around the Heavenly Father because Jesus, the great High Priest [and perfect sacrifice], had once for all opened the way into the holiest of all. These elders are said to be "clothed in white raiment" (Rev 4:4).... When the ancient high priest of Israel on the Day of Atonement prepared to enter the Holy of Holies and the presence of God, he discarded his magnificent priestly robes and put on in their place " the holy linen coat" (Lev 16:4).... In the presence of a holy God...a linen robe was deemed more fitting. The "white raiment" in which the elders were clothed speaks elegantly of their entrance "within the veil" in the presence of their God.61

Rosenthal then spends a few moments showing that the crowns worn by the elders are crowns of victory rather than crowns of a ruler. He also points out the elders' priestly ministry of praise (Rev 4:10, 11). He concludes that whatever the true significance, there

---

[61] <u>The Pre-Wrath Rapture of the church,,</u> op. cit., p

134

has been no consensus among scholars to their identity. Thus their presence cannot be used to prove a pre-trib rapture.

Chapter 9: The Day of the Lord Wrath

The timing of the rapture is inextractibly tied to the Day of the Lord (DOL) and God's wrath. Scripture is clear the church will be delivered before either of these begin. Most pre-millennial scholars agree the DOL begins immediately following the rapture based on passages such as 1Thessalonians 4 and 5, which clearly establishes their relationship. Therefore, every rapture position must carefully consider this.

If it can be demonstrated that the entire seven years is part of this Day, then pre-trib is made strong while all other theories are severely damaged. However, if it can be proven the DOL begins within the seventieth week, then the way is opened for a later view such as pre-wrath.

Most pre-tribs believe the DOL and God's wrath both begin at the start of the week. R.C. Sproule explains:

> If it can be established that (1) God's wrath embraces this entire seven-year period yet to come and (2) that the true church has been promised exemption from that wrath, then pre-tribulationism will be essentially established. Once this proof is established then pre-tribs can rightly claim reasonable explanations of the many *debatable* passages (including those that seem to teach imminency) as support for their system.[62]

I agree. After a brief dissertation on this question, Pentecost concludes:

> Thus it is concluded that the day of the Lord will include the time of the tribulation. (Zechariah 14:1-4) makes it clear

---

[62] In Defense of Pre-tribulationism, revised ed., R.C. Sproul: BMH Books, Winona Lake, IN, 1950, pp 43, 47, 52, Emph mine

that the events of the second advent are included... (2Peter 3:10) gives authority for including the entire millennial age.... If the day of the Lord did not begin until the second advent [at Armageddon], since that event is preceded by signs, the day of the Lord could not come as a "thief in the night," unexpected and unheralded, as it is said that it will come in (1Thess 5:2). The only way this day could break unexpectedly is to have it begin immediately after the [pre-tribulational] rapture.63

Is his conclusion sound? We have already seen considerable evidence that the church will enter the great tribulation. But all of this discussion is null and void if he is correct. In the following pages we will discover that the Day of the Lord and God's wrath both arrive with the sixth and seventh seals, at the same time as the rapture. The first proof is Acts 2:20, quoting Joel 2:31.

*The sun shall be turned into darkness, and the moon into blood, **before** the coming of the great and notable Day of the Lord.*

Notice there will be unmistakable heavenly signs before or when that Day arrives. 1Thessalonians 5 clearly explains that the reason it comes unexpectedly upon the world is because they are in spiritual darkness and so cannot see it coming, just as Jesus warned in the Olivet Discourse (Matt 24:42-50; Mark 13:32-37). Jesus gave similar warning to the end time churches in Revelation. If believers are faithful to Christ and watching we should see signs of the approaching Day.

Walvoord counters this interpretation of Joel 2:31, maintaining that

What is meant here is not that the day of the Lord will begin after these wonders in heaven, but that it will come to its climax when this judgment is actually executed.64

---

63 Things To Come, op. cit., p230
64 Bibliotheca Sacra; "Post-tribulationism Today: Part IX", John

I will allow that this Hebrew word translated *before* can carry that connotation, for it has a wide variety of applications (Strong's # 6440). But we can easily determine what Joel meant by looking at the context, for he uses the word four additional times in chapter two (vv. 3, 6, 10, 11). In each case it carries the idea of being immediately in front of, either in time or physical space. We can safely conclude, then, that a similar meaning is intended here.

Furthermore, this cannot be the *climax* of the Day of the Lord. The only thing in Revelation that fits that criterion is the bowls of wrath and Battle of Armageddon, all contained within the seventh trumpet. The real climax is when Jesus *takes up His great power and reigns* (Rev 11:17).

The word *before*, then, indicates that these heavenly signs are a direct result of God's approaching wrath for the Day of the Lord.

This fact becomes significant when we look at Mark 13 (Matt 24). Here we see the exact same signs in the sun and moon which Joel declared as signaling the DOL - and we find a group of elect gathered from earth to heaven. Then in Revelation 6:12-7:17 we see the same signs at the sixth seal, again with a worldwide gathering to heaven to stand before Jesus. No gaps in the walls of this rapture theory!

The prophet Zephaniah (1:7) tells of another event:

> *Be silent in the presence of the Lord God; for the Day of the Lord is at hand [or, now here]; for the Lord has prepared a sacrifice; He has invited [lit., sanctified or set apart]* **His guests**.

Now turn to the prelude to the trumpets (Rev 8:1-6). John describes a short period of silence when the seventh seal is opened. A perfect fit! This moment of silence shows great respect for the awesome and terrible wrath about to fall upon the earth. *Be silent, all flesh, before the Lord, for He is aroused from His holy habitation* (Zech 2:13).

F. Walvoord: Jan-Mar 1977, p. 7

Two more points in Zephaniah add to the evidence. The last clause declares that God has invited, or set apart, His guests. In light of all we have already seen, this could easily be the rapture of the church. In fact, Jesus even told a parable about a wedding supper in which the saved are guests (Matt 22).

Second, the Lord is about to perform the sacrifice which He has prepared, the objects of His wrath. The Son of Man calls the birds and beast to begin gathering for the great sacrificial feast God is preparing (Ez 39:17-30). In Isaiah 18:3-6, after God blows a trumpet (see Zeph 1:8; 1Thess 4:15; the trump of God at the rapture), He will reap the sour grapes of wrath (Rev 14:17-20) and leave them for the beasts and birds to feast upon. The grapes of wrath in the trumpets are the hors-deourves, if you will. An angel will call them to the actual supper at Armageddon (Rev 19:17, 18), but the feast begins earlier, seeing as the sixth trumpet kills 1/3 of mankind.

Many of the prophetic utterances in this section of Isaiah (chapters 16-21) are dual prophecies, having near (Isaiah's day) and far significance (end time). In 16:1-5 the Lamb is sent, Israel is gathered to Zion after her flight into the wilderness, the spoiler and extortioner, that is, the Antichrist, is at an end, and Christ's throne is established. In Isaiah 17:4-8 man looks to his Maker and has respect for Jesus, the Holy One of Israel, and he turns from his idols. In our text of 18:3-6, the trumpet is blown by God (*He*) at the battle of Jehoshaphat (Zechariah 9:14, explained in later chapters) and the rapture (1Thess 4:16; 1Cor 15:51, 52; Matt 24:31), the sour grapes of wrath are reaped (Rev 14:17-20, relates to the trumpets), and the birds and beasts begin gathering for the feast. In Isaiah 19:1, 18-25 we see Jesus coming in the clouds, and Egypt's repentance following God's wrath. In 21:16, 17 we see the Islamic nations diminished *"within a year"* which is the *year of recompense*, probably referring to the wrath of the DOL (see Is 34:8; Jer 23:12), and initiated by the Jehoshaphat Campaign.

Thus we establish that the Day of the Lord begins with the sixth and seventh seals. It cannot encompass the entire seventieth week. Feinberg concedes this is possible, but still argues:

I think Gundry is probably right in arguing that the Day of the Lord does not begin with the Tribulation, although I would start the Day of the Lord about the middle of the week (see Jer 30:7; Joel 2:1-11; Matt 24:14; 2Thess 2:3-4). Thus the *terminus a quo* of the Day of the Lord is indecisive unless one assumes that divine wrath coincides with the Day of the Lord. Put differently, divine wrath may not be confined simply to the Day of the Lord.65

It need not be *assumed* that God's wrath begins at the same time. 1Thessalonians 5:2-10 teaches that the DOL will not overtake believers as they are not appointed to wrath, but to salvation [deliverance]. Zephaniah 1:14-18 tells us the DOL is a day of wrath, a day of darkness (see Rev 6:12), and a *day of trumpets* (Rev 8 and 9). A very important passage showing this relationship is Isaiah 13:6-13:

> *Wail, for the Day of the Lord is at hand!... Every man's heart will melt, and they will be afraid.... Behold, the Day of the Lord comes,* **with** *both* **wrath** *and fierce anger.... For the stars of heaven ...will not give their light; the sun will be darkened..., and the moon will not cause its light to shine.... Therefore I will shake the heavens, and the earth will move out of its place, in the wrath of the Lord of Hosts.*

Compare this to the sixth seal. The sun and moon are darkened, the heavens shaken so that the stars disappear, every mountain and island moved out of its place, and men mourning with hearts melting in fear at what is coming on the earth (Luke 21:25-27). It is clear they are directly related.

Let's look at God's wrath from another angle. The second, third, and fourth seals in many ways are similar to Old Testament accounts of God's wrath. Most pre-tribs believe his proves they are DOL wrath and so equate wrath with the entire week. But nowhere does the Bible refer to these seals as part of God's divine wrath upon the entire world.

---

65 The Rapture..., op. cit., p.61

Careful study of the use of the various Hebrew words translated as *wrath* in the Old Testament clearly indicates that the strong Hebrew word explicitly used in connection with God's Day-of-the-Lord wrath against the nations is not the same Hebrew word used in relation to God's chastisement of Israel through these natural disasters. Milder terms are invariably used.66 [More on this shortly.]

Some teachers believe the seals are part of divine wrath based on the similarities in *the four severe judgments* of Ezekiel 14:12-21, because of the word wrath in verse 19. Also, the O.T. several times describes God's wrath as manifested in war, famine, pestilence, and wild animals (Lev 25:21-28; Is 9:12; Jer 14:12; 16:4, 10, 11; Ez 4:16, and others). Van Kampen illustrates the logical flaw with this reasoning, here abbreviated:

> The other day I saw two teams competing on the playing field, the object of the game being to hit a ball with the wooden object in their hands. From strictly the given information, there is no way to tell what game is being played (e.g. baseball, field hockey, cricket, etc.). More information is needed to know exactly which. Even though the judgments in Ezekiel 14 seem to correspond to the second, third, and fourth seals, we cannot automatically conclude that these refer to the Day-of-the-Lord wrath until all the data concerning the seventieth week is analyzed. We must first consider the first and fifth seals, as the sixth seal is indeed associated with God's wrath.67

The first seal (Rev 6:1, 2) probably relates to the seven-year covenant (Dan 9:27) setting up the one world government, and a related sudden upsurge in false teachers to ready the professing church to take the mark (Matt 24:5). The fifth seal is the continued martyrdom of God's faithful during the Tribulation (Rev 6:9-11); the martyred souls under the altar must wait a while longer for God's vengeance until their full number is completed. Since

---

66 The Sign, p. 186
67 The Sign, p. 479-480

Scripture never calls these two seals part of God's wrath, it is unlikely the seals in between are wrath. While I admit I argue from silence, this is but the first nail in the coffin.

Associating the first, and especially the fifth, seals with God's wrath maligns God. To attribute false christs and martyrdom of the saints - both of which are largely directed against God's elect (Matt 24:21-24) - would mean God pours out His wrath against His saints. But the DOL wrath is manifested against the ungodly and unrighteous, and those who fight against the gospel (Rom 1:18; 2Pet 2:9). This would surely be a prime example of a kingdom divided against itself (Matt 12:24). While believers are subject to disciplinary anger, which would fit with the seals, they are not subject to condemning wrath which is found in the Day of the Lord.

Notice that the fifth seal martyrs already under the altar are told they must wait yet a while for judgment and vengeance to be poured out. The DOL wrath is also God's vengeance on those who kill His people (Prov 6:34b, 35; Is 59:17; 2Thess 1:8). Thus God's wrathful vengeance must follow the fifth seal.

Some may protest that God sent wrath on Israel in the Old Testament. But that was disciplinary in nature, to correct Israel and restore her to right standing with God. DOL wrath, on the other hand, is condemning wrath, punishment rather than chastisement. The key to understanding this is, as mentioned earlier, the Hebrew words used.

There are several Hebrew words translated as *wrath* in the O.T. Each of these conveys a different degree of anger. *Chemah* (Strong's # 2534) means hot displeasure or indignation; *charon* (#2740) means heat or burning anger; and *qetseph* (# 7110) simply means anger. All of these, however, have a lighter implication than *'ebrah* (#5678), which is the overflowing fury of God. This strong Hebrew word is only used to describe God's DOL wrath against the whole world, such as in Zephaniah 1:14, 15, 18 and Isaiah 13:9-13, which ties to the sixth seal.

141

The key pre-trib passage uses the milder term *chemah* (Ez 14:19-21). God's chemah, while conveying a strong sense of anger, is still disciplinary in nature. Van Kampen explains that:

> The only place that this strong Hebrew word... is used to directly support the view that the entire seventieth week is a time of God's wrath is Ezekiel 38:19-22. This writer agrees that this passage is certainly a reference to God's divine wrath during the Day of the Lord. But like Zephaniah 1:14-18, the use of 'ebrah in the Ezekiel 38 context refers to the wrath of God against THE NATIONS who have come against Israel in the last days (v.16), just before His wrath is poured out, making absolutely no reference to the false messiahs, famines, or wild animals, or the persecution of God's own elect which embody the general focus of the first five seals.68

The similarities of war and pestilence alone are not enough of a match on which to build their case. Other possibilities must be considered to ensure this is not a separate war. And it is.

Several times I have referred to the Jehoshaphat Campaign. This battle happens sometime after the Antichrist comes to power. The armies which control Jerusalem and Israel after the Abomination of Desolation are likely from surrounding Islamic countries. God stirs up an Israeli resistance force that comes to fight them. God Himself blows a trumpet at this battle and leads Israel to victory (Joel 3:1, 2, 9, 12-16; Zech 9:14-16, 12:6; Is 18:3). Notice the Ezekiel 38 passage says God gathers the armies from the mountains to fight and defeat Gog (Russia or Turkey, who lately supports Iran becoming a nuclear power, and is largely Islamic). God will rain down on him fire and brimstone, as the first trumpet judgment (Rev 8:7). This is entirely separate from Armageddon, during which Jesus will come with heavenly armies to slay the beast and his armies with the sword of His mouth (Rev 19:14, 15). I will detail the Jehoshaphat Campaign in chapters 11 and 14.

---

68 The Sign, pp. 480-481

Feinberg offers another hypothesis for making the seals God's wrath:

> While our Lord was on this earth He declared that all judgment had been committed into His hands (John 5:22). The assumption of this judicial and judgmental authority is strikingly set forth in the scenes of Revelation 4 and 5... Christ alone has the authority to take the scroll and to break *its seals. Every* judgment from the first seal to the last judgment comes as the retributive wrath of God.[69]

Remember we saw that the first portion of the week and the great tribulation is called a time of testing, not wrath. The purpose is to prove mankind deserves wrath, and to test the church to separate the wheat from the tares. Mid-trib Gleason Archer adds:

> While it is true that the first four seals of Revelation 6 are components of the book of destiny unrolled by the Lamb, it would be unjustified to label these first four developments of the earlier half of the week as manifestations of the *wrath* of God... even though they may be included in the *plan* of God.... It is these four seals that pertain to the first half of the week, and they do not give expression to the wrath of God on a miraculous or apocalyptic scale. They merely present on a somewhat intensified scale the same sad story that earlier centuries have often witnessed during the history of mankind.[70]

Another problem with making the seals wrath is the fact that the word *wrath* is not found in Revelation until after the signs of the sixth seal appear. This matches perfectly what we learned with the Day of the Lord. When these signs manifest mankind will cry out, *"Hide us from the wrath of the Lamb,"* which caused John to say, *"For the great day of His wrath has come, and who is able to stand"* (Rev 6:16, 17; Is 2:10-22).

---

[69] The Rapture..., pp. 61-62, emphasis his
[70] The Rapture..., p. 108

The debate over wrath and the seals centers on the term *has come* in this passage. Pentecost explains the usual pre-trib understanding:

> The aorist tense in verse 17, elthen (has come), signifies, not something that is about to happen, but that which has taken place. Thus in unfolding the program of the seals, John announces that these represent *the wrath* that has already come.71

Pre-tribs who address this say the aorist tense always refers to past, completed action or single (punctiliar) action. So they say this refers to wrath which already came in the seals.

But that is not necessarily the case. Feinberg admits that Robert Gundry, a respected Greek scholar and a post-trib, may be correct that elthen here is used as a future.

> ...Gundry argues two points with regard to this passage. He contends that the wrath spoken of in this text, as well as others, falls only on unbelievers. Further, the aorist verb elthen is either an ingressive or dramatic aorist. The ingressive...expresses a state or condition just entered. On the other hand, the dramatic... functions like a future, taking place after the realization of some condition. This would mean that with the sixth seal the wrath of God has just begun or is just about to appear. In support of on ingressive or passive aorist interpretation, Gundry argues that "if the wrath of God has already fallen, how could the wicked yet be fleeing for refuge? Rather, the wrath is at the inception of its breaking forth.. or on the verge of doing so..." *Gundry's view is exegetically possible.*72

John Sproule, former head of the Greek department of Grace Theological Seminary and a pre-trib, also admits this:

---

71 Things to Come, op. cit., p. 84
72 The Rapture..., p. 60

If the verb is taken as a constantive, then it speaks of past action and includes the preceding seals. If, however, it is a dramatic aorist, the tense of the verb is indecisive [can be past or future].73

Shortly after his above comment, Feinberg presents his argument for past action:

It may be that with the increased severity of the judgments, people are just beginning to recognize that this is not simply a stroke of bad luck, but the outpouring of God's wrath.74

The aorist tense, in itself, does not specify the time of an action. This is determined by the context. Feinberg bases his conclusion on speculation and doctrinal prejudice rather than on close examination of context and comparing it to related passages.

In considering the issue, the following are noticed: (1) This is the first time the word *wrath* appears in Revelation. (2) The heavenly signs of the sixth seal match those found in Matthew 24:29-31, and are also said to appear before the Day of the Lord (Acts 2:20). (3) Mankind is pictured both here and in the gospels as beginning to flee what is just now coming on the earth (Luke 21:25-28), and the same is in Isaiah 13:6-13. (4) God's *wrath* is mentioned several times after this in direct relationship to events of the seventh seal (which includes trumpets and bowls). And (5), the verse reads that His wrath has come, and *who is able to stand*, the present tense defining the aorist. Based on these clear facts, we can safely deduce that God's wrath is just beginning. The rapture need not be pre-trib on account of God's wrath.

Walvoord comes close to admitting the truth about the DOL, but shies away at the last moment:

---

73 In Defense of Pre-tribulationism, John Sproule: BMH Books, Winona Lake, IN, 1980, pp. 54-55
74 The Rapture..., p. 60

145

It is true that the sixth seal introduces... "the great day of His wrath," but it is also clear that the preceding seals record devastating divine judgments.... While the climax of the wrath of God may very well be introduced by the sixth seal, it is by no means the beginning of the wrath of God on the world. 75... It is quite clear...that the fourth seal...is not at the end, but in the earlier phase.... Certainly the destruction of one-fourth of the population would qualify as a day of the Lord for the earth. 76

I agree the first four seals are, in a sense, judgment, just as recent plagues such as AIDS judge immorality and drug use. The seals are part of His sovereign plan. They are not, however, DOL wrath from which the church is promised deliverance.

Also, the fourth seal does not say one-fourth of mankind is killed, but that Death is given power to come against one-fourth of the earth, Hades following with him. I believe this is the persecution of the saints and Israel by the Antichrist and false prophet (*by the beasts of the earth*). The sixth seal does not announce the climax of God's wrath, but its start. The climax is introduced by the seventh trumpet (Rev 11:18).

To drive home the point about the aorist verb *elthen*, let us consider how it is used elsewhere. In Mark 14:41-43 this verb is used to describe something just then coming:

And He [Jesus] came the third time, and said to them, "Are you still sleeping...? It is enough; the hour has come [elthen]; behold the Son of Man is being betrayed into the hands of sinners. Arise, let us be going; Behold the one who betrays Me is at hand." And immediately, while He was still speaking, Judas....

---

75 "Post-tribulationism Today" John Walvoord, Bibliotheca Sacra, Apr-June 1976, p114
76 "Post-tribulationism Today, part IX," Jan-Mar 1977, p. 9

You can see for yourself that Jesus used the aorist verb in this instance to indicate something that was happening at that very moment.

Earlier I said making the fifth seal wrath would make God directly responsible for the death of the saints. Such a claim is so startling that I think it needs a little more attention.

The souls under the altar (Rev 6:9-11) are those martyred up to this time, and the fifth seal says more must be martyred. There is no judgment associated with this seal, unless it is the martyrdom. But Jesus has already borne God's wrath on Himself for those who come to Him in faith (Is 53:5, 8, 10, 11). The saints living during the great tribulation are said to be saved by faith in Jesus and washed by His blood (Rev 7:4; 12:17; 14:12), so are covered by this promise. Plus, we have seen strong evidence that these saints are the church, evidence which must be carefully considered before proclaiming these seals God's wrath. [Post-tribs need to heed this as well, concerning trumpets and bowls which are wrath.] Those who are washed by the blood are promised exemption from wrath.

The murder of the elect is not a result of God's wrath, but of another's: *Woe to the inhabitants of the earth and sea! for the devil has come down to you, having great wrath, because he know that he has a short time* (Rev 12:12). It is clear this relates to the Abomination of Desolation, for *when the dragon saw that he had been cast down to earth, he persecuted the woman [Israel]*, who flees into the wilderness for three-and-a-half years. Then Satan turns against the rest of her offspring *who keep the commandments of God and have the testimony of Jesus Christ* (12:17). This fits perfectly what we have seen in the fourth and fifth seals.

The fact is, the first five seals are largely a result of the actions of mankind. Walvoord admits that "the judgments of War, Famine, and Death, and the martyrdom of the saints have largely originated in human decisions and in the evil heart of men."77

---

77 The Revelation of Jesus Christ, John F. Walvoord: Dunham Publishing Co., Findlay, OH, 1966, p. 136

These are not God's overflowing fury but mankind's inborn wickedness and stupidity unloosed.

There is an even more ominous problem in attempting to make the entire seventieth week, or even the great tribulation prior to the sixth seal, be part of God's DOL wrath. If it were so, then Satan, through his beast, would gain ground against God for a significant portion of the Day of the Lord; While God was pouring out fierce vengeance the Antichrist's kingdom would be thriving; While God was busy humbling everyone, they would instead grow ever more arrogant. The beast will even set up his throne or image in the temple or on the temple mount to receive worship and adoration from the world. All while God was pouring out His wrath. In contrast, the great flood immediately brought the unrighteous to their knees in terror, even if not in repentance. If Satan is to prevail against God and His holy saints on GOD'S OWN DAY, God would end up looking a mite bit foolish. **Ain't gonna happen!!!**

Isaiah tells us what to really expect of that Day:

(Is 2:11, 12, 17) *For the Day of the Lord of Hosts shall come upon everything proud and lofty, upon everything lifted up – and it shall be brought low... The loftiness of man shall be bowed down, and the haughtiness of men shall be brought low; THE LORD ALONE SHALL BE EXALTED IN THAT DAY.*

If YHWH God, the Mighty God, the Holy One alone is to be exalted on that terrible and glorious Day, as Isaiah so confidently proclaimed, then it would be a contradiction of inspired holy Scripture to have the beast and the dragon gaining ascendancy within the DOL. The Antichrist's power will be curtailed with the sixth seal coming, considering the church will be removed from his reach and the Israeli resistance will gain victory at the Jehoshaphat campaign. At the same time, the wrath of God will begin upon the earth. Then God alone shall be exalted, even as mankind desperately and with futility gathers to fight Him at Armageddon a short time later. Amen.

Chapter 10: Imminency and the Early Church

So far we have concentrated on what the Bible says concerning the rapture question. Let's take a short break from our intensive study and see what the early church believed, before we examine the final scriptural testimony. While any doctrine must fully depend on the Bible, sometimes it is interesting and helpful to see what the most reliable early church fathers believed on various issues.

It is only relatively recently that the rapture question has been discussed and studied in such detail. The roots of pre-trib can be traced back to the early 1830's, and only arrived in America about 60 years later. Mid-trib didn't become prominent until 1941, and modern post-trib is about the same age as pre-trib. We will see, however, that most of the writing of the first 300 years of the church firmly taught that we would face the Antichrist.

Some pre-tribs claim the early church believed in an any-moment, pre-trib rapture. They offer ambiguous quotes like Jesus' statement that He is coming at an hour we do not expect or that the Day of the Lord is coming like a thief. From these they conclude that the early church believed Christ's coming was imminent, could come immediately.

The truth is, they overwhelmingly believed the church would suffer through the depredations of the Antichrist. They had no problem with the church entering the great tribulation. Robert Gundry explains [78]:

> The antiquity of a view weighs in its favor, especially when that antiquity reaches back to the apostolic age. For those who

---

[78] The Church and the Tribulation, Robert Gundry: Zondervan, 1973

received their doctrine first hand from the apostles and from those who heard them stood in a better position to judge what was apostolic doctrine than we who are many centuries removed. (p.172)

Until Augustine in the fourth century, the early church generally held to a premillennial understanding... and it was post-tribulational. Neither mentioned nor considered, the possibility of a pre-tribulational rapture seems never to have occurred to anyone in the church. (p.173)

Every Ante-Nicene writer who touches in any detail upon the tribulation, resurrection, rapture, or second coming displays a post-tribulational persuasion. The number of those is about equal to those whom we can quote directly in favor of premillennialism... (p.178)

...And who among the outstanding early fathers is missing from the list of post-tribulationists? Only Clement of Alexandria and Origen, whose names have become trademarks for the mystical, allegorical method of interpretation, and who strongly opposed premillennialism....The evidence that the early church was post-tribulational needs no apology for lack of numbers. (p.179)

Even though Gundry believes in a seventh trumpet rapture, while pre-wrath is somewhat earlier at the sixth seal, we completely agree the church will enter the great tribulation. But the early church universally held to believers entering the great tribulation. So while post-trib has better support in the fathers, pre-wrath is not excluded. But no support whatsoever is found for pre-trib.

Also, Daniel 12:9 says the meaning of the prophecies God gave him was to be sealed until the end time. Now that the end is near, greater understanding should come to those open to receive it, and it has been so. Even in the process of editing the final draft of this book little pieces of the puzzle have suddenly become clearer to me. The early church, I believe, had partial understanding, but many of the details were hidden from them still. Thus they could understand the church must face Antichrist without realizing we must be removed before God pours out His wrath.

But some pre-tribs insist the early church writings support them. Let us look and see who has better support. I include a few Scripture references in brackets, for it is the Bible that ultimately determines truth.

Justin Martyr (100-168 A.D.): The man of apostasy...shall venture to do unlawful deeds on the earth against us the Christians. (Dialogue with Trypho the Jew, 110) [see 2Thess 2:3-8; Rev 13:7]

Iranaeus (140-202 A.D.): "And the ten horns which thou sawest are ten kings, who have received no kingdom as yet, but shall receive power as kings one hour with the beast. These have one mind, and give their strength and power to the beast. These shall make war with the Lamb, and the Lamb shall overcome them, because He is the Lord of lords and the King of kings." It is manifest, therefore, that of these [potentates], he who is to come shall slay three, and subject the remainder to his power, and that he shall be himself the eighth among them. And they shall lay Babylon waste, and burn her with fire, and shall give their kingdom to the beast, and put the church to flight. (Against Heresies, V, 26, 1). [Rev 13:7; 17:12ff]

But [John] indicates the number of the name [of the beast, 666] now, that when this man comes we may avoid him, being aware who he is. (Against Heresies, V, 30, 4). [Rev 13:1-18; 14:9-12]

Iranaeus also placed the resurrection of the church and the Old Testament saints after the revelation of the Antichrist. (Against Heresies, V, 34, 3; V, 35, 1; see also The Didache ca. 100 A.D.)

Melito of Sardis (100-170 A.D.): Now concerning the tribulation of the persecution which is to fall upon the church from the adversary [he has been speaking of the beast and so continues]...that refers to the one thousand two hundred and threescore days during which the tyrant is to reign and persecute the church. (Treatise on Christ and Antichrist, pp 60-61) [Dan 12:7; Rev 13:5; 12:6]

Tertullian (150-220 A.D.): ...that the beast Antichrist with his false prophet may wage war on the church of God....Since, then, the Scriptures both indicate the stages of the last times, and concentrate the harvest of the Christian hope in the very end of the world.(On the Resurrection of the Flesh, xxv; see Scorpiace, xxii)

Now the privilege of this favor [to go without dying at the rapture] awaits those who shall at the coming of the Lord be found in the flesh, and who shall, owing to the oppressions of the time of Antichrist, deserve by instantaneous death [the rapture], which is accomplished by a sudden change, to become qualified to join the rising saints [the dead in Christ]; as [Paul] writes to the Thessalonians." (On the Resurrection of the Flesh, xli) [1Thess 4:13-18; 1Cor 15:50-54]

He equated the rapture of the church in 1Thessalonians (Against Marcion, iii, 25) and the resurrection of the church (On the Resurrection of the Flesh, xxiv) with Christ's coming to destroy the Antichrist. [see 2Thess 2:8]

Lactantius (240-303 A.D.) believed that the coming of the Lord to resurrect the righteous was to take place after the great tribulation. (Institutes, VII, xv-xxvii; see Institutes, IV; and Epitome, lxxi-lxxii).

Commodianus (200-270 A.D.) did likewise. (Instructions, xliv, lxxx)

Cyprian (200-258 A.D.), commenting on the tribulation in the Olivet Discourse (Matt 24), said:

With the exhortation of His foreseeing word, instructing, and teaching, and preparing, and strengthening the people of His church for all endurance of things to come, He predicted and said that wars, and famines, and earthquakes, and pestilences would arise in each place; and lest an unexpected and new dread of mischiefs should shake us, He previously warned us

152

that adversity would increase more and more in the last times. Behold, the very things occur which were spoken; and since those occur which were foretold before, whatever things were promised will also follow; as the Lord Himself promises, saying, "But when ye see all these things come to pass, know ye that the kingdom of God is at hand."(Treatise, VII)

He later discusses the persecution of the Christians by the Antichrist from the text of Matthew 24, and others. (Treatise, XI, 12)

These last two references include portions claimed by pre-tribs to teach an any-moment, imminent rapture:

The Constitutions of the Holy Apostles: Be watchful for your life. Let your loins be girded about, and your lights burning, and ye like unto men who wait for their Lord, when He will come, at even, or in the morning..... For at what hour they think not, the Lord will come; and if they open to Him, blessed are those servants, because they were watching...

Gundry notes that "Walvoord breaks off... in an endeavor to make the passage teach imminence" (p.177). Read on:

...And then shall appear the deceiver of the world, the enemy of the truth, the prince of lies, whom the Lord Jesus shall destroy with the Spirit of His mouth, who takes away the wicked with His lips; and many shall be offended at Him. But they that endure to the end, the same shall be saved. And then shall appear the sign of the son of Man in heaven; and afterward shall be the voice of a trumpet by the archangel; and in that interval shall be the revival of those that were asleep. And then the Lord shall come and His saints with Him. (Constitutions, VIII, ii, xxxi-xxxii)[Matt 24:29-31; 1Cor 15:51-52; 1Thess 3:13; 4:16, 17; Jude 14; Rev 6:12-7:17]

This next quote is very similar, and uses the same Scripture references:

The Teachings of the Twelve Apostles: Watch for you life's sake. Let not your lamps be quenched, nor your loins

153

unloosed, but be ye ready, for you know not the hour in which our Lord cometh...

"Here Walvoord, Stanton, and Pentecost break off the quotation in an endeavor to make the passage establish a belief in imminence by the early church" (p155). Again, look at the context:

...But often shall ye come together, seeking the things which are befitting soul: for the whole time of your faith will not profit you, if you be not made perfect in the last time. For in the last days false prophets and corrupters shall be multiplied...and then shall appear the world deceiver as the Son of God, and shall do signs and wonders, and the earth shall be delivered into his hands, and he shall do iniquitous things which have never yet come to pass since the beginning.... And then shall appear the signs of the truth; first, the sign of an outspreading in heaven; then the sign of the sound of a trumpet; and the third, the resurrection of the dead; yet not all, but as it is said: "The Lord shall come and His saints with Him. Then shall the world see the Lord coming upon the clouds of heaven." (Teachings, XVI)

In Chapter IX and X of this same work, Matthew 24:31 is twice quoted with the substitution of the word *church* for *elect*. This is precisely what the pre-wrath rapture teaches.

Rosenthal notes in his study guide[79] that the following early church fathers also held to a similar view: Clement of Rome (30-100 A.D.), Ignatius (50-115 A.D.), Polycarp (70-167 A.D), Papias (80-163 A.D.) Pothinus (87-177 A.D.), Hegisippus (130-190 A.D.), Tatian (130-190 A.D.), and others.

It should be obvious that the early church believed we would enter the great tribulation. So let's return to our study.

---

[79] Examining the Pre-Wrath Rapture of the Church, p. 118

The Theory of Imminency

Pre-tribs use several different angles attempting to defend their theory of imminency. They claim the N.T. authors, and even Jesus Himself, taught an any-moment coming for the church. They say the frequent use of phrases such as *look for, be ready,* or *no-one know the day or hour* in relation to the rapture and the DOL demonstrate it could come immediately. The second issue is that the church is never mentioned by name in Revelation after chapter three until the marriage supper in chapter nineteen - the church being the Bride of Christ. They also argue that the church is never told to look for signs, but for Jesus Himself; thus, they say, we must be raptured before the seventieth week or else there would be signs. Last is the frequently raised cry that God would never make the church suffer through the persecution of the great tribulation. While it would be unfair to say this last is a major point for all pre-trib teachers, nevertheless many do focus on this. Each of these will be considered.

I have frequently heard the objection that God would never make the church suffer through the great tribulation. Ohh... and why wouldn't He? God allowed the early church to suffer severe persecution: they were crucified, like Peter, exiled, like John, beheaded, tortured, covered with tar and tied to a stake to be burned alive, thrown to wild animals, impaled, and more. In modern times, it has been said that more Christians have been martyred in the twentieth century than the rest of church history combined! Do believers in relatively free nations think they are somehow better or more deserving of protection than these? Are we better than the Apostles, all of whom suffered for their faith? Actually, I believe the free church needs some good, old-fashioned persecution to purge it of the dead weight of wishy-washy Christianity so prevalent today.

The Christian life is sometimes compared to warfare (see Eph 6:10-13), as also is the great tribulation (Rev 12 and 13). Would God remove His earth-based, experienced army just before the greatest spiritual battle ever to take place, the seventieth week, and leave behind a brand-new, untaught army, the so-called post-rapture tribulation saints, to fight the war? That would be comparable to a modern army going AWOL just before the most important, deciding battle while leaving the unprepared civilians to form an untrained army at the last moment.

2Thess 1:4-8 explains that one of the evidences to the world why God's DOL wrath is perfectly righteous is the world's severe persecution of the saints. Another passage shedding light on this issue is Romans 8:35-39:

> *Who shall separate us from the love of Christ? Shall tribulation, or distress, or persecution, or famine, or nakedness, or peril or sword? As it is written:* **For Your sake we are killed all day long; we are accounted as sheep for the slaughter.** *Yet in all these things we are more than conquerors through Him who loved us. For I am persuaded that neither death, nor life, nor angels nor principalities nor powers, nor things present, nor things to come...shall be able to separate us from the love of God which is in Jesus Christ our Lord.*

Here we are specifically told that Christians are subject to persecution and murder. And Paul was not teaching a new thing, but merely expounding on what Jesus Himself taught (Matt 5:11, 12; 10:16-39; Luke 6:22, 23; John 15:18-25; and others). When persecutions come we need to remember Peter's and James's exhortations to rejoice, for tribulations have spiritual value (James 1:2, 3; 1Pet 4:12-14; see Acts 5:41). While it is true that these passages refer to general tribulations and provide no direct proof the church will enter the seventieth week, they do argue against the above pre-trib complaint.

Richard E. Orchard brings up an interesting point:

> If the saints are going to have to go through the Tribulation it would be better for us to die than to live until Jesus comes. So terrible will be the storm of the Tribulation...80

---

80   Look Who's Coming, Richard E. Orchard: Gospel Publishing

He has a valid point, for it will be a difficult time – even for those few who are promised some kind of divine protection in Revelation 3:10. Even God openly agrees, for He explicitly says so in Revelation 14:13: *Then I heard a voice from heaven saying to me, 'Write: Blessed [happy, to be envied] are the dead who die in the Lord from now on.' 'Yes,' says the Spirit, 'that they may rest from their labors, and their works follow them.'* This is said concerning saints who keep the faith of Jesus under the Antichrist (v.12).

Next is the question of signs. The theory of imminency states that no prophecies need to be fulfilled before the Lord comes for His church, and *requires* that no recognizable signs precede it, as well. How else could the Day of the Lord come like a thief? If it were preceded by signs, it could no longer be considered unexpected. Titus 2:13 is frequently raised up under this category, which declares we are *"looking for the blessed hope and appearing of the glory of our great God and Savior, Jesus Christ."*

> Gundry's presentation makes it clear that if one believes in post-tribulationism as he presents it, the hope of the Lord's return is a vain illusion, and what we are looking for is not the Lord's coming, but the great tribulation. Because this is hardly a blessed hope, pre-tribulationists continue to insist that their point of view is quite different from the post-tribulational view in its expectation. If there are well-defined events that must occur before the rapture of the church...then the concept of imminency can no longer be properly applied to the rapture.81

> The real issue, as pre-tribulationists state it, is that the hope offered them in the New Testament is the hope of the rapture before the tribulation, not the hope of survival through the tribulation.82

House, Springfield, MO 65802, 1975, p. 36
[81]   Bibliotheca Sacra; "Post-tribulationism Today," John F. Walvoord, Apr-Jun 1976, p. 112
[82] ibid. p. 110

Their view which is *quite different* is also quite unscriptural and flawed. The blessedness of our hope has *absolutely nothing* to do with the timing of the rapture. This does not say we are looking for the resurrection; It says we are looking for Jesus Himself. There is not one single aspect of true Christianity which is about an event or a written doctrine. It is the New and Living Way. In every respect it is about a Person, Jesus Christ. He is our hope of glory. He is the Author and Finisher of our faith. Jesus is our strength and our righteousness. Jesus is the Way, the Truth, and the Life. He is the Living Word. And Jesus is the Resurrection and the Life.

Did you catch that? *He* is our resurrection. The rapture is not an event but His Person. Our hope is not in the rapture, but in Christ. This is true no matter when He comes to get us.

I like how Rosenthal answered this:

> ...It does not follow that the *blessed hope* is no longer the blessed hope because a period of severe difficulty is to precede it. The blessed hope is the certain prospect of deliverance from God's wrath and of spiritual union between Christ and the church...in spite of all possible obstacles. A strong case can be made for the thesis that the blessed hope is enhanced if a time of difficulty were to precede it (Rom 5:2-4, 9). The greater the suffering, the more glorious the deliverance.... A blessed hope is literally a living hope, and difficulty and testing does not invalidate that prospect.[83]

Also, what believers are looking for is the *appearing* of Jesus and His glory. This is the *epiphaneia,* which implies visibility and conspicuousness (Strong's # 2015). Why would believers be told to look for a glorious, visible advent if they are to be raptured pre-trib, at a *secret* coming?

The purpose of signs is largely to testify of the truth to unbelievers (John 4:48; 1Cor 14:22). The same is true of the

---

[83] <u>The Pre-Wrath Rapture of the church</u>, op. cit., p. 247

heavenly signs at the sixth seal and in the gospel accounts - they are *signs of the truth*, for they will testify that mankind rejected the only Savior and abide under God's wrath.

We are not supposed to look for signs, but for Jesus. Some of the false prophets will perform miracles, as will the Antichrist, to even deceive the elect if possible (Matt 24:24; 2Thess 2:9, 10; Rev 13:13, 14). Many times over the centuries the church has seen characteristics of the Antichrist in individuals and named them so. Sometimes certain events seem to line up with prophecy. But Jesus has not yet returned. We are not to look for signs, but wait for Jesus!

But Jesus did tell the disciples that if they watched they would see signs. In Matthew 24:32-35 He said when we see the things He just described begin to happen, particularly the Abomination of Desolation, we will know His coming is at the very doors. Luke's adds that when we see the signs of the sixth seal we should *lift our heads, for our redemption draws near* (21:28). These signs, will be noticed around the world and cause the ungodly to flee in terror. The Day of the Lord has caught them by surprise, like a thief, and stolen away the church. Nevertheless, we are told when we see these signs to look beyond them for Christ our Deliverance.

Let me illustrate the effect signs should have on the believer. It is well into spring; summer is drawing near. The children in school, anxious for summer vacation to arrive, are restless and easily distracted. They look through the windows and see the trees covered with leaves, the birds and insect flying about, the sun brightly shining. They can feel the warmth of summer, smell the scent of flowers in the air. In short, they see the signs of the approaching summer vacation. However, they must still look through the classroom window, must keep on going to school, must keep on working; *they still have final exams*. They must continue to wait, come what may. But…they keep looking and waiting anxiously for summer vacation. Dear brothers and sisters in Christ, children of the Most High God, keep looking for that blessed and glorious Christian *summer vacation* with Christ that will never, ever end – even while in the midst of final exams!

159

Supposedly, the fact that the church is not named in Revelation after chapter three proves they cannot then be present. After all, John did not have a problem talking about the church in the first three chapters.

There are numerous logical and scriptural errors with this line of thinking. First, every time the word *church* appears in Revelation, apart from 1:4, John directly quotes Jesus as He dictates the letters. Through the remainder of the book John narrates what he sees and hears rather than being told what to say. John rarely used the term in his writings, and the few times he did it referred to the local congregation rather than the universal body of believers. Also, in Revelation Jesus referred to seven specific congregations of John's day (and congregational groupings of the last days). Not only that, most of the times the word *church* is used in the N.T. it refers to local congregations. Thus this is consistent with Scripture. Feinberg admits this, but asks:

> ...Why is there no mention of local assemblies in the last 19 chapters of Revelation? There are references to saints and elect. They are not said to be the church, however.84

Easy to answer: Because Jesus already gave personal instructions to the seven types of churches in the seventieth week. No individual congregation has any more significant role than what He already told them.

On the other hand, the *saints of Jesus* are named three times in these chapters, always in relation to the rise of the beast and the persecution they must endure (Rev 12:7; 14:12; 13:10). We saw earlier the problems with the hypothetical, post-rapture revival so they cannot be saved during the Tribulation. The 144,000 do not appear on the scene until the sixth seal, the same time the saints of Jesus appear in heaven, so these saints of Jesus cannot be them. The only group left is the church.

---

84 The Rapture..., p. 83

Additionally, it should be observed that the term *church* never occurs in any of the main Rapture passages either (1Cor 15:51-57; 1Thess 4:14-18; Tit 2:11-14).. Since all agree that the church is nevertheless the subject involved in these passages, this argument from silence is robbed of any possible validity.[85] Also, Revelation 4 and 5 are said to describe the heavenly scene just after the pre-trib rapture, and the church is conspicuously absent there, too. Not even saints of Jesus are mentioned there.

If we accept at face value that Matthew 24:29-31 is the sixth seal and that the trumpets and bowls follow it, two more significant points appear. First, these saints of Jesus are always mentioned in relation to the Abomination of Desolation and great tribulation. They are never described, however, in any earthly event following the sixth seal, such as during the trumpets and bowls. Second, Israel is never mentioned in Revelation prior to the sixth seal in time - apart from the flight into the wilderness at the Abomination (Rev 12). Besides these two times, Israel is hardly mentioned at all (Rev 14:1-5; 11:13). If the entire seventieth week concerns primarily the restoration of Israel while the church is absent, then why are they not mentioned more often? While I admit I argue from silence, so do the pre-tribs..... Only this silence is louder.

But doesn't Scripture warn us that Christ could come for the rapture at any moment? Most pre-tribs insist that the answer is yes, seeing imminence in passages such as John 14:2-3; 1Cor1:7; Ph'p3:20-21; 1Thess 1:9, 10; 4:13-18; 5:5-9; Tit 2:13; Jam 5:8-9; Rev 3:10-11; 22:17-22, and others.

The truth is the majority of these simply state Christ will certainly come for the church. They say nothing of the timing of His coming. Pre-tribs whine that they do not mention the great tribulation or signs to support a later rapture view. This argument is based solely on silence and is worth exactly nothing. After all, no passage describes the rapture prior to the seven years, either. Also, a few imply coming out of a time of testing (Rev 3:10, 11),

---

[85] The Rapture..., Gleason Archer contrib., p. 135

or tell believers to wait for his appearing or revelation (which imply visibility). Others exhort us to endure to the end. 1Thess 5:5-9 merely promises we will avoid the Day of the Lord and wrath, which starts with the sixth seal. So once again pre-tribs base their entire case on silence. "If Scripture does *not* say something then it must be true!"

Pre-tribs argue for imminence in 1Thess 4:13-18 in three ways. First is that this does not explain that the great tribulation comes first.86 Paul's purpose was not to explain the end times. It was to reassure them that those who died in Christ would not be left out, but would actually be resurrected first. He did conclude by promising Christ would come before the Day of the Lord, before God's wrath (1Thess 5:1-11).

Feinberg argues:

> I think that the belief in an any-moment imminency grows out of these three lines of argumentation: Paul's inclusion of himself and his readers among the potential participants in the Rapture... in a number of places Paul writes as though he and his readers might participate in the Rapture....87

He points out the first person pronoun "we" in 1Thessalonians 4:13-17 and 1Corinthians 15:51-53. After admitting that Paul might have been identifying with the church as a whole, he states, "but one cannot escape the impression that Paul thought that he and the Thessalonians might participate in the rapture."

Perhaps Paul did think he might participate in the rapture in his lifetime. This does not mean, however, that he did not understand the Antichrist would come first and he would have to survive the great tribulation. In Philippians 3:10-11, Paul expected at this time to attain to the resurrection of the dead rather than be alive for the rapture. This argues against a belief in imminence by Paul.

---

[86] Bibliotheca Sacra; "Post-tribulationism Today," John F. Walvoord: Oct-Dec 1976, p. 301

[87] The Rapture..., pp. 155-156

Walvoord explains the third argument:

> The hope of the Lord's return is presented as a comfort to the Thessalonians sorrowing for their loved ones who have died. The hope of a rapture after a literal great tribulation would be small comfort to those in this situation.[88]

He misses the entire point. The comfort has absolutely nothing to do with the timing of the rapture. The comfort is the promise that the dead in Christ will be resurrected at the same time the living are snatched away. Moreover, the Thessalonians were already facing severe persecution, so there was no need to tell them that persecution comes first.

Prophetic Delays

> As a pre-tribulationist I want to see an occurrence of one of the terms in a passage that I understand as relating to the Rapture (e.g. John 14:1-3 or 1Thess 4:13-18) that requires intervening events or time delay. Simply to appeal to passages which are non-eschatological or relate to the second coming [Armageddon] will not convince me.[89]

You must take all of what Scripture says before arriving at truth. He asks that we only use the passages he picks out. If we pick and choose which verses we will accept, we are as likely to arrive at error as truth. In other words, if we form a theory then pick only those passages which agree with us, and bypass or explain away those which don't fit our theory, we will probably be wrong. Those who use this method should quote the old adage, "Don't confuse me with the facts."

While I cannot provide evidence *requiring* a delay or signs using his verses, I can show some which strongly suggest it. Titus 2:13

---

[88] Bibliotheca Sacra, Oct-Dec 1976, op cit., p. 301
[89] The Rapture..., Feinberg, p. 153

tells us to wait for *the appearing of the glory* of Jesus (literal rendition of the Greek). The word *appearing* means something visible and noticeable. After the sign of the Son of Man appears (phaneroo, closely related to epiphaneia) the world will see Jesus coming in glory (Matt 24:30). I challenge Feinberg to show a point where Jesus appears in glory in a passage which places His coming at another time. Simply saying no such information is provided does not prove it must be pre-trib.

Several passages say we are waiting for the apokalupsis (revealing) of Jesus. The earliest it can be demonstrated in the book of the Apocalypse that Jesus appears is the sixth seal (Rev 6:16-17). Several passages tell us to *wait for* His coming (Ph'p 3:20), which at least suggests the possibility of a delay. Also, in some of Jesus' kingdom parables the principal character leaves for a *long time*, then comes back to see how his servants have done to reward them accordingly (Matt 25:14-30).

1Thessalonians 4:15-17 also suggest the possibility of a delay with the phrase, *we who are alive and remain*. This appears to be redundant in English, for of course those who are alive at the rapture are remaining. But it is not mere repetition.

The Greek word translated *remain* is *perileipo* (Strong's #4035), which means *to leave all around, survive*. It carries the idea of passing through circumstances and is related to our word *peril*. Also, the word *and* is not in the Greek, but was added by the translators. They were mistaken to add the word here for it weakens the impact of this phrase. It would be better translated *then we the living ones, the ones surviving*. This suggests the possibility of an ordeal which the church must survive through to go without dying at the rapture. While I will admit it does not require an ordeal or period of time, it certainly does not suggest imminency, either.

We have seen that their case for imminency is without support. There is also additional direct evidence against the idea that the church believed in it, evidence requiring a gap before Jesus could come. In 1895 Arthur J. Pierson noted that "the imminence of the

Lord's coming is destroyed the moment you locate between the first and second coming... any period of time whatsoever that is a definite period, whether 10, 100, or 1,000 years. I cannot look for a thing as an imminent event which I know is not going to take place for 10 years to come..."90 So if a necessary gap can be proven to exist, then the theory of biblical imminency can no longer stand.

First gap: Peter was told he would live to be an old man before he died by crucifixion (John 21:18, 19). Second gap: Paul was convinced he should live long enough to carry out an extensive ministry (Ph'p 1:21-26). Third gap: The temple first had to be destroyed and completely dismantled before Christ could come (Matt 24:1, 2) - which was fulfilled forty years after Christ spoke this prophecy and *after* most of the New Testament was written. Fourth gap: Several passages suggest quite a program for the church age (Matt 13:1-50; 28:19, 20; Luke 19:11-27; Acts 1:5-8), for the gospel had to be preached to all nations before Christ could return (Acts 1:8).

Herman A. Hoyt offers this rebuttal:

> While the above objections...are valid up to a point, the matter is made more serious by the fact that nineteen hundred years have elapsed, suggesting that it was the purpose of God to carry out a providential ministry over a long period of time. Is there an answer for these objections which would have satisfied first century Christians, and will satisfy those today who believe in the imminent return of Christ?

> In reply at least three points can be made. At the very outset it needs to be pointed out that these very things that are cited as objections...are not necessarily objections in themselves. In the perspective of these utterances, these things were intended to be parts in the normal unfolding of events, apart from unforeseen interruption. The imminent return of Christ, however, would be an unforeseen interruption. Being on such

---

90 cit. in The Rapture..., p. 20

a grand and catastrophic scale, it would not only interrupt but also supersede all other events.

Second, it must be remembered that almost all the things alluded to as objections disappeared during the first century....

Third, in the midst of passages recording the so-called objections, as well as outside of them, there are numerous exhortations for constant expectation of the coming of Christ....91

First he claims that these prophecies are not valid evidence because the rapture could supersede their fulfillment. Does this satisfy you? Would it have satisfied the first century church? Jesus said that His Word would never pass away (Matt 24:35). Thus, at the very least, those prophecies made by Christ must be fulfilled.

Among these were Peter's death, the destruction of the temple, and the preaching of the gospel to all nations. Since the Americas were already inhabited by various tribes when Christ spoke, this last prophecy could not be fulfilled until the gospel had reached them. I can hear some stubborn protesters argue that the early church did not know of these and could thus believe in imminency once their known world was evangelized. But Jesus spoke only what the Father told Him to, and God certainly knew (John 8:28).

Hoyt's second point is that most of these were fulfilled in the first century and cease to be problems. Douglas Moo explains the logical fallacy of this thinking:

It is not sufficient to say that all of these COULD have been fulfilled in the first century and therefore represent no barrier to an *any moment* Rapture NOW. For the point is to determine what the statements about the nearness of the Parousia would have meant to those who first heard them. If the original speaker did not intend and the original hearers did not understand a particular statement to require an *any moment*

---

91 The End Times, Herman A. Hoyt, op. cit., pp. 88-89

Rapture, that statement can hardly have such a meaning NOW.92

Daniel 9:27 prophesies a seven year covenant which pre-tribs agree triggers the start of the seventieth week. But from the destruction of Jerusalem in 70 A.D. until Israel became a nation again in 1941 this would have been impossible because the Jews had no central government through whom to make such a treaty. While they could potentially have been restored in any generation, it had to precede the rapture. Also, based on some prophecies, it seems the temple must also be rebuilt, for the Antichrist sets up his image in the holy place of the temple at the Abomination mid-week.

John H. Dobson, in discussing the usefulness of learning the Greek language, made this comment regarding the scriptural evidence for a delay in Christ's coming:

> If we can trust the evidence of Mark 13 and some of the parables, Jesus did not expect His return to be soon. Of course, an attentive reading of a good translation will also show this, but it is sometimes the careful attention to the Greek text necessary for the task of translation that makes us more sharply aware of what it actually says.93

The parable of the virgins (Matt 25:5) says the Bridegroom took long enough that they fell asleep. The parable of the minas (Luke 19:12-17) suggests a delay while the servants make a profit. In the parallel parable of the talents it specifically says the Lord would be gone a long time (Matt 25:19), right in the context of the parousia and the gathering of the elect. The parable of the wheat and tares also suggests a long time while the crop and weeds grow together until harvest (Matt 13:24-30); Likewise the parable of the workers in the vineyard (Matt 10:1-16). And James (5:7-9) compares waiting for Christ's coming to a farmer waiting for his crops to grow and ripen for harvest - hardly any moment. As Gundry concludes, "If a delay in the Parousia...was compatible with

---

92 The Rapture..., p. 210
93 Learn New Testament Greek, 2nd Ed, op. cit., pp. 276-277

167

expectancy in apostolic times, a delay for the several years of the tribulation is compatible with expectancy in the current time."94

It is interesting that even pre-tribs often turn to various prophecies that describe the world and the church in the last days (1Tim 4:1-5; 2Tim 3:1-9; 2Pet 2 and 3) and rightly note how they seem to be fulfilled today. But they ignore the fact that these qualify as prophecies which must be fulfilled before the rapture! If only one prophecy clearly requires a delay in Christ's coming, biblical imminency is destroyed. We have seen many.

Pre-tribs beat around the bush, totally oblivious to the tiger waiting to jump out and devour them; they quietly step over the log lying in the path, failing to see the rattlesnake coiled right beneath their foot. If these things must be fulfilled before the rapture, and they must, then the theory of biblical imminency cannot be true. The tiger, tired of running before his pursuers, has pounced; the rattlesnake, disturbed in his nest, has struck. The theory of imminency has died as a result.

The early church clearly could not believe Christ could return at any moment, without any prophesied events or signs preceding it. On the other hand, they did believe Jesus could potentially return in any generation. Scripture repeatedly advises the church to wait for, look for, and expect Jesus (Luke 12:36; Tit 2:13; Matt 24:50; 1Thess 1:10), to await Him eagerly (Rom 8:23; Gal 5:5), and so to be ready and alert (1Thess 5:6, 8; Matt 24:42, 43; Rev 16:15); for the coming of the Lord has drawn near (Ph'p 4:5; Jam 5:8, 9). That is the true and simple meaning behind these verses.

After considering these arguments against imminency, I am certain you will find John Sproule's comments interesting:

> However, another question arises. Is pre-tribulationism proven by the doctrine of imminency or does the doctrine of imminency drive from an exegetically proven pre-tribulationism? To find help, the researcher will be

---

94 The church and the Tribulation, op. cit., p. 37

disappointed in his search for pre-trib literature on the subject of imminency. Walvoord...refers to imminency as the "heart of pre-tribulationism." Yet he is able to muster only a few vague quotations for the Early Church Fathers plus a few debatable Scriptures (John 14:1-3; 1Thess 1:10; 4:13-18; 5:6; and 1Cor 1:7) to support his statement. However, a contextual examination of these quotations shows them more supportive of post-trib than pre-trib....

Pre-tribulationism can ill afford to rest on the shaky foundation of traditional and eisetelogical [reading into the text] statements. If its "heart" is a debatable and inductively determined doctrine of imminency then, perhaps, an exegetical "heart transplant" may be in order.95

You've got to love these more honest pre-tribs. For every one that claims a certain doctrine or theory proves pre-trib, another one comes along and admits that either the true doctrine can be aligned with any of the rapture theories, or else agrees that the given pre-trib argument is questionable at best. Throughout this book I have shown this true of nearly every major point.

Since many pre-tribs spend a number of pages trying to explain imminency, its death alone weakens the pre-trib theory. And when you consider just how many of their claims have been destroyed by this simple study, there are no safe grounds on which to base the pre-trib theory. Note that Sproule realizes the context of these passages show more support with post-trib, yet he insists on defending pre-trib. Perhaps it is all these problems which caused Feinberg to begin his defense of imminency by stating:

There is no question that pre-tribulationists have and do make a great deal of an any-moment imminency and its practical consequences. Nevertheless, I think it is important to see that an any-moment imminency could be wrong and pre-tribulationism could still be right. The minimum requirement for the truth of pre-tribulationism is simply that

---

95 In Defense of Pre-tribulationism, op. cit., pp 18, 23

the Rapture of the church must PRECEDE the Tribulation. That is all.96

The fact that the various other pre-millennial views all have problems is admitted by some adherents. Mid-trib Gleason Archer concludes that "as we draw this whole discussion to a close, we must confess that the data of Scripture do not lend themselves to any clear and unambiguous pattern which is completely free of difficulties."97   Post-trib Douglas Moo likewise admits that "the simple fact is that each of the views possesses some problems – what will be ultimately decisive is the question as to which view can most satisfactorily handle the most directly relevant texts."98

John Walvoord was challenged to cite a verse of Scripture that clearly promised the church would be raptured prior to the seventieth week. In reply, he admitted that "the fact is that neither post-tribulationism nor pre-tribulationism is an explicit teaching of the Scriptures. The Bible does not, in so many words, state either. Pre-tribulationism is based on the fact that it allows harmony of the Scripture relating to the Second Advent." He makes an even more revealing statement earlier in the same book: "It is therefore not too much to say that the rapture question is determined more by ecclesiology [word of the people; tradition] than eschatology [study of last things]."99

Every passage I have discussed is relevant to the issue, for you do not have truth until all the pieces fit. None of the other views can successfully harmonize them while maintaining a literal method of interpretation.   Pre-wrath, on the other hand, does harmonize these passages.   It easily answers the key post-trib problem of placing the church on earth during God's wrath.   It explains why no passage shows Jesus returning before the great

---

96 The Rapture..., p. 152
97 The Rapture..., p. 144
98 The Rapture..., p. 167
99 The Rapture Question, 1st ed.: Findlay OH, n.p., 1957, p. 148, quote removed from later editions.

tribulation, a major problem with pre-trib and mid-trib. When you line everything up, the rapture just naturally falls into place at the sixth seal, when the great tribulation is cut short and God's wrath is introduced.

One wonders, seeing how many serious problems the other theories have, why nobody considered searching for a view which solves them until recently. Instead, they continued trying to explain them away with weak, unconvincing, illogical arguments through much fast talking, like a used car salesman trying to sell a piece of junk. Expositors seem to be continually stuck in a rut, always churning the same dirt roads, looking at the same tired view. They keep pushing the same positions, always finding the same bumps and potholes and never truly finding satisfactory answers.

The pre-wrath view pulls the rapture wagon out of its rut to find smoother riding, searching for and finding the answers to those problems. It affirms those points which are correct in the other theories. It finds the balancing point. We insist on a consistently literal method of interpreting Scripture, and have no need to fast talk our way past rough spots. We don't have to strain at a gnat and swallow a camel to explain our view.

In the next chapters we will consider a few additional, brief points, then begin inspecting our doctrinal house. Are their any leaky faucets or missing windows? Several books and articles have been written by those who would critique the pre-wrath view. We will examine their case and see if pre-wrath holds up to close scrutiny.

Part II
Answering the Critics

Chapter 11: Last Points and Most Common Critiques

Dispensational Theory

A few points must still be addressed before this study can be considered complete. First, pre-tribs often raise up dispensational theory as the key proof for their position. For example, Pentecost says because God is turning His attention to the restoration of Israel during the seventieth week, the church must be absent. He further argues that

> ...since the church did not have its existence until after the death of Christ (Eph 5:25-26), until after the resurrection (Rom 4:25; Col 3:1-3), until after His ascension (Eph 1:19, 20), and until after the descent of the Holy Spirit at Pentecost (Acts 2), the church could not have been in the first sixty-nine weeks, which are related only to God's program for Israel, it can have no part in the seventieth week, which is again related to God's program for Israel after the mystery program for the church has been completed.100

The most glaring point is that the church did not yet exist during the sixty-nine weeks, so it is impossible to have been in them. But the church does exist now, so it is possible to be in the seventieth week. This could admittedly create an overlap between the church age and God's program for Israel. Is this impossible to reconcile? Consider these points.

God did not immediately cease working with Israel when the church age began. Many dispensationalists concede that the book of Acts describes a transition period between them. In Acts 3:1 the early Jewish believers in Christ still gathered at the temple to worship the Lord. In fact, for more than five years after Pentecost

---

[100] Things to Come, op. cit., p. 194

the church consisted almost exclusively of Jewish believers. Paul, the apostle to the Gentiles, routinely presented the gospel to the Jews first during the early years of his ministry. Later he stopped and presented it to only the Gentiles. Also, the church did not really begin to understand the unity of Jewish and Gentile believers until Acts 15:6-18.

Furthermore, it's impossible to defend the position that a righteous Jew under the Old Covenant would suddenly be under God's condemnation after Pentecost. What of those who had never heard of Jesus? God is just, so surely there would be a transitional period - perhaps the forty years between Christ's death and the destruction of Jerusalem in 70AD. Don't misunderstand me. Once Jesus fulfilled the Law the old system passed away. But I am convinced God would not automatically condemn righteous Jews, allowing time for the gospel to spread. It is not God's will to send anyone to hell, and it is His heart to save those He can without violating His holiness (2Pet 3:9; Heb 8:13).

Feinberg, paraphrasing Gundry, asks: "How would Israel and the church coexist since both have different regulations (Law and Gospel)? Would the Tribulation church be exclusively Gentile, or could some Jews be a part of it? Would each group preach a variation of the gospel...?" 101

First, the 144,000 firstfruits of Israel do not appear until the sixth seal. It is impossible to show that they put faith in Jesus any earlier than this point, which Matthew 24 clearly places after the appearance of the Antichrist. Second, the purpose of the seventieth week as it relates to Israel is to bring them to acceptance of Jesus as their Messiah. It is to usher in the millennial kingdom with Christ directly ruling the earth, not to restore the Old Covenant. While the kingdom will have ties to O.T. promises of God, it will be different in many ways. Third, few conversions to Christianity take place during this time period.

---

101 The Rapture..., p. 49

Feinberg feels "what should at least be noted is that dispensationalism has more often than not led to pre-tribulationism."102 John A. Witmer makes an even stronger assertion in a review of the book When the Trumpet Sounds:

> A second foundation of the pre-tribulational rapture, therefore, is the literal interpretation of the Bible. This leads both to consistent dispensationalism and to pre-tribulationism, which are inseparably combined.103

Does consistent dispensationalism require a pre-trib rapture? Actually, as pre-trib is usually presented it ends up contradicting this doctrine. They claim because the seventieth week concerns God's program for Israel, the church as a mostly Gentile institution must be removed before it can begin. But then, because Revelation 7:9-17 leaves no other choice, they turn around a say God will save many millions of Gentiles from around the world during this period. Pre-tribs say God will not extend the Gentile church age into the week, yet assert that a vast number of them will put faith in Christ for salvation during those seven years. Why would God remove the Gentile church only to save a huge number of Gentiles by the blood of Christ immediately afterward? Sort of defeats the purpose, doesn't it?

Some attempt to avoid this by having the multitude obtain salvation through the witness of the 144,000 and subject to the Law, placing them under the dispensation of the seventieth week.

The first problem, already mentioned, is that the 144,000 do not appear on the scene until the sixth seal (Rev 6:12-7:8). We have seen that this seal opens after the great tribulation is amputated (Matt 24:29-31). To claim an earlier salvation requires they argue from silence, for no scripture teaches it. Remember that the saints of Jesus are attacked very quickly after the Abomination of Desolation (Rev 13:7; 14:9-13). Even assuming for argument's sake that the sixth seal precedes the Abomination, there would still

---

102 The Rapture..., p. 49
103 Bibliotheca Sacra; Vol 153, Apr-Jn 1996, p. 237

be insufficient time in the severely restrictive environment of the seventieth week for the 144,000 to preach to the entire world (Matt 24:14) and produce such fantastic results. But this is what Stanton stands on in his critique of Rosenthal's book:

> A more normal view is that Israel is beginning to turn back to the Lord, and that these are sealed for service and evangelism to fulfill their destiny as God's witnesses and a "light to the Gentiles" (Is 42:6; 43:10, 12; 49:6).104

The problem is they are NOT sealed for ministry. The angels holding the four winds are told not to harm the trees, water, etc. until after the 144,000 are sealed. Thus it is to protect them in the first four trumpets. The first trumpet, fire and hail, falls on the enemy at the Jehoshaphat Campaign, and the seal protects the Jewish army from the hail as they pursue the enemy. As for his Scripture references, Isaiah 42 and 49 both relate to Christ's first advent as a light to the world, not to Israel's role as witnesses to the world. Isaiah 43 does concern Israel - during the millennial kingdom. Most importantly, nothing in either passage concerning the 144,000 says anything about an evangelistic ministry for them (Rev 7:1-8; 14:1-5). The pre-trib case argues from silence and is unjustified from all angles. It is based solely on their rapture theory rather than on a clear pattern from Scripture.

When we realize that the rapture and the sealing of the 144,000 firstfruits both occur with the sixth seal, the true dispensational doctrine is revealed. The pre-wrath position better fits the requisites for this than does pre-trib. As Feinberg confesses:

> ...There is a certain logical independence between the two views.... It will not follow that an argument FOR dispensationalism will necessarily be an argument FOR pre-tribulationism....105

---

104 Bibliotheca Sacra; "A Review of The Pre-Wrath Rapture of the Church": Jan-Mar 1991, p. 102
105 The Rapture..., p. 49, emph. his

The Last Trump

Still to be identified is the last trump of God which sounds at the rapture (1Cor 15:51, 52; 1Thess 4:15-17). Some pre-tribs say it is the voice of Jesus (Rev 1:10; 4:1), based partly on when Jesus raised Lazarus from the dead (John 11:43). Others believe it is a literal trumpet like those in the Old Testament. For example, Paul Van Gorder notes that while Israel was in the wilderness two trumpets were used, one calling them to gather and another move on.106   Another view is that there are two trumps, one for the resurrection of the dead and one for the catching away of the living - thus the *last trump* at the rapture. Still others see the first trump starting the church age and the last concluding it.   Other suggestions have also been offered.

Most of these would work as well for the pre-wrath view. However, none has any support in prophecy. Before we look at one which is supported, let's examine these. First is the claim of two trumpets, one for the resurrection and one for the rapture. 1Corinthians 15:52 clearly states, *For the trumpet will sound, and the dead will be raised incorruptible, and we shall be changed*, speaking of only one trumpet. A trumpet marking the start and end of the age is mere conjecture. Scripture says we gather at the last trump, not that we move on at that trump. And finally, relating it to the voice of Jesus is largely based on Revelation 4:1 describing the rapture, which I already thoroughly refuted. Furthermore, it says Jesus *will descend from heaven with a shout ... and with the trumpet of God,* clearly separating the two.

Robert Van Kampen makes a suggestion which has some prophetic support. Here is his glossary definition, followed by a summary of what he taught.

---

106   Waiting, Working, Watching, Paul Van Gorder: Radio bible Class, Grand Rapids, MI, p. 6

179

TRUMPET OF GOD: A heavenly trumpet that is blown by God Himself on two distinct but parallel occasions. The first blowing occurred before God delivered Israel from Antiochus Epiphanes [a type of the Antichrist who ravaged Israel during the 2nd century B.C.] and his armies and is recorded by the prophet Zechariah [9:14] in a near/far depiction of His second coming and last blowing. The second time God blows His trumpet will occur just before Christ raptures the church and begins to execute His Day-of-the-Lord wrath...107

This trumpet sounds at the Jehoshaphat Campaign. This is a separate, prophetically important major battle from Armageddon and follows the Abomination of Desolation. The Jews will be stirred up to fight the Islamic coalition whose armies control Israel under the Antichrist's authority. This battle is centered in the valley of Jehoshaphat, which lies between Jerusalem and the Mount of Olives (Ps 46; Joel 3:1, 2, 9, 12-16; Zech 9:14-16; 12:6; Ez 38:18ff). It begins when the Day of the Lord is *near* (Joel 3:14). God Himself blows a trumpet and leads Israel's armies to victory against her enemies. This contrasts with Armageddon when Jesus comes with the heavenly armies and destroys the armies of the *world* gathered against Himself with the sword of His mouth.

This same event is alluded to in Isaiah 18:3-6 as an oracle against Ethiopia, but here directed for the entire world to notice: He will blow a trumpet immediately before the sour grapes [of wrath] are harvested as a sacrifice (see Zeph 1:7; Rev 14:17-20). Psalm 47:5-9 mentions all three stages of Christ's parousia: At the first God goes up with a shout, YHWH with the sound of a trumpet (v.5, see 1Thess 4:16); In the second God is proclaimed King of the earth (v.7, see Rev 11:15-19); And Armageddon and the sheep and goat judgment, when He judges the nations is third (vv. 8-9; see Matt 25:31-46; Rev 2:26, 27; 20:4). This demonstrates all are seen as parts of a single parousia.

---

107 The Sign, op. cit., p. 441

Also, Ezekiel 38:18-23 prophesies against Gog. Likely the Islamic countries controlling Israel will be joined or headed up by Gog (probably Russia or Turkey, which are heavily Islamic). There will be a great earthquake that causes all men to shake in fear, after which God rains fire and brimstone on his troops and thus magnifies Himself (see Rev 6:14-17; 8:7; Luke 21:25, 26; Is 2:12, 17). This is clearly the sixth seal, followed by the first trumpet. In this time frame Jesus gathers the elect at the rapture and seals the 144,000, who are probably the Israeli armies at Jehoshaphat. I break down this battle in greater detail in a later chapter.

Some mid- and post-tribs identify the last trumpet as the seventh trumpet judgment (Rev 11:15-19). They base this on Revelation 10:7, which says this trumpet finishes *the mystery of God.* They take this to be the mystery program of the church.

I discussed some critical problems with this in chapter 3. In addition, there are at least four more. For one, the church is expressly promised complete deliverance from God's wrath and the Day of the Lord (1Thess 1:10; 5:1-11). The Bible clearly says that the trumpets are part of His wrath, so the church must be gone.

Second, Paul informed us in 1Corinthians that the rapture is at the *last trump.* This book was written thirty years before Revelation. Logic says this last trump would have to be something already known or searchable to the church, so it seems unlikely it could refer to the seventh trumpet.

Third, this leaves no room for the judgment of the saints. The seventh trumpet says they receive their rewards (Rev 11:18), so they must have been judged before this.

Finally, the last trumpet is apparently blown by God Himself (1Thess 4:15-17), whereas the seventh trumpet is blown by an angel. The only other place in history in which God is said to have blown a trumpet is when He brought victory to the Maccabees over Antiochus Epiphanes (see <u>The Sign,</u> for more on this), a type of the Antichrist. This provides a first trumpet to go with the *last.*

181

What is the *mystery of God* completed with the seventh trumpet, if not the church age? It is the mystery of the hardening of Israel. Romans 11:25-26 shows us a mystery concerning the temporary hardening of Israel *until the fullness of the Gentiles has come in. And so all Israel will be saved.* According to pre-wrath understanding, most of Israel who survives the ravishment by the Antichrist will begin repenting in the interval between the sixth seal and seventh trumpet (Rev 11:13; Acts 3:21). At this point Jesus returns for the second part of His parousia, standing on the Mount of Olives and splitting it in half so the Jews may flee to safety (Azal) from the grand finale of God's wrath in the bowls (Zech 14:4, 5). The seventh trumpet also marks the end of the seventieth week and the 1260 days Antichrist is given to rule. The bowls fill up the next 30 days (1290 days, Dan 12:11), concluding with Armageddon.

The Most Common Critique Points Answered

We have clearly seen the evidence for the pre-wrath rapture. Several books and articles have been written attempting to refute this view. I am not afraid to face the scrutiny of others. This chapter will address some of the most common critiques. Then the following chapters answer two other writers, each of whom has a different approach.

The majority of the questions in this chapter are taken from articles in the Bibliotheca Sacra ("A Review of The Pre-Wrath Rapture of the Church," Gerald B. Stanton: Jan-Mr 1991, pp90-111; "Another Look at Rosenthal's Pre-Wrath Rapture," John A. McLean: Oct-Dec 1991, pp387-398); and Arnold Fruchtenbaum's contribution in When the Trumpet Sounds.108

---

[108] When the Trumpet Sounds, Thomas Ice and Timothy Demy: Harvest House Publishers, 1995

Objection (1): "Rosenthal is in serious trouble when he limits the Great Tribulation to the third quarter of the seven year period [when the DOL and rapture cut it short]....This event [Abomination of Desolation]...is the sign for the Jews to flee from the wrath of Satan, from whom they must be protected three-and-one-half years...(Rev 12:14)" {Stanton, p.96}. "Daniel 12:6-7 speaks of the length of this period of time: '...it would be for a time, times, and a half time [3 ½ years]'" {McLean, p.390}. The objection is that the Bible indicates the great tribulation will last the entire last half of the seventieth week.

Answer: Matthew 24:22 explains that the great tribulation will be amputated only as far as the elect are concerned. As the Jews will still be on earth following the rapture, the church is the elect covered by this promise. The beast will undoubtedly still exercise his authority and conduct his reign of terror against the Jews and the world after this; But even in that his influence will be reduced following the Jewish victory at Jehoshaphat and the disappearance of the church. No problem.

Objection (2): A further question... is whether Revelation 4:1-6:11 should also be included as part of God's tribulation judgment of wrath on the world? Christ... will take the scroll with seven seals (Rev 5:4-7) and open the seals (6:1), which will usher in the judgments of the seven seals (6:2-17). However, Rosenthal argues that since the first five seals are carried out by man, the seals are not part of God's judgment. This logic sets up an artificial principle of interpretation that ignores the plain teaching of God's control and execution of events throughout the book of Revelation.... Therefore, since the seals contain God's judgments executed by Christ [see John 5:22, 23, 27] (and not by man), the church must be removed before the seal judgments. (McLean, pp 392-393)

Answer: I already addressed this in the book, but will briefly summarize it one last time. We agree that God is ultimately in control of these seals - just as He is ultimately in control of everything happening today. God uses the nations to bring corrective anger against Israel and the saints. The seals are similar to these cases and are designed to show forth the wickedness of mankind. On the other hand, the trumpets and bowls introduce God's condemning wrath. Once the signs of the DOL appear with the sixth seal, man will know how puny his efforts have been in denying God (Psalm 2).

Objection (3): "There shall be cosmic disturbances, according to Joel 2:31.... Rosenthal identifies this with the sixth seal and uses it to date the rapture and the beginning of the Day of the Lord. But that can hardly be dogmatized, for the predicted Tribulation will not be limited to one display of cosmic power (see Rev 8:10-12; 11:19; 16:8, 21). In Matthew 24:27, Christ placed yet another great cosmic disturbance after the seventieth week when He stated that He shall appear with clouds and great glory and Israel shall mourn as they finally identify Him as the long-awaited Messiah (v.30).

"Indeed if there must be a cosmic disturbance before the day of the Lord can commence, let it be during a brief transitional period after the rapture but before the announcement of the Antichrist..." (Stanton, p.100)

Answer: This is so full of garbage it is hard to decide where to start cleaning. Stanton neither examined his arguments nor understood what Rosenthal teaches on this point. First of all, three of his Revelation references absolutely cannot be the cosmic disturbances to which Joel alluded (Rev 11:19; 16:8, 21). The first and third have nothing to do with the heavenly lights, but concern instead lightning, thunder, and hail. The second reference is a heating up of the sun, not a darkening. The presence of *other kinds* of cosmic disturbances cannot help us identify Joel's specific account. Only Revelation 8:12 otherwise comes close to matching it, but there is enough difference to make it doubtful. The sixth seal, on the other hand, is virtually identical. This dissolves the possibility of the fourth trumpet. This is also what we see in Matthew 24.

Second, the *sign of the Son of Man* and Christ's parousia are said to cause *all the tribes of the earth* to mourn (Matt 24:30; see Luke 21:25). Revelation 1:7 says that *every eye will see Him, and they also who pierced Him*, not just Israel. Again, this is perfectly described in the sixth seal, which aligns with Joel's prophecy. I demonstrated in chapter three that the trumpets and bowls must follow the seals, proving Matthew 24:27-31 cannot be Christ's coming at Armageddon. This passage cannot possibly be fulfilled at the end of the seventieth week. Stanton fails to acknowledge that this is what Rosenthal taught so he could place Matthew 24:29-31 at the end of the seventieth week as a separate match to Joel's prophecy.

In fact, sadly, Stanton frequently and seriously misrepresented Rosenthal's position throughout his review, as I have seen others also do. I don't know if this was intentional to raise more straw-man arguments and keep people from looking into pre-wrath, or whether he just didn't pay attention to what Rosenthal said. I lean to the former because he also maligned Rosenthal's character, integrity, and motives. Rosenthal admitted he had difficulty giving up the pre-trib view he had taught for thirty years, causing sleepless nights and lost friendships. Stanton says this is hardly the mark of God's leading.

It can be difficult to give up a wrong position held for years. I also resisted for a time because I thought the problems I saw might have been due to my own misunderstanding. It is human nature to resist admitting we are wrong. We do not want to look foolish by reneging on something we used to wrongly proclaim as true. And as for lost friendships, I am certain the disciples did not remain close friends with everyone they knew who rejected Christ. Matthew 10 says Jesus' message brings division and a sword, not peace. Well, the pre-wrath view is not particularly well received in a pre-trib church, and strong feelings can lead to division. That is part of the reason we have so many denominations.

Stanton also falsely accuses Rosenthal of placing the rapture in essentially the center of the second half of the week. But in truth he, like all pre-wraths, places it at an indefinite time within that period - it could be six months in or it could be six months from the end. A couple of passages suggest God's wrath lasts about a year, but we do not know for sure.

Stanton accuses Rosenthal of "distortion of prophetic truth, sometimes curious, sometimes strange, and frequently false" (p. 111). Yet he is guilty of that exact charge. He says if there must be cosmic signs before the DOL, let them follow the pre-trib rapture during a transitional period. There is absolutely no scriptural authority for placing such signs at the start of the week. His argument is patently false, based on sheer argumentativeness. We have an exact match to Joel with the sixth seal, and Joel plainly states these signs must precede the DOL. Jesus described these same exact signs when the great tribulation is cut short. Where is the distortion in that?

Objection (4): Even a casual reading of Revelation 6:12-17 reveals that the cry in verses 16-17 is a scream of terror from the wicked, rebellious human leaders who have endured war and famine, death and destruction, a shattering earthquake and a frightful disruption of heavenly bodies under the earlier seal judgments. Obviously they are responding to past judgments and not judgments yet to come, for wicked men have no ability to speak a prophecy.... It is a major error to force the translation to declare, 'the great day of His wrath WILL COME.' One can only conclude that this strong reference to the wrath of God is the direct response of the wicked to their shattering experience under the first six seals, and not a veiled prophecy of coming trumpet judgments. (Stanton, p.102)

Answer: I agree that, if this is spoken by the people, it is as a result of something that has happened rather than a prophetic utterance on their part. However, it is not in response to the first five seals. They do not panic and despair until after the terrifying cosmic signs and earthquake of the sixth seal. Mankind will see these awe-inspiring signs (Matt 24), and instinctively know God's wrath has come. With the sudden, global disappearance of the surviving saints they have been persecuting, it will strike home that what the saints told them is true. Mankind is not so much prophesying that God's wrath will come as they are recognizing it has begun. Sadly, most will still refuse to repent (Rev 9:20).

Stanton asserts that after undergoing several years of God's wrath in the first five seals, the world cries for the mountains and rocks to fall on them and hide them from the wrath of the Lamb, for His wrath came. Hide them from the wrath which was already completed? That does not make any sense.

Such a view is not only illogical, but unscriptural, too. Look again at 6:17: *For the great day of His wrath has come, and who is able to stand.* This is present tense. Luke 21:26 says it is not past judgments, but the immediate calamities which causes them to run in *fear and EXPECTATION of those things WHICH ARE COMING on the earth.*

Perhaps Stanton should do more than a *casual reading* of texts such as Rosenthal's if he intends to review them. It is clear that is all he did. Most of his objections would have melted away if he had looked more closely at what Rosenthal actually taught with an open heart to seriously consider it.

For myself, I was very careful when examining critiques of pre-wrath. First I read through the entire examination, pausing frequently to consider what was said. Then I went back through and highlighted the summary point of each argument and made preliminary notes on them. After that I went through it again and began writing out my answers, carefully considering every point. Finally, I re-wrote and re-worked it several times, each time carefully examining the critique and my answer. The entire time I was open to be convinced and corrected. In fact, a couple of points by Brainard and Showers (next three chapters) caused me to make a few minor changes to my own understanding. I would personally prefer pre-trib to be true, but I must base my doctrine on God's Word, not on my preference.

Objection (5): It is likewise strange, if [the great multitude does] indeed represent the church, that John could not recognize them,

187

for John was...a member of the early church and a part of its essential foundation (Stanton, p. 103). In fact, John Himself did not know who they were! If they had been Old Testament believers, or the church, John would have recognized them. That the elder had to tell John who they were suggests that they are a special people, which, indeed, they are.109

Answer: Note that the previous verse (Rev 7:13) says the elder first asked John if he knew who they were, suggesting that the elder thought he should have recognized them. He would have no reason to identify them as the end-time-revival saints, for the *entire* case for them is based on what John is witnessing at that moment. Yet he did know they were washed by the blood of the Lamb through faith in Christ. So the same argument can be turned back on Stanton and Wiersbe.

Why should he have recognized them, anyway - even if they are Old and/or New Testament saints? Certainly he has personally known only a very small number of saints, so there was little chance of him picking them out among so many. Picture this: Take all of the people currently in the United States and group them together. Now take the couple of hundred people you know well enough by sight and mix them in randomly. Now you have about one minute to locate someone you know in the midst of this 300,000,000 people. Sound practically impossible? You're right!

What about the white robes they wore? Shouldn't that have identified them as resurrected saints? Actually, outside of Revelation references to saints as clothed in white are not found. Several say our sins can be washed white, but I found none which say the saints wear white. In contrast, angels were frequently described wearing white raiment - but John had already seen the angels and knew these weren't them.

In fact, since John did recognize that they were washed in the blood and came from all nations, it is possible he suspected that these were the resurrected saints and was over-awed by the number.

---

109 Be Victorious, p. 71

I know if I had lived in a day when the world population was less than 500,000,000, and had never seen a crowd larger than maybe a couple hundred thousand during the Passover in Jerusalem, I would be shocked to see maybe a billion saints standing before Jesus. John was a humble man. It would be in perfect keeping with humility if he did not venture his uncertain guess, but rather asked the elder to explain them. And having been told they come out of the great tribulation would remind him of a group Jesus said would come out of this time (Matt 24). He had his answer! Of course, any arguments concerning his thoughts must be based on speculation, regardless of which rapture position you hold. So, no problem.

Objection (6): Rosenthal argues that the aorist tense *elthen* [His wrath *has come*] is about to occur, thus making God's wrath come after the sixth seal.... Granted elthen may occasionally have a future sense, as perhaps in Revelation 19:7. But it normally refers to a past action. In Revelation 5:7; 7:13; 8:3; 11:18; 17:1, 10; 18:10; and 21:9 elthen is used of events that will have already occurred. (McLean, p.392)

Answer: In four of his cited verses (5:7; 8:3; 17:1; and 21:9) elthen is used as a dramatic past; in other words, it is a past that functions like a present, as is used in novels to describe the action (e.g. He *said*, "Hello."), explaining what is happening at that moment in the story, not what was done previously. Revelation 11:18 parallels 6:17, and represents the wrath to be fulfilled in the bowls as a part of the seventh trumpet. Revelation 18:10 functions similarly, describing something that in the context is just now happening. In 17:10 elthen is used for something that had not happened at the time of writing (a) but in the future would (b). That leaves only 7:13 as a true past aorist usage. McLean is without support here; like a one-legged centipede, he can get nowhere.

Objection (7): Some pre-tribs argue that any later schedule comes dangerously close to saying, *My Lord delays His coming.* (Matt 24:48)

Answer: This passage in Matthew says the servant starts living a worldly life and harassing faithful servants because he believes the

Master has delayed His coming. These are the ones who reject the true gospel, which promotes holiness, and choose Hades over Death in the fourth seal by betraying others. It says nothing of signs one way or the other. Also, we should always try to live as if Christ might come in our lifetime. Anyone of us could die today and face Christ in our current spiritual condition. That is the spiritual application of the passage.

Moreover, the context is the coming in Matthew 24:29-31, as no other coming is mentioned in this passage. It is always amusing when some pre-trib teachers quote one of these verses in Matthew 24 and 25 to argue against later rapture views, while ignoring the context which explicitly says He comes after the great tribulation is amputated.

Objection (8): Some give another reason they don't think Matthew 24:31 can be the rapture. They say Jesus doesn't need the help of angels in gathering His church, pointing out that He didn't need their help in raising Lazarus from the dead. They also note that the main rapture passages (1Cor 15:51-54; 1Thess 4:13-18) make no mention of angels.

Answer: I made several points addressing this issue in other chapters. Pre-tribs misunderstand what role the angels will play in the rapture. They are not there so much to help Jesus raise them as to be an escort of honor. Look again at the accounts of the resurrection of our Lord. In His case, angels were sent to open the tomb and to greet their risen King; Jesus could just as easily have told the stone to move, as He had told the storm and waves to *cease, be still,* and it would have had no other choice except to obey its Creator. But instead, the Father had the angels come and open His tomb to greet Him.... And to think, we will receive this same honor!!

Objection (9): McLean notes that in the context of one being taken and the other left (Luke 17) the disciples asked, *Where, Lord,* and were told, *Where the body is, there will the vultures be gathered.* McLean explains that this clearly indicates that the ones taken will be killed and their bodies will be eaten by vultures, a further reference to the time period of the Battle of Armageddon (Rev 19:17-18). (McLean, p.395)

Answer: When a creature dies or is dying, and it is discovered by vultures, they gather in the air above it before they swoop down to claim their reward. When the church is raptured, or *"taken to Himself,"* we will be caught up into the air while the spiritually dead remain on the earth as a sacrifice for the beasts and vultures (see Ez 39:17-21; Is 18:3-6), who have been called to gather for the occasion. This is not a parable but a simile, so the vultures do not directly represent the church, as some have said; rather just as vultures gather in the air, so will we, and as 1Thessalonians 4 also agrees. This is in line with Matthew 24:28, which indicates that Jesus will appear suddenly in the air like vultures over a dead body.

Objection (10): Rosenthal tries to parallel Matthew 24:4-8 with the first five seals of Revelation 6, but there are three problems here. First, the similarities are quite superficial and the differences outnumber the similarities. Nowhere in Matthew does it mention a destruction of humanity, and there is no mention of martyred saints. Revelation does not mention the Antichrist. There are other dissimilarities. Second, even if there were a greater level of similarities, it would not prove his point since similarity does not mean sameness, and a more exact linguistic correlation...is necessary to prove sameness. Third, Rosenthal has not actually proved that verses 4-8 are part of the seven years...[they] can also refer to prophetic events preceding the seven years, with the seven years only beginning at verse 9... (Fruchtenbaum p. 385).

Answer: It is Fruchtenbaum's case which is superficial. He argues that Matthew 24:4-8 does not mention martyrs. I agree, for these only describe the first three seals. The fourth and fifth seals begin with verse nine, describing the persecution of the saints by the beasts of the earth, and their continued martyrdom until God finally brings vengeance. Fruchtenbaum also alludes to the fourth seal as destruction of humanity which is not found in Matthew. But this seal does not say one-fourth of mankind is killed, but that the rider (Death) has power over one-fourth of the earth to kill with the sword (war) and with hunger, and *by the beasts of the earth. This is the persecution of believers and Jews, as I have already explained.*

The third difference, he claims, is that the first seal does not describe many false christs, while Matthew does not mention the Antichrist. Again his case is faulty, for the first seal does not specifically name the Antichrist – that is just the usual interpretation. There is no reason that this cannot carry the idea of an upsurge in false christs, rather than just referring to the beast. For that matter, the beast is given authority for only 3 1/2 years by the kings of the earth after Satan is cast down, so at this point he is not yet officially the Antichrist. He is merely one of many who confirms the covenant (Dan 9:27). Thus this may be the signing of the covenant rather than specifically relating to the beast.

Some also say that the second seal describes one great war while Matthew mentions multiple wars. Again, the second seal says the rider has power to take peace from the earth, not that there is one big war.

In fact, the first three seals are all fulfilled in the plural. One rider of the white horse brings many deceivers, probably including the start of Antichrist's rise to power and the founding of the one world government. One rider of the red horse brings wars and rumors of wars. And one rider of the black horse brings famine - a result of all the warfare and the earthquakes and pestilences - in diverse places. This is consistent at all times. In fact, in the same book Fruchtenbaum voices this complaint John McLean ties the seals to the Olivet Discourse in his essay,110 as do many from all rapture positions.

Matthew 24:8 provides a final piece of evidence that, taken with the rest, virtually proves the connection with the seventieth week. This verse equates the seals as described in Matthew with the birth

---

110 When the Trumpet Sounds, John McLean contrib., pp. 323-324

pains of a woman (see Mark 13:8). This analogy has several times been used to describe the seventieth week (1Thess 5:3; Is 13:8 as the DOL approaches).

Objection (11): Furthermore, the four horsemen of the apocalypse in the first four seal judgments are initiated by the four living creatures; so these judgments do not only concern 'man's activity under the controlling influence of Satan.' (Fruchtenbaum, p. 385)

Answer: The living creatures did not initiate the seal judgments – they merely told John to come and see what is taking place. If I am walking in the woods with a friend and I spot a deer drinking from a pond, do I initiate the deer's action by pointing it out to my friend?

Objection (12): [Rosenthal] wants to limit *the Day of the Lord* to the last quarter of the seven years....but the facts are the Day of the Lord cannot be limited only to the last quarter; it actually covers the whole seven year period. How the Day of Jehovah affects the Gentiles is detailed in Isaiah 2:12-22; 13:6-16; Ezekiel 30:1-9; Jowl 1:15-20; Obadiah 1:10-20; Zephaniah 1:14-18; and 2Peter 3:10-12. How the Day of Jehovah affects Israel is given in Ezekiel 13:1-7; Joel 2:1-11; 3:14-17; Amos 5:18-20; and Zephaniah 1:7-13. It is mere assumption to limit all this to the last quarter. (Fruchtenbaum, p.390)

Answer: He again fails to carefully examine his argument. Many of these describe the heavenly signs of the sixth seal and their effects, which pre-wrath adherents agree directly relate to the Day of the Lord (Is 2:12-22; 13:6-16; Zeph 1:14-18, sixth seal and *"day of trumpets"*; Joel 3:14-17). Others state that the Day of the Lord is coming or is at hand (Joel 1:15-20; 2:1-11; Obadiah 1:10-20). Ezekiel 30:1-9 combines both, regarding the destruction of Egypt (see Is 19). Zephaniah 1:7-13 describes the seventh seal, whereas Amos 5:18-20 offers virtually no details suitable for setting a time aside from mention of darkness, and may refer to the fourth trumpet or the fifth bowl. The final passage offered by Fruchtenbaum, Ezekiel 13:1-7, has nothing to do with the

193

seventieth week but concerns the Babylonian captivity 2,500 years ago. The passages he claims create problems for pre-wrath are the very verses that prove it is correct.

Objection (13): Another point is ignored by Rosenthal. If this great multitude is the church, then, of necessity, this is only a partial rapture.... Verses 13-17 [Rev 7] state that these saints came out of the Great Tribulation. This would exclude all church saints who have died since Acts 2, or who will die before the Great Tribulation. This shows that the great multitude simply cannot be the church, the whole body of Christ. (Fruchtenbaum, p. 404)

Answer: His logic is faulty. Nothing in this text states or requires that they all live during the great tribulation, only that they appear in heaven from the midst of this time. This is true whether they were still alive and raptured, or whether they were the resurrected dead, who are raised in the earthly realm in the midst of the Tribulation to meet the Lord in the air. In either case, they have come to heaven in their new bodies from within the great tribulation.

Objection (14): Part of Rosenthal's scheme is to distinguish between the Great Tribulation and the Day of the Lord. However, a comparison of the Scriptures on the *Great Tribulation* and the *Day of the Jehovah* shows that these are not separate time frames, but that they all refer to the same thing. The key is to compare the Scriptures that describe a period of time which is unparalleled and worse than any other time in human history, past or future. (Fruchtenbaum, p. 407) He then quotes the two major Old Testament passages on the time of Jacob's Trouble (Jer 30:7; Dan 12:1). He next quotes Joel 2:1-2 which *he says* describes the DOL as a Day *the like of whom has never been; nor will there ever be any such after them.* He argues that the similar descriptions prove that they are one and the same.

Answer: A closer look, however, reveals that the Day of the Lord "is coming" in Joel 2; it is not yet here:

*1) Blow the trumpet in Zion, and sound an alarm in My holy mountain! Let all the inhabitants of the land tremble: for the Day of the Lord **is coming**, for it is at hand [imminent]: 2) a day of darkness and gloominess, a day of clouds and thick darkness, like the morning clouds spread over the mountains.*

A people come, great and strong, the like of whom has never been; nor will there ever be any such after them....

Joel chapter one warns of the coming Babylonian invasion of Judah by comparing it to a swarm of locusts which destroys everything. Babylon is one of the previous beast empires. Joel 2 is a dual prophecy, with near/far implications of both the Babylonian empire and the final beast empire under the Antichrist. This passage goes on to describe the ransacking of Jerusalem and Israel by these empires, demonstrating how the invasion will be like the plague of locusts in the earlier segment. In the case of the Antichrist empire, it happens when the DOL *is coming*. Moreover, this does **not say** that the DOL is like no other, but **the army** which goes forth when that Day **is near**.

Joel tells us what he is about to describe takes place when the Day of the Lord is coming, when it is impending. There will be darkness and gloominess because of clouds, which the following description suggests is overhanging smoke from weapons of war. An army comes upon Israel the like which has never been seen (see Matt 24:15). What follows sounds like a description of modern warfare, with fighter jets, tanks, and guided missiles and other weapons, blasting away such that the earth shakes and the heavenly lights are obscured by the smoke and debris. Like Babylon before (Joel 1), God has sent this army to shatter the people of Israel (Daniel 12).

In verse 11 the Lord utters His voice before His army at Jehoshaphat, introducing the Day of the Lord. What follows (2:12-29) is a call for repentance, the rapture (Bridegroom and bride leaving their chambers), the destruction of the surrounding Islamic (Joel 3:12; Zeph. 2) and Russian/Turkish armies (Gog, king of the north, Daniel 11; Joel 2:20) controlling Israel, at the Jehoshaphat

Campaign, and the ultimate restoration of Israel. Joel's prophecy lines up perfectly with the pre-wrath schedule. Remember it is Joel who said that the heavenly signs of the sixth seal MUST appear BEFORE the Day of the Lord (2:31). Following the sixth seal prophecy, Joel breaks down in greater detail the Jehoshaphat Campaign. We will look at this later.

Objection (15): This reviewer sincerely questions...the necessity of adding a fifth position to an already overcrowded rapture debate. (Stanton, p.90) He asserts that the pre-wrath position contributes nothing particularly new to the debate. (p.91)

Answer: The real question here is: Do any of these other theories do justice to *all* of the pertinent Scriptures? Each of these views has battled each other for over a hundred years by noting the glaring problems of the competing views. The answers offered are usually weak and unconvincing, or else they would cease to be problems. Pre-tribs resort to *the Jewish waste-paper basket,* 111 while post-tribs keep the church on earth during God's wrath. Mid-tribs often admit their view is an attempted compromise. And the other theories use an allegorical method of interpretation which allows them to make Scripture say what they want it to.

Furthermore, adherents of these theories widely disagree among themselves on various key points. One of the most obvious is on the order of the Revelation judgments - I showed several in chapter two. They cannot even agree which part of the week each is fulfilled, because their basic assumptions do not allow the Bible to order them itself.

Pre-wrath adherents do not have such wide-ranging disagreements. Our schedule follows clear, scriptural guidelines. Pre-wrath is *not* a compromise or combining of views, but a systematic study which acknowledges the strong points of both pre- and post-trib. We insist on a consistent, face-value method of interpretation. While we have a few differences on tangential

---

111 The Hope of Christ's Second Coming, S.P. Tregelles: orig pub. 1864

issues, such as the identity of the beast empire or the nature of the millennial kingdom, we mostly agree on the major points as regarding the time line of events.

Stanton feels there is too much confusion already due to the plethora of rapture views. Perhaps he would be happier if the very real problems with pre-trib were ignored and the position uniformly held. Perhaps we should not follow the example of Luther and the other reformers, who rejected the traditions of a corrupt Roman Catholic Church because they seriously compromised the teaching of Scripture. Perhaps he disagrees with the philosophy of the Bereans who checked what they were taught against Scripture to ensure they were receiving the correct doctrine... Then, what if pre-trib turns out to be the wrong choice? No-one would be ready when Antichrist appears and all would be confused when what they had been told as truth turned out to be error.

I maintain that the addition of the pre-wrath position does not add to the confusion, for God is Truth and is not the author of confusion, and everything lines up with His Holy Writ. In fact, this view will hopefully clear up the tangled thoughts of those who cannot decide on a position because of all of the problems with the other views. There IS a necessity of solving those problems, for our goal is to *find* truth, not invent it, and the pre-wrath position succeeds fully and completely.

Chapter 12: Answering Showers

In 2001 Renald E. Showers attempted to discredit the pre-wrath rapture in a book called The Pre-wrath Rapture View: An Examination and Critique.112 He used some of the same arguments already addressed, which I will typically bypass.

On a positive note, for the most part Showers correctly represented the pre-wrath position as explained by Rosenthal and Van Kampen, whose works he critiques. I also admire the godly tone he used in presenting his case.

In his first chapter Mr. Showers addresses whether it is acceptable to call the entire seventieth week *the Tribulation Period*. I agreed in the beginning of this book that it is acceptable, even though Scripture does not use the term. I even use it a couple of times myself. But this can cause confusion with the *great tribulation*, which is a biblical term. That is why I usually call it the seventieth week.

In chapter two (pp. 19-35) he argues that the great tribulation lasts the entire second half of the seven years, while pre-wraths conclude it with the sixth seal. We say the rest of the week is the Day of the Lord, distinct from the great tribulation. Showers correctly observes that Daniel and Revelation say Antichrist will reign the full 1260 days. But as I pointed out, no passage says the great tribulation lasts the entire time.

As it concerns the elect it is amputated, for the church is gathered from earth to heaven (Mark 13). As it concerns the Jews it is greatly reduced because God gives them the victory at the Jehoshaphat Campaign. They will remain on earth and

---

112 Kregel Publications, a division of Kregel, Inc., P.O Box 2607, Grand Rapids, MI 49501

undoubtedly still face some troubles, but it will be greatly curtailed. In fact, the Antichrist's influence will be reduced to the point that demons must go forth and perform wonders to draw the kings of the earth to Armageddon (Rev 16:14).

Showers next argues that the term *shortened* in Matthew 24:22 is in the aorist tense. He says this signifies past action and indicates God limited the great tribulation to 1260 days by past prophecy, or else it would destroy all flesh. We saw in chapter nine that the aorist tense is determined more by context, and does not always refer to past or completed actions. In this case, the cutting short is directly associated with Matthew 24:29-31, which clearly matches the sixth seal. Therefore, whenever the sixth seal gathering of elect takes place is when the great tribulation is cut short for their sake. I believe I have adequately shown this seal happens well before Armageddon.

Chapter three (pp 36-56) presents Showers' case for the significance of the seven seals, where he suggests the sealed scroll is the deed to the earth. I have little dispute with this chapter and it is mostly tangential to the issue at hand. He agrees on several important points with pre-wrath, though. He accedes that the first four seals apparently correlate to the first part of Matthew 24. He also agrees that the seventh seal contains the seven trumpets and seven bowls (p. 54), which instigates the total bombardment of divine wrath against the domain of Satan and his forces. But he fails to realize it is this from which the church is promised deliverance, not the kinds of things we see in the first five seals.

The Significance of the Seals

In chapter four (pp. 57-81) he explains the significance of the seals. His first point is that because it is Jesus Himself who opens the seals to initiate their judgments, this qualifies them as divine wrath. I already explained that this only shows they are part of God's plan, not His wrath.

200

Showers says the rise of Antichrist is directly attributed to God, as are the rest of the seals. He concludes "that the events that will transpire when all seven seals are broken will be expressions of divine wrath poured out on Satan's domain." (p. 58) So the rise of Antichrist, Satan's creature, is wrath upon Satan's domain? The devil's wrath is poured out on Himself (Rev 12:12)? This reminds me of a game adults sometimes play with children where they take the child's hand and make them hit themselves while telling them to stop hitting themselves. God's wrath is not a game! Biblical testimony, on the other hand, says the devil is released by God to pour out His unholy wrath upon the chosen of God - Israel and the saints of Jesus - to fill up the wickedness of mankind and demonstrate the righteousness of God's wrath (2Thess 1:6-8).

On page 75 Showers says the fifth seal martyrs, the tribulation saints, have been witnessing God's wrath in the seals as they as they continue to be killed. They ask when God is going to avenge them. God responds that He will delay only until all of the saints to be martyred have been killed. Showers concludes that "the...way in which the fifth seal will be related to the wrath of God is by its guarantee of further outpouring of God's wrath after the first four seals."

Problem 1: *Why* do they ask *when* God will pour out His wrath, if He has been doing so for some time? The O.T. says the DOL is a Day of vengeance, and according to Showers they have witnessed the first four seals and recognize them as wrath. By this reasoning, then, they should have realized God was already in the process of avenging them. But God told them to rest a little longer, *and then* vengeance will come.

Problem 2: Showers assumes that the souls under the altar consist exclusively of seventieth week martyrs. But nothing in the text requires this. They are martyrs for upholding the Word and having a testimony. This is the reason most of the saints have been killed throughout history. Won't their blood be avenged on earth, also? 2Thessalonians 1 says we will receive rest from persecutions when Jesus appears with His angels to take vengeance. It also says this proves God's judgment is just. This was said to a church then undergoing persecutions. Thus the martyrs of the past are also under the altar.

Showers next debates Rosenthal's claim that wrath begins with the seventh seal. He argues that Isaiah 2:11-22 makes the sixth seal God's wrath, both because the heavenly signs are supernaturally caused and because Isaiah describes the same earthquake and man fleeing. He insists this proves the sixth seal is within the DOL wrath, not before it.

Pre-wrath adherents all agree the sixth seal is directly related to God's wrath. Men run to hide in the rocks *when the Lord arises to shake the earth mightily* (Is 2:19, 21). This does not say that after several years of wrath mankind finally decides to hide, but rather *when* He arises. This is clearly the inception of the Day of the Lord rather than within it.

Showers concludes this chapter complaining about the unexpectedness of the DOL. How can it come as a thief if the first six seals forewarn that Day? And how can it come while the world cries *peace and safety* if the world is hiding in the rocks in fear before it arrives?

First, most of the world will not see the first five seals and rise of a world government as signs of God's approaching Day. According to 1 Thessalonians 5 believers should not be caught by surprise if they are watching. However, to the unsaved these things will appear only as the natural progression of society. Most likely because of the difficult problems arising in the first three seals, worldwide famine and widespread war, they will agree on the need of a single ruler over the nations to bring peace and resolve these problems. Thus when the sixth seal is opened they are caught completely off guard.

Second, just because the world cries peace and safety does not make it a reality. They have a supreme government coming together to solve the world's problems, giving the world a false hope. The only true hope for mankind is found through Christ.

This antichrist government latches on to the Jews as cause of much of the world's problems, just as Hitler did in Nazi German.

Then when many flee to safety in the wilderness after the Abomination, the Antichrist turns his attentions to *the rest of her offspring, who have the testimony of Jesus*, that is, the church. Why? Because we take a stand for righteousness and refuse to accede to the ungodly demands of the antichrist government, and many will protest the actions taken against Israel, among other reasons. The beast will conduct an apparently successful war against the saints and the Jews (Rev 12:6; 13:7). The world sees everything the government is doing to resolve the world's problems and believe that soon there will be *peace and safety*.

Then the sixth seal is opened with its mighty signs of the truth, the surviving saints are caught up with the resurrected in the rapture, and Israel gains an impossible military victory at Jehoshaphat. So while the world is crying peace and safety, destruction comes upon them suddenly!

In chapter five (pp. 82-92) Showers addresses issues related to the second coming. Most of his complaints here come from a failure to understand the unity of Christ's single parousia, which includes three closely interrelated phases, as I already explained.

Showers points out that pre-wraths rightly understand that after the rapture we will be with the Lord forever (1Thess 4:17), and that the church remains in heaven until the millennial reign begins. "If the church will go wherever Christ goes, and if Christ will go back and forth between heaven and earth several times, then how will the church remain in heaven...?" (p. 85)

Easily answered. When a husband and wife are married, they are to stay together for life - that is God's plan. But this does not mean the wife follows her husband to work, to the golf course, etc. This is a normal figure of speech used similarly even today. We are spiritually espoused to Christ, and raptured to attend the wedding feast. During the millennium many will have responsibilities of rulership throughout the earth. Thus while we will always be with the Lord, there is room for physical separation.

Showers next repeats the oft cited complaint of how the DOL can come like a thief if preceded by the sixth seal. We supposedly contradict ourselves when we say the unsaved will have no sense of impending doom until that Day arrives, but then say the sixth seal signals them to hide in the rocks as a precursor to the DOL.

But since it is this seal which announces the arrival of the Day of the Lord, there is no problem. God wants mankind to know that His Day has come just as soon as He brings it. God alone will be exalted on His Day as He systematically humbles all the loftiness of man. Pre-trib, on the other hand, says mankind slowly realizes through the seals that they are in the Day of the Lord. Their view also includes the Antichrist gaining power and being worshiped by the world as a god. And while the world will be required to bow to his idols (Rev 13), Isaiah also says mankind *throws away his idols* as they flee at the inception of God's Day at the sixth seal, though most do not actually repent. What a contrast between pre-trib and what Scripture says!

Showers complains that we say Antichrist will rule for 1290 days while Scripture gives him 1260. Several passages in Daniel and Revelation say he rules 3 1/2 years.

According to the pre-wrath schedule, the seventh trumpet sounds on day 1260. From God's point of view this is the end of his reign, for *the kingdoms of this world have become the kingdom of our Lord and of His Christ* (Rev 11:15-19). But Daniel 12:11 says from the Abomination of Desolation there will be 1290 days - an extra thirty days for which we must account. It goes on to pronounce a blessing on those who continue to 1335 days - an additional forty-five days to determine. If the seventh trump marks the end of the 1260 days, then the thirty days are logically the bowls of wrath.

Unlike the trumpets which sound, all told, over perhaps a year or two, the bowls take place very quickly. Now that Jesus has received His earthly crown He is not going to waste much time establishing His authority. The bowls are poured out rapidly, perhaps even all on the same day. As severe as these judgments are, mankind could not survive if they continued very long, so their brevity is logical. Three demons will be sent forth to the kings of the earth to gather the armies of the world to Armageddon (Rev.16:12-16). The following forty-five days allow the sheep and goat judgment (Matt 25) - thus those who continue to this point are blessed to enter the millennium. In this manner every Scripture is fulfilled consistently and logically.

*** I've got a question for pre-tribs: How do you reasonably explain the extra days in Daniel 12:11-12? I have never seen this directly addressed and reasoned out - apart from a lame attempt by Mr. Brainard in the next chapter. I suppose I could have missed it in the fifty-some books I have examined. It is not enough to conjecture maybe's and could be's, and conclude you don't know for sure (Brainard's method), while insisting it could not be the logical, scriptural progression expressed by pre-wrath adherents.

In 2Thessalonians 2:8, Van Kampen taught from the Greek that the Antichrist will be paralyzed or rendered useless at the brightness of Christ's parousia (sixth seal, Matt 24:29-31) (The Sign, p. 496). He will then be finally consumed by the breath of His mouth at Armageddon. Showers asks how the Antichrist is rendered useless if he can still prompt the kings of the earth to gather for Armageddon.

I agree this interpretation is debatable. I did not include it in the main study, though I believe it is true and sometimes refer to it. This verse could refer to only Armageddon and not weaken pre-wrath in the slightest. However, we believe at the sixth seal the church is removed, Israel gains a major military victory at Jehoshaphat, and God's wrath is announced by the heavenly signs and earthquake. Add to this mix that Jesus appears in glory, and suddenly the world knows they made the wrong choice by following Antichrist. But messengers from God warned them to fear God and give Him glory, and to refuse the mark or be lost for eternity (Rev 14:6-13). Most ignored them, thus choose to gather in desperation when the beast calls, seeing it as their only hope.

Here is a return question: Why do demons need to go forth to convince them to answer the call to fight, if the kings are still fully supporting the beast? We see again a logical, scriptural progression. He is rendered useless at the sixth seal, but able to gather the armies for Armageddon in a futile, last ditch effort to keep Christ away.

Showers also takes issue with the Jehoshaphat Campaign. Van Kampen explains there will be a gathering of an Israeli resistance force just before the sixth seal. How can the DOL come as a thief if this precedes it?

Simply, it still surprises them because they are unbelievers. They have no reason to be familiar with this prophecy because they mostly think the Bible is stories made up by control freaks. For that matter most Christians are not familiar with this battle as the only view I see teaching it is pre-wrath. So it is not even common knowledge in the church. Also, God blinds them to the significance of this gathering just as He sends strong delusion to continue believing the lie to those who rejected the love of the truth (2Thess 2). Furthermore, it would seem only natural that Israel might attempt to regain control of Israel at some point. No problem!

Matthew 24

Showers looks at Matthew 24 in chapter six (pp. 93-138). He first notes that Jesus says the heavenly signs appear after the tribulation and charges pre-wrath with changing it to say *when* the tribulation is cut short.

This is a serious charge, if true, but it evaporates under the heat of scrutiny. The moment the sixth seal is opened the great tribulation cuts short. Then heavenly signs, the earthquake, the gathering of elect, and the sealing of the 144,000 just before God's wrath are all results of the amputation of the tribulation. After a person slip on a banana peel, she falls down. Cause and effect.

Showers points out that Matthew 24 does not describe the effect the signs produce in the population, while the sixth seal does. He ignores Luke 21:25-28 which includes that information.

Showers also complains that the sixth seal signs are not the only cosmic disturbances in the seventieth week. I addressed this lamest of arguments in the previous chapter.

He then grumbles again about the Jehoshaphat Campaign. He points out that Scriptures indicate Christ will fight against them with Israel. He then points out that the sixth seal says everyone, including the military, will be fleeing as a result of the signs of the seal. Who then would Christ fight?

The armies assemble on the field of battle before the sixth seal is opened. Within minutes after it is opened Christ appears and leads Israel's armies to victory. Here is the order: The armies begin to battle, the seal is opened and the signs appear and Christ appears. The armies flee what is coming. Israel is sealed then pursues. As the enemy flees, fire and brimstone from the first trumpet begins falling on them, and Israel's armies, who are untouched by the brimstone, defeat them.

Showers insists that the heavenly signs in Joel 3 cannot be the same as the sixth seal. The military is seen fighting in Joel while they are fleeing in the sixth seal. He concludes that there must, therefore, be another like disturbance in addition to the sixth seal, then suggests Matthew 24 (as at Armageddon) lines up with Joel rather than the sixth seal.

Revelation details the seventieth week and clearly describes several different cosmic disturbances. But these exact signs only appear at the sixth seal, and not at Armageddon. Thus Showers argues from silence, based solely on his rapture theory, rather than from Scripture. Pre-wraths see the heavenly signs at the Joel 3 / Zechariah 14 battle as the same signs with the sixth seal. We can logically and scripturally place these in the time line revealed by Matthew 24. Every piece falls easily into place.

Showers also complains that if the armies of the world are destroyed at this campaign, then who is left to fight at Armageddon?

First, not every single military person of the world will be present at the Abomination or the Jehoshaphat Campaign. Second, those controlling Israel after the Abomination will most likely consist of Islamic nations which surround Israel, though other nations may have some representation there as well. That leaves plenty of military for Armageddon. I will thoroughly cover this Campaign in the next chapter.

Most pre-wraths teach that the parable of wheat and tares (Matt 13) relates to the rapture. Most pre-tribs relate it to the sheep and goat judgment (Matt 24), as does Showers. He points out that nothing in the passage specifically shows the tares were set aside until the wheat was put into the barn, then burned - which is what we teach. In reply, neither does it state the tares were burned first, so both sides must argue from silence. But pre-wrath follows a certain logic. It makes sense the wheat would be put in a safe place so they don't catch fire and burn with the tares.

The basis for the pre-trib view is that this seems to say the tares were gathered before the wheat was put in the barn. This relates to the fourth seal and the time of testing which comes upon the whole earth (Rev 3:10). Wheat represents true believers. Tares look a lot like wheat, but don't produce the head of grain which wheat produces. Scripture teaches that true believers bear spiritual fruit, and that if no fruit is ever produced then they are not saved. They may go to church and profess faith, but genuine faith will produce at least some real change in a person's life. Jesus said we will know them by their fruits.

That means tares represent fruitless, professing Christians. God sowed the good wheat, while the enemy sowed tares among the wheat. The tares do not represent the world, for Jesus clearly said the field is the world. The time of testing is the time of the harvest (Rev 14). Jesus said let the wheat and tares grow together until harvest. Matthew 24 says many will become offended and fall away, and 2Thessalonians warns of a great apostasy - both in relation to the appearance of Antichrist. The fourth seal says the rider of the fourth horse, Death, comes against one-fourth of the earth to kill with sword and with famine and by the beasts of the earth. Hades follows after to collect the tares which are separated out. The same pattern is in the following parable of good and bad fish. Thus the wicked are removed from among the just by betraying Christ during the great tribulation, then the wheat is gathered into the barn and the tares burned. I will bypass any further arguments based on these parables.

On page 118 Showers discusses the example of Noah. I already addressed every point he makes, so will bypass it.

I showed in Matthew 24:39-41 that two different words are translated as taken or take away, *airo* (to take) and *paralambano* (to take alongside or with). Showers argues that the presence of two different verbs does not necessarily indicate two different events of taking, one for wrath and one fore the rapture. He presents the case that the individual are taken by angels in wrath to the lake of fire, rather than taken with Jesus in the rapture.

Several problems appear. First, the context is the gathering of elect by angels (Matt 24:31), and the term elect is **never** used for the unsaved in Scripture. Second, Noah was put in the ark of safety before wrath fell, which fits perfectly the rapture scenario. Third, those taken or left behind are surrounded on both sides with warnings to be ready for Christ's coming or face the consequences. And last, nowhere does Scripture describe angels gathering the unsaved and throwing them in the Lake of Fire - but only the beast and his false prophet. The wicked are merely slain and left for the vultures. Also, the unsaved are not thrown into the Lake until the end of the Millennium, while this is at the end of this age. This leaves only the rapture for the individual taken.

Showers points out that the heavenly signs of Matthew 24 are from the Old Testament, concluding this proves the gathering of elect relates exclusively to the nation of Israel, and not the church (p. 125). This logic is faulty because the church was still a hidden truth at the time these were written. Furthermore, these same signs are found in Revelation, a book specifically addressed to the churches. Third, Peter preached from Joel 2 on Pentecost, and declared the filling of the Holy Spirit began fulfilling the prophecy. Using Showers' logic, then the baptism of the Spirit had nothing to do with the church either, for it is prophesied in the O.T. alongside the heavenly signs. Yet we read in Acts that Gentile believers also received the Spirit, and in 1Corinthians 12 that it was for the edification of the church.

After noting Israel is the elect in the Old Testament - which I already thoroughly discussed - Showers looks at the clause which says the elect are gathered *from the four winds, from one end of heaven to the other.* He points to several O.T. passages telling of Israel scattered to or gathered from the four winds, the four cardinal directions. Now if pre-trib were true, then this would be a correct correlation.

However, I provided a strong case for the rapture, which I will just briefly summarize here. In Revelation 7 the angels holding the four winds are told to wait to harm earth and sea until the 144,000 are sealed. In the same context a great multitude from all nations appears in heaven. Then note the first four trumpets harm the earth and sea. Thus the gathering of elect is away from the wrath in these trumpets. Mark 13 adds that they are gathered from the farthest parts of earth to the farthest parts of heaven, which matches the great multitude. This creates a problem for Showers' thesis, because Israel is not gathered to heaven but to her homeland.

On page 127 Showers notes Israel will be gathered after Armageddon by the sound of a *great* trumpet (Is 27:13), and Matthew 24:29-31 literally says a great trumpet. While this single point could tie them together, in chapter four I provided about twelve ties. I'll let you weigh the evidence.

On page 129 he says that Matthew 25:31-32 refers to another gathering of people at Christ's second coming with His angels. Because this group of Gentiles consists of both saved and unsaved that are gathered for the judgment, and because the unsaved are never called *elect*, the sheep and goat gathering cannot be of the elect (Matt 24:31) Yet both gatherings are in conjunction with Christ's second coming with angels. Since the gathering in Matthew 25 consists of all Gentiles, saved or unsaved, so the gathering of elect must consist of all Jews, saved or unsaved.

First, Matthew 24:29-31 seems to take place at the sixth seal. Showers even admits this seal precedes the trumpets and bowls. No passage repeats these same signs at Armageddon. Without that corroborating evidence its difficult to place this first gathering at the end of the week.

Second, the angels come at both the sixth seal and at Armageddon. At the sixth seal their primary task is to gather the saints and to seal the 144,000 before wrath falls. At Armageddon the angels come as a military force to conquer the beast and his armies. In this time frame the sheep and goat judgment also takes place. It is all a part of Christ taking over the kingdoms of the earth.

Finally, the great multitude (Rev 7), whom pre-tribs relate to the sheep, is saved by the blood of Jesus. But the sheep in the sheep and goat judgment are not said to be saved through faith in Christ. Quite the contrary, they are specifically those who had compassion on even the least of Christ's brethren - visiting them in prison, feeding and clothing them. I believe this includes mercy on both Christians and Jews during the great tribulation. In fact, the sheep seem surprised to be counted as sheep in this story (*When did we...*). It seems probable that these are the ones who heed the advice of the proclaiming angels (Rev 14) - one who proclaims the everlasting gospel, specifically to *fear God and give Him glory,* and another who warns not to take the mark of the beast. They do not necessarily put faith in Christ since that is not how the angel presents it. Thus the sheep do not require a post-rapture revival of faith in Christ, which is at the root of Showers' case.

Next, Showers compares Matthew 24:30, 31 to 1Thessalonians 4:15-17, claiming there are more differences than similarities. You cannot prove the point with two incomplete contexts when there is so much more information on the topic. I gave a complete picture in chapter four.

The Great Multitude

In chapter 7 (pp. 139-151) he focuses in on the great multitude (Rev 7). Van Kampen argued that these must be resurrected saints because they appear to have bodies, rather than merely being the spirits of slain martyrs. He explained because they wore robes, waved palm branches in their hands, and stood before God's throne, they must have resurrection bodies. Showers presents a solid case this does not necessarily prove the point. He cannot, however, disprove the point, so this is a straw man complaint.

Van Kampen also contrasts the saints under the altar at the fifth seal with the great multitude resurrected at the sixth seal.[113] This is based on Revelation 20:4, which seems to say those martyred by the beast are raised up on the first day of the millennium rather than at the sixth seal. This would tie them in with the fifth seal martyrs. Shower's insists this must be true for pre-wrath to be correct, for we cannot allow that the great multitude comes out individually by martyrdom rather than all at once at the rapture. If the great multitude is martyrs under the beast, then according to pre-trib they come out individually and continuously. Showers says pre-wrath adherents recognize the fifth seal martyrs as saints, and that we cannot explain the reason for them to not be raptured. His third point is that all believers in Christ are part of the church and have part in the rapture.

Fourth, Showers contrasts the martyrs under the altar (Rev 6:9-11) with those in Revelation 20:4. He says they do not directly describe

---

[113] *The Sign*, pp. 296-298, 502

the same group of people. He notes those under the altar were merely slain for their testimony, while those in 20:4 were specifically beheaded. The fifth seal also does not describe saints being martyred but those slain before the great tribulation, while 20:4 describes those specifically slain during the great tribulation. He says this is because the souls under the altar represent those killed prior to the Abomination rather than throughout history, while those in 20:4 are those yet to be martyred (Rev 6:11). He is defending the post-rapture revival required by pre-trib.

It is possible those who are martyred under the Antichrist will not be resurrected until the start of the millennium. However, I admit such a view is difficult to reconcile with the key rapture passages which say we will all be raised up at the same time.

There are other possible answers. There is a little room in the pre-wrath view for some to repent and trust Christ after the sixth seal rapture as long as they have not taken the mark - though the vast majority of mankind will not repent (Rev 11:20). It will not be the great revival required by pre-trib, but perhaps some will be saved. The beast will still be on the scene and the world unrepentant, so these new saints who profess Christ will still face persecution and beheading. Remember, the proclaiming angels tell the world to fear God and refuse the Mark (Rev 14). After Jesus appears, some of those who obey could then extend to faith in Jesus. Thus this passage promises those who do trust Christ after the rapture and are killed for it will have part in the first resurrection. Isn't God's grace glorious!!!

Furthermore, the pre-trib view *requires* that the great multitude consist of martyrs, for they *appear in heaven* from the midst of the great tribulation. But nowhere are they identified as martyrs, whereas 20:4 are specifically martyrs. Thus their view is based solely on their rapture position. In contrast, pre-wrath shows direct, contextual evidence that the multitude is the resurrected church.

Revelation 6:14 says *these are the ones who come out of the great tribulation*. Showers notes the phrase *come out* is in the

213

present tense. He then presents a lengthy argument which essentially concludes the present tense indicates the number of the multitude is continually being added to. Greek scholars are divided as to whether a present tense typically indicates a continuous action or can also be a point action. If pre-trib is true then Mr. Showers' thesis here would be correct. But the pre-wrath view that this happens all at once is just as possible. When all the rest of the evidence is put together, pre-wrath is validated.

The Day of the Lord

In chapter eight (pp. 152-171) Showers explains his concept of the Day of the Lord. He first unjustly accuses pre-wrath adherents of claiming there is only on DOL referred to in Scripture. We fully understand that some of the past judgments on Israel were called the Day of the Lord, such as the Babylonian captivity (Ez 7:19 and others). We are pretty much in agreement with Showers and others as to which prophecies relate to the end of this age. We primarily differ on when that Day starts.

Rosenthal claimed that the end-time DOL wrath is characterized by God's direct wrath against man in Scripture, not by man's wrath against man as seen in the first five seals. Showers argues that He does use the nations in apocalyptic wrath. But instead of quoting Scriptures showing this, *all he does* is quote other theological works which also make this claim. Mr. Showers, while it is certainly okay to support a claim by referencing other scholars, you will not convince me without clear scriptural testimony. I base my doctrine on the Word, not on theologians.

He next discusses the various Hebrew words translated as *wrath*. He quotes a single Old Testament scholar who apparently, from the brief quote, believes *'ebrah* is actually a weak word, claiming that the other three are "probably" the stronger words. He secondly contests the idea that DOL wrath is only against the Gentile nations and not against Israel.

214

Regarding the first point, one scholarly opinion out of many is not enough to convince me. I notice he does not deny that 'ebrah is *only* used in the context of the end time Day of the Lord. Since this is true, and this Day will bring wrath only paralleled by the great flood and the destruction of Sodom, how can he claim this is the weaker word for wrath? Especially in light of the fact that the other words are also used for anger expressed through warfare, pestilence, and other disciplinary anger? Nor do I have a problem with some of God's 'ebrah coming on Israel, as they appear to be mostly unrepentant still at the start of the trumpet judgments, apart from the 144,000 firstfruits. However, they are exempt from the completely unrestrained 'ebrah contained in the bowls, for by the seventh trump they have repented and are provided a path to Azal before the bowls are emptied on the earth.

Next he claims there are two kinds of the DOL in the end time, a broad meaning which covers part or all of the seven years and a narrow sense which is Armageddon. He notes that the beast gathers the armies of the world to Israel (Rev 16:12-17). He compares this to Joel 3 and Zechariah 14 which describe the armies of the world gathering in Israel when that Day is near.

First of all, no prophecy shows both of these supposed *Days* in a single context to show there are two distinct DOL's. Nor do any refer to the *Days of the Lord*. It is always found in the singular. Pre-tribs seem to have a problem with seeing two where there is only one - two parousias, two DOL's - because only then is their theory defensible. Their arguments are so confusing and convoluted it makes their own eyes cross [grin]. This is the only way they can make the heavenly signs, the gathering of the armies, and the coming of Elijah all (Joel 3; Zech 14; Mal 4:5) precede the DOL. These precede only their narrow Day of Armageddon, but not their broad Day including the seventieth week.

Notably, the armies in Joel 3 and Zechariah 14 gather in the Valley of Jehoshaphat whereas the armies in Revelation 16 gather to Mount Megiddo - distinct locations located more the 60 miles apart. The prophecies are quite clear and specific where the armies are gathered. I go into greater detail about the Jehoshaphat Campaign in the next chapter.

Again, Showers looks at the examples of Noah and Lot. He states that neither passage (Matt 24; Luke 17) specifically mentions the rapture. He concludes since neither the church nor the rapture are specifically named, "the pre-wrath Rapture view must draw this parallel by implication on the basis of its beliefs concerning such things as the divisions of the seventieth week, the length of the Great Tribulation, the significance of the sixth seal, the time that the Day of the Lord begins, and the relationship of the Rapture to the Matthew 24 and Luke 17 coming of Christ, not on the basis of explicit textual reference. Thus it reads more into the Matthew 24 and Luke 17 texts than what those texts specifically state." (p.169)

His second point is that Jesus illustrates the suddenness of God's wrath when Christ comes, which happens to parallel the day Noah was shut up in the ark; He was not illustrating the deliverance of the righteous before wrath. Showers compares the groups of those taken and those left behind. Noah entered the ark under his own power and Lot chose to leave Sodom, whereas the individuals taken from the field, etc. is in the passive voice, meaning they are taken by others. He then refers back to arguments made in the sixth chapter, which I already addressed.

ANSWER: In Matthew 28 Jesus gave the great commission to the disciples. Strangely enough, He didn't call the church by name here, either, so maybe it does not apply to the church. Yes it does! Just because he did not specifically mention the church or the resurrection does not mean the context does not refer to the church. He does refer to the *elect* (Matt 24), which in the New Testament is almost always the church. And Showers says there is no mention of the rapture, refusing to see it in Matthew 24:31. This is the immediate context to which Christ's coming refers in the example of Noah. Also, a plain reading of Scripture establishes all of those things on which he insists our interpretation relies.

Shower's second point was that Noah and Lot each went to safety of his own volition. Well, Christians choose to receive salvation when God offers it, and so escape God's wrath. Noah entered the ark on his own two legs, but God shut the ark (Gen 7:16). So we see that God secured Noah's deliverance from the flood, just as He will doours before His wrath. And Lot was escorted out by angels - likewise we see angels escorting the elect to Jesus. There are so many obvious parallels; you have to choose to be blind to not see them. As for that passive voice, as angels gather us together to meet the Lord there is no problem.

We have had eight chapters of no real problems. Let's move to the next one.

2Thessalonians

Chapter nine (pp. 172-199) concerns 2Thessalonians 2. Showers explains the background, making several correct observations. He first notes the Greek construction of 2:1 indicates this coming of Christ and the gathering of the saints are part of a single, great event. He agrees with pre-wraths that Paul referred to the coming of Christ that involves the rapture. He concludes that the real issue in this letter was not the *fact* of Christ's coming but the *time* of His coming in relations to the judgment phase of the DOL. Showers then explains the pre-wrath view that this Day must be preceded by the apostasy and the revealing of the Antichrist. Rosenthal taught the apostasy is the covenant with many offered by Antichrist (Dan 9:26-27). All pre-wraths identify the revealing of the beast with the Abomination of Desolation. Thus the DOL must follow this point.

Showers insists that because Paul did not identify this apostasy nobody can be sure to what it refers. Thus Rosenthal's suggestion it is the covenant is uncertain. Second, when it says the apostasy must come first, the verb translated *come* merely says this will happen at some point in the future. It does not say how long

217

afterwards until Christ comes, so it could be at the very beginning. Third, Showers emphasizes that this is *the* apostasy in the Greek. He argues from several *theologians* that: 1) This indicates it is worldwide or universal in scope, distinct from limited apostasies in the past; 2) It is a sudden event, not over a period of time; and 3) This apostasy is in the absolute sense, implying it will be complete - it will not be diluted with a mixture of that which is not apostasy. He then establishes that *apostasy* is rebellion against God, a characteristic of the unsaved. What follows is his theory of the apostasy, which we shall examine shortly.

I agree it is uncertain that the apostasy relates to the covenant with Antichrist. In fact, I present another possibility which has better textual support. To review, Matthew 24:10 says many will be scandalized and fall away just before or in relation to the Abomination. This relates to the fourth seal. When the persecution increases worldwide, many professing believers will rebel against God and follow the beasts of the earth to save their own lives. No place will be safe. Thus pre-wrath meets his arbitrary criterion that the apostasy is worldwide or large scale.

Second, all Showers does is demonstrate that Rosenthal may or may not be correct in his assertions that the apostasy is the covenant.

Third, his three criteria for *the* apostasy are completely arbitrary. He again argues from theologians rather than from the Bible. Showers reads meaning into it which has no scriptural justification. That is like saying *the* carnival is a sudden event, when it takes days to set up and usually lasts for several days. I agree that the apostasy is rebellion against God and is large scale.

He explains his scheme for the apostasy: At its beginning it will be a worldwide or universal rebellion against God's rule. Just before the seventieth week the Spirit's work of restraining lawlessness will be taken from the earth when the church is raptured. Instantly the total human population will change from a mixture of saved and unsaved co-existing to unsaved only. All those who were in rebellion will be left on earth. As a result of the rapture a sudden, worldwide apostasy will occur. He then compares this favorably with his arbitrary criteria above.

Quite the curious and imaginative scenario. First, *apostasia* is related to the Greek *apostasion*, which is a writing or bill of divorcement. Thus the apostasy are those who become rebellious rather than those who remain rebellious, just as a person becomes divorced but is not in a divorced state prior to marriage. Matthew describes a falling away because of offense which meets this central idea of becoming apostate. Reading the Early Church Fathers, they held a person as apostate who has fallen away from the faith or fallen into serious sin, not someone who has never believed.

Second, this apostasy of Showers would last all of - oh, let's be generous and say thirty minutes. As soon as the shock wore off a little and people began to realize what had happened, there would naturally be a great revival. Thus a pre-trib rapture would not initiate further rebellion, but the exact opposite - a restoration. If he can claim the word *the* makes it a sudden and complete event, with equal validity I can say it makes it too significant to be such a brief event. That is one of the major weaknesses of pre-trib. They must often infer things which are not there based on the requirements of their theory, rather than rely only on the testimony of Scripture.

Showers sees two ways the word *first* (2Thess 2) could be interpreted. He admits the pre-wrath understanding that both the apostasy and the revealing must come first is possible. But he then suggests this could be saying that the apostasy must precede the revealing of the man of sin, not that they both precede the Day of the Lord. Thus he makes this mean that the rapture induced apostasy precedes the revealing of Antichrist. He makes this passage say, "Don't worry, the time for Christ's coming and the rapture on the Day of the Lord has not arrived. Now don't be deceived, for the rapture-induced apostasy must come before the revealing of the man of sin."

The main point Paul is explaining is the timing of the rapture and the Day of the Lord. Some of the Thessalonians thought Christ's coming was imminent, and Paul told them it's not, so get back to work (2Thess 3). If we interpret this the way Showers does, then Paul fails to make the point.

According to pre-wrath, the man of sin is revealed by the Abomination and related events. Showers contends that Paul did not identify what reveals him in 2Thessalonians 2, but only said that he would do those things. Second, he argues that the apostasy and the revealing could come either at the same time or else one immediately after the other, which "conflicts with the pre-wrath view teaching that the apostasy will come at the beginning of the seventieth week." (p. 185) Third, he points out that all of the things the man of sin is said to do - sit in the temple, declare self as God, etc. - use active verbs in the Greek; On the other hand, his revealing uses a passive verb, meaning that someone else reveals him. Pre-wrath asserts that it is his actions which reveal him, while the passage says something or someone else does it.

His first point has some validity, for Paul did not say those actions would reveal him, only that he would do those things. However, neither did he say what *would* reveal him. The things Paul said he will do could, then, be that which reveals him. While pre-wraths can surmise from existing information, Showers can only speculate. Further, Matthew 24 describes a scandalized falling away in relation to the Abomination, which matches what we see in 2Thessalonians. Also, while Rosenthal associates the apostasy with the seven year covenant (Dan 9:27), most pre-wraths associate it with the persecution later in the week.

Second, when the Antichrist commits the Abomination he will not announce himself as the man of sin, but declare himself as God. God has told us beforehand this would happen, so it is God who revealed Him by telling us what he would do. I can also suggest the two witnesses. Revelation 11 says they will prophesy for 1260 days and are killed a few days before the seventh trumpet - which trump ends the 1260 days for the beast. Thus they apparently come on the scene just before the Abomination. Perhaps they reveal him and give warning, which allows some of the Jews time to flee. Then there are the proclaiming angels (Rev 14) who appear at this time. Any of these explain the passive verb.

In a lengthy discussion Showers next tries to demonstrate that the Antichrist will be revealed by earlier action. He claims the first four seals will probably be recognizable, particularly the first seal and the signing of the covenant.

First, these events could only be recognized by watchful believers who are expecting them. Most unbelievers and many untaught believers are unfamiliar with these prophecies except for a few minor details. Even that recognition is debatable. There is already a seven year treaty in the E.U. which has been re-ratified (confirmed) once of this writing - the Stockholm Accord. The future seven year treaty could be another re-confirmation of this accord or something similar, perhaps with more countries signing. This would not be so obvious, then. In this case it would be a progressive revealing as more prophecy was fulfilled.

However, the first seal may not even refer to the covenant with Antichrist, though that is the most common view. It may just be a sudden upsurge in false christs and false prophets mentioned in Matthew 24. The key sign in the Olivet Discourse is the armies surrounding Israel and the Abomination - not the wars, pestilence, and false prophets - which have appeared throughout history. Jesus emphasized the Abomination as a sign of His coming.

Now I realize a pre-trib rapture at the same time as this covenant would reveal its true nature to those left behind who have had this teaching. Also, the so-called tribulation revival would cause many to seek for answers about the end time, and so many would learn the truth. But this has its own problems.

How many would reasonably still choose to follow the Antichrist after the pre-trib rapture proved to the world that God's Word is true? How could the beast invalidate the testimony of hundreds of millions of people who were left behind and the thousands of readily available books explaining what had happened? While many would rebel and still follow the Antichrist

221

in hopes he can win, there could be no skeptics or atheists after such a miracle as the rapture. 2Thessalonians says mankind will be deceived by the Antichrist when he comes on the scene. But if it is the rapture and covenant which reveal him it is difficult to imagine most of mankind believing he is God.

Most telling, the Antichrist does not sit in the temple declaring himself God until after the Abomination, some years after the covenant. He will be only one of many individual rulers who are part of the covenant, for he is is given authority by the ten kings for 1260 days only just before the Abomination. So how would he be in a position to deceive the world after the rapture?

But in the pre-wrath view there will be no amazingly fulfilled prophecy of the rapture to hinder the world from following Antichrist if they so choose when he fully comes on the scene. Messengers or angels of God will warn mankind to fear God and refuse the mark of the beast (Rev 14). Some will heed the warnings, though they do not necessarily put faith in Christ - that is not the message the angels preach. Those who refuse the mark and survive until the sheep and goat judgment will enter the millennial reign of Christ. These points essentially answer all of Showers's other complaints about the revealing of the man of sin, though I could show more.

Showers also disagrees with our identity of the restrainer in this passage. He agrees that Daniel 10 describes the Archangel Michael as the defender of Israel. He also agrees Daniel 12:1 says he does something at the middle of the week. But he contends that Michael is not the restrainer in 2Thessalonians that moves out of the way. Showers asserts that in the seventieth week Satan begins his final and greatest attempt to totally annihilate Israel. This requires Michael to go into full action to prevent that total annihilation. (p. 191)

Pre-wraths say Michael will *stand still* rather than stand up (Dan 12:1). Showers admits the Hebrew word can be translated either way. He then quotes a Hebrew lexicon which states it especially means to arise or come on the scene in this verse. He explains that the Septuagint (Greek translation of O.T.) uses the middle voice form of *anestemi*, which always means *to arise*. His final point on this word is that the context describes Michael as *the great prince which standeth for the children of thy people*, using a form of 'amad. He says this emphasizes why Michael arises at the abomination, to protect Israel from total annihilation. I will first address these three points.

First, it does not make sense that Michael - pictured as defending Israel throughout her history against Satan - has been sitting down on the job taking it easy, so to speak, so he can be said to arise at this time. Based on 2Thessalonians, the early church asserted the great tribulation is to be without restraint. Daniel was told the *purpose* of Jacob's troubles is to completely shatter the holy people (Dan 12:7). How does this testimony line up with Michael arising to defend Israel?

I've got a question for Mr. Showers: Did Satan hold himself back in the previous beast empires and desolations of Israel- such as the Nazi holocaust? The Great tribulation will be more severe than any before. Matthew 24 says it will be so bad that if God did not amputate it no flesh would survive. This supports the idea of no restraint.

It makes more sense that Michael has been restraining even until now, and that he will back off at the midpoint of the week to allow Satan to *shatter* Israel. I mean, does Satan somehow become more powerful that he is able to overwhelm Michael and his forces to bring this great tribulation against Israel and the saints of Jesus? Michael and his angels prevail against Satan and cast him to earth. Satan then is allowed to vent his wrath - for a short time. (Rev 12) Michael stands back so Satan can vent his rage. This position is 100% supported by Scriptural testimony.

Showers quoted a Hebrew lexicon which stated 'amad in Daniel 12:1 especially means *to arise*. This is an opinion of the scholar who wrote it. The meaning must be determined by context, not by personal opinion. Daniel 10 pictures Michael already up and defending Israel. This contrasts to Daniel 12:1 when Michael does

223

something. He is already fighting, so how can he arise at this time? Rather, the angel says when Michael stands still will come the greatest time of trouble for Israel in history. Its the law of Cause and Effect. Michael shall 'amad and trouble shall come.

Showers also quotes from the Septuagint which uses the word *arise*. We must remember that this is a translation of the original language and thus subject to occasional inaccuracies - especially of words which have a wide variety of meanings such as this one.

Showers then presents his case against Michael as the restrainer. 1) This restrainer restrains *lawlessness*, while Michael restrains enemy attacks against one nation, Israel. 2) This uses the neuter gender participle (*what* restrains), as well as the masculine (*until he is taken*), while the Greek word for archangel is only masculine. 3) Michael is said to stand still, while the restrainer is taken out of the way. Showers concludes the restrainer is the Holy Spirit, which I have already addressed..

I already addressed all three points in my chapter on 2Thessalonians, but feel I should briefly review them. 1) It is not lawlessness which is restrained, but *the mystery of lawlessness*, the spiritual forces behind Antichrist, thus matching Michael's ministry. 2) The neuter can reference the armies under Michael while the masculine refers to the head of the army. Not really a problem in light of all the other evidence. 3) Do you mean to suggest, if it is Michael, that he stops defending Israel on his own authority? Certainly it is by God's command and in God's timing. Thus he stands still when God takes him out of the way.

The last point actually creates a problem with Showers' hypothesis that the restrainer is the Holy Spirit. This taking out of the way is passive, implying someone else removes him. The Spirit is God Himself. Who would move God out of the way? That is difficult to reconcile, but Michael is easy to see as the restrainer.

For his final case in this chapter, Showers argues that the Thessalonians thought the Day of the Lord was already upon them.

He asks how they could think they were in that Day if God's wrath was not being poured out. Logically, it was because of the persecution they endured. Showers believes they understood the DOL would include both persecution of believers and wrath. Paul had previously taught them about the DOL (1Thess 5), so apparently taught them this. Thus, because the first half of the seventieth week is characterized by persecution (Matt 24:8-14), and because Paul taught the DOL would be characterized by persecution, so Paul taught them that the first half week is part of that Day.

He makes two assumptions in this circular reasoning. First, He assumes that Paul taught them the DOL would be characterized by persecution of believers. Where does it say that? In the first letter Paul only told them they would not enter that Day, so take comfort in this truth. He said nothing of persecution.

Second, he assumes their error was thinking they were already in that Day. While the phrase *as if the Day of the Lord had come* (2Thess 2:2) could be understood that way, the previous letter shows the error of this assumption. They had already been told they would not enter that Day.

It seems more likely they thought that Day was about to come at any moment. Interestingly, in the next chapter Showers argues the same concept. He agrees some of them had stopped working in excitement and anticipation of Christ's coming (2Thess 3). Thus they probably understood that persecution would come just before Christ came for the church, and Paul was explaining that some other things had to happen first.

Imminency

In his final chapter (pp.200-232) Showers defends the theory of imminency, which he defines as an event which can literally happen at any moment. He further clarifies that an imminent event cannot rightly be said to be coming soon, for that implies a short time must take place first.

225

He first argues that the pre-wrath expectancy of Christ's coming - that Scripture says to watch for Him - does not rule out the thought that He could come immediately. This is true. But if they knew of things which must happen first, they could not have held to imminency, which by definition means nothing *must* happen first.

Over the next few pages he presents several *theologians* who claimed the early church believed in the imminent return of Christ. On the contrary, we saw earlier that the most reliable early church teachers clearly taught the Antichrist must come first. I take us directly to the source rather than the vague, out-of-context quotes of theologians.

He then counters pre-wrath claims that the Bible nowhere teaches imminency by quoting scholars who say it does, including many who are not pre-tribs (p. 205). Just because they say it does not mean they are right. It is interesting that at least one of his sources is considered either a post-trib or historicist. This means Showers ignores that his definition of imminency still allows the Antichrist to come first. We do not say the church fathers did not look for Christ to possibly come during their lifetime, only that other things had to happen first. We will look at a few of Showers' arguments to give him a fair hearing. (Refer to Showers' book for most references. I just summarize the points here.)

J. Barton Payne114 argued from Scripture that the early church desperately longed for Christ's coming and that the lack of evidence for any postponement suggests a *perhaps today* mentality. You can argue almost anything from silence. It would be tedious to always refer to Antichrist and other events every time we discussed the coming of Christ. Plus, as either a historicist or post-trib Payne apparently had no problem with events preceding his concept of an imminent coming.

---

114 The Imminent Coming of Christ, Eerdmans, Grand Rapids, MI, 1962, pp.95-103

In 1Corinthians 1:7 Paul expressed an ever present concern about Christ's return. *...That you come short in no gift, eagerly waiting for the revelation of our Lord Jesus Christ, who will also confirm you to the end, blameless in the day of our Lord Jesus Christ* (1Cor 1:7, 8). Where does this say Christ could come immediately? It rather says we are waiting for the *apocalypse* of Jesus.

Showers argues that the word *maranatha* (1Cor 16:22) was a sort of code word, establishing the importance of the doctrine of Christ's second coming in the church. I agree. But how does this establish that they believed it could happen at any moment? Rather it was an exhortation to stand firm in their faith and a prayer for His coming.

And to wait for His Son from heaven... (1Thess 1:10). Showers insists the Greek phrase *wait for* implies waiting for someone who could arrive at any moment. He argues that if you knew it would be several hours yet before the guests arrived, they would not have to wait up for them - they would go to bed and set their alarms to wake them at the known time of their guest's arrival.

Christ gave us an alarm clock. In Matthew 24 Jesus said when we see ALL THESE THINGS (context, the great tribulation) we know that His coming is at the very doors. *Blessed is that servant who, when the master knocks, opens to Him immediately,* having been watching and ready. When we see the Abomination we know Christ is due any time. When Christ knocks on the door, the very earth shakes and the sun and moon darken in obeisance. Then we lift our heads for our redemption is at the door. This statement (1Thess 1:10) does not preclude the idea of events happening first.

Showers also concludes the reason some had stopped working (2Thess 3:10-12) was excitement in the belief Christ's coming was imminent. I agree. But he cannot have it both ways. If they thought Christ's coming was imminent then that was the false teaching Paul was correcting - not that they were already in the Day of the Lord.

Titus 2:13: *Looking for that blessed hope, and the glorious appearing of our great God and Savior, Jesus Christ.* Showers says the word *looking* carries the sense of awaiting. The word *hope* means assurance. The word *blessed* refers to the joy of salvation. And the final clause is better translated as *the appearing of the glory....* Thus the Christian's hope is the appearing of the glory that belongs to God and Christ - so the Christians will certainly see that glory in Christ when He comes to rapture the church. In context, this hope is a catalyst for holy living while we wait. With all these I agree completely. But then Showers asks, "Why should Christians always be prepared for Christ's coming, unless that coming could take place at any moment?"

ANSWER: First, because we could also die at any moment and not have the chance to get right with God. Second, because God promises extra protection in tribulations to those who are faithful (see Rev 3:10). Third, because God also promises especially hard times in the great tribulation for certain, unrepentant believers (Rev 2:22). Fourth, because Christ exhorted us to be faithful servants and not wicked so as to be alert to the signs of His coming (Matt 24:45-51). Fifth, because we must make our calling and election sure, demonstrated by the evidence of growing to maturity in Him. I could go on. Also note we are *looking for the appearing of the glory* (doxys) of Jesus. In Matthew 24:29-31 Jesus appears in clouds with glory (doxys).

James 5:7-9 *"Be patient therefore, brethren, unto the coming of the Lord.... Be ye also patient; stablish your hearts: For the coming of the Lord draweth nigh. Grudge not one against the another, brethren, lest ye be condemned: behold, the judge standeth before the door."* I will address only one issue here, which renders his following arguments moot. Read the portion he cut out to abbreviate the passage: *"...See how the farmer waits for the precious fruit of the earth, waiting patiently for it until it receives the early and latter rain. You also be patient. Establish your hearts, for the coming of the Lord is at hand [draws near]."* A farmer waiting for the turns of the seasons for his harvest hardly suggests imminency in the passage.

228

1John 2:28 28 *"And now, little children, abide in Him; that, when He shall appear, we may have confidence, and not be ashamed before Him at His coming."* Showers argues that the Greek word "when" introduces an element of uncertainty as to the timing of Christ's coming. Thus, Christ's coming might be while they all still lived. He says we can conclude that John's statements imply Christ could come at any moment and so we should be continuously ready.

First, John's focus is being ashamed or confident at Christ's coming. Second, the word *appear* is a form of the Greek *phaneroo* (Strong's # 5319), which is openly, shiningly visible. It is a strong verb. In contrast, pre-tribs say we await a secret coming where Christ will not yet be openly manifested. What's more, this *coming* is the parousia, which Matthew 24 places after the Abomination at the sixth seal. Then the sign of the Son of Man shall appear (another form of phaneroo), and Christ will come in glory.

Revelation 3:11 *"I come quickly."* Showers asserts that this word means swiftly, all at once. The context of this is the letters of Revelation, and particularly v.10 which is a promise of divine protection within the great tribulation. We saw the significance of this in my chapter on the letters to the churches. This is a time of testing which shall come on the whole earth to prove those who are earth dwellers. Jesus promises He is coming swiftly. Don't get discouraged, but hold fast to our faith. This is one of the great promises of Scripture. We must remember it and cling to it during the great tribulation. Matthew 24 and others warn that many will not cling to this hope, but be offended and fall away - even to the betrayal of others. We must be overcomers by seeking Christ for strength (Rev 2:7, 11, 17, 26; 3:5, 12, 21; 12:11). **CLING TO THE PROMISE!**

Chapter 13: Answering Brainard, part one

In 2001 Lee W. Brainard wrote a book critiquing the pre-wrath view.115   His approach is different from other critiques.   He focuses most intently on the Day of the Lord, the nature of the seal judgments, and Revelation 3:10, which comprises nearly half his book. He states in his introduction that he once believed similarly to the pre-wrath view, but was forced to back down point by point by a pre-trib brother until he backed into pre-tribulationism.

I do want to take a moment to thank Brainard for his book. Some of his reasoning forced me to weigh and sift a few things carefully, helping me make an even stronger case for pre-wrath. I can honestly say his critique challenged me more than any other I have seen.   The majority of his points, though, were easy to answer.

Chapter one (pp. 15-17) is a short section in which Brainard states the promise of the rapture is an anchor for the soul.

> The rapture keeps us from drifting into sin. When we fix our eyes on the recompense of reward we find the strength to keep from falling back into the pleasures of sin for a season (Heb. 11:25-26)...The rapture is a purifying hope (1John 3:3)....

> But not every believer has a full and clear view of the church's promised deliverance from the trials that shall beset the world at the end of the age. Several truncated rapture teachings in circulation today teach that it occurs after the church has passed through half or more of the seventieth week. This is a tragedy. That which was meant to be an anchor for

---

115   The Pre-wrath Rapture Answered: From the Testimony of Scripture   (Gospel Folio Press, 304 Killaly St.   West, Port Colborne ON L3K 6A6 Canada, 2001)

the soul is bereft of much of the stabilizing effect it was intended to have. Multitudes of Christians drift with various winds of doctrine that nurture concerns, anxieties, and worries about undergoing the time of tribulation and being on earth for the visitations of the seventieth week. (p. 17)

First, the rapture is not a *recompense of reward.* It is the completion of our redemption. This passage says Moses looked forward to the reward as he endured and obeyed God. Moses looked for the resurrection of the O.T. saints, not the rapture. Also, the Hebrews passage does not support Brainard's idea of escape before the Tribulation, but of suffering for the faith in expectation of God's reward.

> *Choosing rather to **suffer affliction** with the people of God than to enjoy the passing pleasures of sin, esteeming the reproach of Christ greater riches than the treasures in Egypt; for he looked to the reward.* (emph. mine)

Second, nowhere does the Bible say our hope is in a rapture before the Tribulation, contrary to his assertion above. Our hope is in Christ.

In his next three chapters Brainard focuses on the Day of the Lord as revealed in both Testaments. He correctly explains that the seals, trumpets, and bowls occur sequentially and each continues to the end of the seventieth week. He notes, for example, that the wars of the second seal is not just a short period of time until the third, but continue through the seven years. He also believes the Day of the Lord begins at Armageddon. Therefore he overlaps the Revelation judgments so he can manipulate things to have the sixth seal signs appear just before Armageddon.

I can agree to a point. Certainly the wars and famines of the second and third seals will continue throughout the time, as will the persecution of martyrdom of the fourth and fifth. Problems arise, however, in the way he applies this to the sixth seal. The first five seals release mankind to ever greater wickedness and show what results when opened. But with the sixth seal the very nature of the judgments changes from man-caused events to supernaturally caused disasters and heavenly signs. The judgments of this seal appear to happen all at once, bringing great terror to mankind. It is because of these things that they cry out for the rocks and mountains to fall on them and hide them from the wrath of God.

Brainard agrees with pre-wrath that the sixth seal is opened before the seventh seal and the trumpets and bowls. However, he must change the order of the text so that the 144,000 are sealed and the great seventieth week revival of the great multitude take place before the heavenly signs and earthquake. Then, just before Armageddon, the judgments of the sixth seal appear and mankind will flee. He argues that it does not make sense to have mankind hiding well before Armageddon at the pre-wrath sixth seal, but then gather together to fight the Battle later. I will give his theory this much credit that if pre-trib happens to be true, then the DOL must happen much as he projects. This view is completely different from what most pre-tribs teach, though. In fact, this chronology is more in line with the post-trib position.

The most obvious problem is the change in order - sealing, revival/martyrdom, then heavenly signs. Whey didn't Jesus present them in this order when He sent the vision to John? For example, just before the seventh trumpet He told John that the prophecy was about to back up and change focus to the important peoples in the end time drama (Rev 10:11). He wants us to understand the basic principles of this prophecy, seen by statements to read and obey it, and to understand it. If we look for the contextual clues, understanding the order of events is fairly straightforward. First are things pertaining to the churches (Rev 1-3). Next is a heavenly prelude to the main body of the prophecy (Rev 4-5). Revelation 6-11 is the first time through the seventieth week, concluding with the seventh trumpet when Jesus takes up His authority.

John begins prophesying again in Revelation 12, detailing the war between God and Satan from the beginning of Israel through the death and resurrection of Jesus, then the Antichrist as he wars against Israel and the saints of Jesus. We also see other major players, such as the witnesses and the false prophet. Then in Revelation 14 we see the two harvests, the rapture which is first and the trumpets which are second. This brings us back to the end of the seventieth week.

Revelation 15-19 describes the manner in which Christ assumes control of earth - the bowl judgments, judgment on Babylon, and Armageddon. These happen quickly, for He is not going to waste a lot of time. The last two chapters tell of Christ's millennial reign, the great white throne judgment, and the new creation.

So, Brainard claims the sealing of the Jews and the martyrdom of the tribulation saints happen first with the opening of the sixth seal. Then just before Armageddon the heavenly signs appear and mankind suddenly realizes Christ is coming to destroy them and flee. By this logic, they were unfazed by the deaths of billions through the trumpets and bowls (at least 1/3 of mankind, and up to another 1/4 in the fourth seal) - following the disappearance of perhaps another half billion Christians before it all began. Christ shows up at Armageddon, and suddenly they are afraid. It does not add up.

Brainard case is based on the fact that most of mankind does not repent during the wrath of God (Rev 9:20). Instead they still rebel and gather to fight at Armageddon. Isaiah 2 says the Lord alone is exalted in the DOL. Because the sixth seal shows mankind being humbled rather than rebellious, he contends this must be at Armageddon.

I contend that they can flee at the sixth seal before the other judgments and still refuse to repent, but continue in rebellion. Many who are on death row for their crimes fear the coming penalty and seek to postpone it any way they can - but are unrepentant of their deeds and hate the cops who keep them (humbled) in jail. Many are in tears when sentence is pronounced, yet do not change while in prison. A few do repent, but many do not. The same happens when God's wrath is introduced by the sixth seal - most will curse God and work to break His chains off (Psalm 2). Because they made their bed with the Antichrist in spite the warnings, they know they are stuck and gather to fight at Armageddon like rioting prisoners. God knows how to *rescue the godly and reserve the unjust under punishment for the day of judgment* (2Pet 2:4-9). With the sixth seal God exalts Himself and continuously humbles man, even in his rebellion.

The DOL in the Old Testament

In chapter three (pp. 29-64) Brainard lists 24 things related to the DOL from Old Testament passages. I agree everything he lists is associated with that Day. But he fails to establish that they must all happen essentially at the same time. They can just as easily be events which unfold over a period of time as God's plan progresses. Let us examine his case, which he believes is fatal to pre-wrath.

Now these eschatological events and circumstances fall into four main categories.

Those events which occur *well before the advent*. Here we find only the coming of Elijah before the coming of the great and dreadful day of the Lord to prepare the way of the Lord in turning the hearts of men (Mal.4:5-6). [I agree with this]

Those events which occur *very shortly prior to the advent*. Here we find only the gathering of the nations for the battle commonly called Armageddon (Joel 3:9-14; Zeph 1:7). [I disagree, as I will show later.]

Those events which no one denies occur *in immediate connection with the advent* [Armageddon]. Here we find the Lord's descent to the Mount of Olives (Zech 14:4), the descent of the heavenly host (Isa 13:3, Joel 2:2-11), deliverance in Mount Zion for the believing remnant (Joel 2:32, Zech 14:4-5), the Lord fighting against the gathered multitudes (Joel 3:13, Isa

235

34:2-3, Zech. 14:3, 12-13, 15), the birds of the air gorging themselves on the flesh of the fallen multitudes (Ez 32:4), the devil bound and cast into the abyss (Isa 24:21-22, Ez 32:2-4, 7), the judgment of the sheep and goats (Joel 3:12), the gathering of all Israel back to her land (Joel 3:1, Zeph 2:7), the Lord reigning in Jerusalem (Obad 21, Isa 24:23), the millennial blessings bestowed upon Israel (Joel 3:14-18, Obad 17, 19-20), and the fountain that flows from the temple of God (Zech 14:8). [I agree with his basic concept, but not the way he puts it together.]

And those events which *some might deem to be either general enough that they could pertain to the entire seventieth week, or flexible enough that they could occur any time therein.* Here fall such things as the shaking of the earth (Isa 2:19-21, Isa 13:13), the signs in the heavens (Isa 24:23, Joel 2:10, 30-31), the clouds which blanket the earth (Joel 2:2, Ezek 30:3), the darkness which covers the land (Exek 32:8, Zeph 14:6-7), the destruction of the land (Zeph 1:16-18, Joel 2:3, Isa 2:13-16), the destruction of the ungodly Mal 4:1, Obad 15, 16), the destruction of Israel's enemies (Zeph 2:4-15, Joel 3:19), the nation of Israel fighting against her enemies (Zeph 2:4-7, Zech 14:14), the heavens opened (Isa 2:10, 19-21, Isa 13:7-80, and the exaltation of the Lord alone (Isa 2:11-18, 20, Zech 14:9).

Now it is to the events of the latter category and to the gathering of the nations in the place called Armageddon that we must and shall give our attention in the following pages....The fact is, these events readily evidence - either by their nature or by their intimate association with one of the events which obviously pertain to the advent - that they too are among those terrors and sorrows which the world will drink at the advent. And several of them, moreover, insist that we embrace the advent as the *terminus a quo* or beginning of the day of the Lord. (pp. 35-37, Emph. his)

A few errors should be noted before we continue. He says that Jesus descends to the Mount of Olives in Zechariah 14:4, and also that deliverance for Israel in Mount Zion is found here. Zechariah does not mention Zion. This is found in Joel 2:32, and refers to salvation after the signs of the sixth seal (Joel 2:30, 31) for the remnant of Israel who calls on the name of the Lord. This corresponds exactly with the pre-wrath schedule.

Zechariah says Christ will stand on Mt. Olives, which will split in two so Israel can flee to Azal, or safety. Brainard, in his next paragraph, points out that Israel will fight against her enemies. Furthermore, at Armageddon the Antichrist and his armies will be struck with a terrible plague at a word from Jesus (Rev 19:21), their eyes and tongues dissolving (Zech 14:12-13). This also says Judah will be at the Battle.

So we have a contradiction. When Christ stands on the Mount of Olives Israel flees to safety. Then it says the Lord will come with His saints (Zech 4:4-6) and *in one day* will set up Jerusalem and destroy the armies of the beast, with Judah present at this battle. Furthermore, Brainard says the gathering of Israel is in immediate connection to the advent. So, while Israel is fleeing away from Jerusalem (loc. of Olives) to safety, Jesus is at the same time gathering the Jews back to Israel (his view Matt. 24:31). And Israel is fleeing to safety when there is no need, as Jesus strikes the enemy with a plague which renders them defenseless. Or perhaps there is a short delay... Jesus first sends Israel to safety, then renders the armies defenseless, then gathers Israel back to fight - all in *one day*. This does not really make much sense.

I do agree all these occur at the advent, or parousia, of Christ. When we understand the advent includes all the events from the sixth seal rapture onward, and His coming is in several stages, all the contradictions are wiped away.

Brainard begins presenting his case:

It is the clear testimony of Scripture that the armies of the nations are gathered very shortly prior to the advent that they might be crushed in the winepress of the wrath of God. For it is not until very late in the seventieth week, even the pouring out of the sixth vial (Rev 16:12-16), which is the sixth of *"the seven last plagues"* (Rev 15:1), that *"the spirits of devils, working miracles, go forth unto the kings of the earth and of the whole world, to gather them to the battle of that great day of God Almighty... and he gathered them together into a place called in the Hebrew tongue Armageddon."*

But the Scriptures testify with just as much clarity that this gathering of the heathen multitudes occurs very shortly prior to the Day of the Lord. Joel 3:9-14 says:

9. Proclaim ye this among the Gentiles; Prepare war... let all the men of war draw near; let them come up... 11. Assemble yourselves, and come, all ye heathen... 12. Let the heathen... come up to the valley of Jehoshaphat... 13. Put ye in the sickle, for the harvest is ripe: come, get you down; for the press is full, the fats (i.e. vats) overflow; for their wickedness is great. 14. Multitudes, multitudes in the valley of decision: for the day of the Lord is near in the valley of decision.

And Zephaniah 1:7-17 says:

7. Hold thy peace at the presence of the Lord God; for the day of the Lord is at hand; for the Lord hath prepared a sacrifice, he hath bid his guests... 14. The great day of the Lord is near, it is near; and hasteth greatly, even the voice of the day of the Lord; the mighty man shall cry there bitterly... 17. and I will bring distress upon men... because they have sinned against the Lord; and their blood shall be poured out as the dust, and their flesh as the dung.

These passages are clear enough that their testimony cannot be misunderstood. When the armies of the nations are gathered and waiting to be crushed in the winepress, the day of the Lord is not already in process, but hanging overhead as a Damoclean sword. It is immediately at hand. And in the light of such distinct testimony, all debate on when the day of the Lord begins ought to be laid to rest. The Lord of hosts descending from heaven in glory and judgment to trample the winepress is one and the same with the arrival of the day of the Lord. (pp. 37, 38)

Pre-wraths understand Joel and Zephaniah to be a separate battle explicitly centered on the valley of Jehoshaphat, distinct from Armageddon. Brainard knows this and tries to destroy our case. He is easily answered.

The Jehoshaphat Campaign

First, Zephaniah 1 does not describe the gathering of the world's armies before the DOL. He describes silence in Heaven when it is at hand (see Rev 8:1), when it arrives. God has prepared or examined His sacrifice, so now it it time for it to begin. He has bid (invited, set apart, raptured) his guests. Under Jewish law a number of things had to be prepared before a sacrifice was made - most notably inspection of the animal to insure it was suitable for the sacrifice. The great tribulation is a time of testing/inspecting the earth-dwellers (Rev 3:10), the ones to be sacrificed in the wrath of God. Therefore, God has prepared His sacrifice.

Zephaniah then tells some of what will happen *in the day of the Lord's sacrifice* (v.8). He says the DOL is near in the valley of decision (Zeph 1:14), a day which *is bitter. Then the mighty men will cry out* (see Rev 6:12-17; Luke 21). *That day is a day of wrath... of trouble and distress... of darkness and gloominess.... A day of trumpets and alarms... The land shall be devoured by the fire of His jealousy* [first trumpet]. Chapter two warns *...before the day of the Lord's anger comes upon you. Seek the Lord, all you meek of the earth, who have upheld His justice. Seek righteousness, seek humility. It may be that you will be hidden in the day of the Lord's anger.* Notice the last is addressed to the entire earth **before** the DOL. In Revelation 14:6-11 proclaiming angels go forth warning man to fear God and refuse the mark of the beast.

239

Zephaniah continues, describing things that happen in that Day to specific places - Gaza, Canaan, Ethiopia, and others. These are probably the nations whose armies sit outside Jerusalem in the valley of Jehoshaphat under authority of the Antichrist.

It is not until Zephaniah 3:8 that the Lord is determined to gather the nations of the entire earth to pour out His indignation, devouring the whole earth and restoring Israel. There is plenty of room here for the DOL to precede Armageddon, while the trumpet and bowl judgments take place. Then the nations are gathered for Armageddon and the sheep and goat judgment. These things are told from the perspective of just before the Day of the Lord. God is telling us what that Day will be like and what will happen on that Day, so repent before it comes.

Joel gives us the most information about the Jehoshaphat Campaign as it relates to the DOL. He first describes the sixth seal announcing that Day (Joel 2:31). Verse 32 says those who call upon the name of the Lord will be delivered. This refers to the 144,000 who will follow the Lamb wherever He goes (Rev 7 and 14) and those in Israel who eventually repent before the seventh trumpet - since they will finally recognize Jesus is their Messiah.

Joel 3 then explains in greater detail what is happening. The Jews will be led captive and dispersed, some sold to the Greeks (v. 6) to reduce their population after the Abomination (Rev 12; Dan 12:1; Matt 24:15-24). They will be stirred up, bringing a counter-attack against the armies which occupy Israel. The occupying force consists largely of Islamic nations surrounding Israel. (Tyre, Sidon, Philistia, Gaza, others. See Zeph 2 for a list of likely nations, whom the DOL falls heavily upon.) It appears the Antichrist gives control of Israel to an Islamic coalition.

At the sixth seal the Lord takes up the cause of His people. There will be a battle at Jehoshaphat, the Valley of Decision. Ultimately, Israel will do to these people as they did to Israel - sell them as slaves. While this passage uses the phrase *all the nations*, which leads some to believe this is Armageddon, verse twelve explains it is *the surrounding nations* at Jehoshaphat, not the armies of the world as at Armageddon. Mount Megiddo is located about 60 miles north of Jehoshaphat.

It is time to put in the sickle and reap the harvest (Joel 3:13). You will recall that after Jesus reaps the first harvest of the rapture another angel comes with another sickle to reap the grapes of wrath (Rev 14). I relate this to the trumpets. Here we see the same command. The time of testing the earth-dwellers is past. They have shown their character - whether they are the meek of the earth as the sheep, or whether they are really goats (Matt 25). Now that the rider of the fourth horse, Death (martyrdom of saints), has passed Hades (hell, judgment) follows after to claim his trophies. The reaping of the grapes of wrath begins with the armies holding Jerusalem captive from Jehoshaphat.

The reaping begins at the Jehoshaphat Campaign. *The Day of the Lord is near in the valley of decision. The sun and moon are darkened,* it is time to stick in the sickle and reap. The trumpets reap the grapes of wrath, while the bowls pour out the resulting sour wine on mankind.

Brainard's lengthy attempt to equate Jehoshaphat with Armageddon comes to naught. This should clearly show why we believe they are separate.

On page 46, Brainard discusses the great earthquake associated with the Day of the Lord. He argues that only one earthquake is described in DOL passages, not quakes in diverse places. But according to pre-wrath those in diverse places are in the first half of the week, relating to the famines and shortages of the third seal.

The DOL is initiated by a worldwide earthquake at the sixth seal, with another at Armageddon, according to our schedule. He points out that Hebrews 12:26 says God will shake *once more* not only the earth, but also the heavens. He insists this proves that these are one and the same earthquake. If so, this creates the first difficulty for pre-wrath.

There are a couple of ways this can be answered. First, earthquakes have aftershocks, which sometimes (though rarely) can be stronger than the initial quake. These can be considered part of the same quake, even though they may take place some time apart. At the sixth seal the earthquake is said to move islands and mountains, while at Armageddon it flattens mountains and sinks islands. So these could be seen as all part of a single shaking. Also, the seventh bowl does not describe the heavens shaken, only the earth. Thus Hebrews 12 may refer only to the sixth seal shaking.

In fact, it could be argued that all of the end time events are part of that shaking, not just the earthquakes. I believe it even includes some of the things which lead up to the seventieth week. God is going to shake *everything* that can be shaken, both heavenly and earthly, so only that which cannot be shaken remains (Heb 12:27). The time of testing those who dwell on the earth, then, could easily fit these criteria. Thus this supposed difficulty is really not all that difficult.

The Lord is Exalted

One of my favorite arguments against the entire seven years being the DOL is that *the Lord alone shall be exalted in that Day* (Is 2:10-21). Brainard uses this against pre-wrath. He points out that the things named in this passage are merely representative of the calamities on earth, not everything that happens. I agree.

> The Lord will overthrow all man's engineering marvels - his dams, skyscrapers, bridges... automobiles... universities... etc. The Lord has determined that He alone will be glorified in that day, and all else that is gloried in will be reduced to heaps of rubble.

> Now the exaltation of the Lord alone cannot be reconciled with the doctrine that the last two years of the seventieth week, much less the whole, is the Day of the Lord.... Right up until the advent the inhabitants of the earth obstinately refuse to give ear to the everlasting gospel. They are not brought low. Their

242

haughtiness is not bowed down. Right up until the advent men glory in themselves, in their shame, in the pleasures of sin, in the pride of life, in the devil, and in the antichrist. Right up until the last day men glory in their military might, in their wonderful cities, in their commercial and financial institutions, in every vain and passing pleasure.

Man's day and the Day of the Lord are in stark contrast.... (page 49)

Pre-wraths believe this will be a continuous humbling of man. God begins by shaking the entire earth, darkening the heavenly lights, showing up in glory to remove the church from the clutches of the beast, and supporting the Israeli resistance force. This will topple much of man's glory. Through the trumpets and bowls God will continue to destroy all of man's delusions of grandeur.

True, mankind as a whole does not repent. But the sixth seal passages and Isaiah 2 say nothing of mankind repenting, either. These only say they run away in fear as God utterly abolishes their idolatry - whether it be humanistic and evolutionary sciences which deny God, or false religion, or engineering marvels, or their riches and things money can buy. For a time Antichrist has been allowed to usurp God's authority on earth and overcome the saints. But suddenly God thwarts him by delivering the saints. God frustrates his efforts to destroy Israel at the Jehoshaphat Campaign. Mankind will know there is a God who is fed up with them. Yet they still rebel. Just as sometimes the naughty child strikes back when the parent disciplines, so mankind tries to strike back at Armageddon rather than repent. While God is humbling man in His anger, taking away their toys and spanking them - looking for any sign of repentance - they continue to kick and scream to the very end. Brainard continues:

When we compare Joel 2:31 and Joel 2:1-11 we find a further argument that the advent [Armageddon coming] is the inception of the day of the Lord. Joel 2:31 says, *"the sun shall be turned into darkness, and the moon into blood, before the...day of the Lord come."* And in Joel 2:1-11 we read, *"the*

243

*day of the Lord cometh...a day of... a great people and a strong...**before them**... the heavens shall tremble, the sun and moon shall be dark, and the stars shall withdraw their shining... the Lord shall utter his voice before his army...that executeth his word."* Now if the signs in the heavens which herald the day of the Lord transpire *in the presence of* the heavenly host at the time of the advent, then the day of the advent is the day of the Lord. ...Not even the simplest comforts of life, as the glow of the sun, the gleam of the moon, and the twinkle of the stars will be allowed to maintain their radiant testimony to the beneficence of God. (page 50, emph., and skips his)

First of all, Joel 2 does not describe the angelic hosts, but the armies of the nations arrayed against Israel at the Abomination, when the Day of the Lord is near.

Then look at the portion he bypassed (Joel 2:15-16). This looks like the rapture, followed by the ultimate repentance of Israel in the next few verses. Verse fifteen commands a trumpet blown in Zion, just as one sounds at the rapture when an angel tells Jesus to reap the harvest (1Cor 15:52; Rev 14:15). Then 2:16 says:

Gather the people, Sanctify (set apart) the congregation, Assemble the elders, Gather the children and nursing babes; Let the bridegroom go out from his chamber, and the bride from her dressing room.

Here we see a gathering of a set apart congregation, including all from old to young. Jesus is called the bridegroom and the church His bride in several prophecies. The bridegroom leaves His chambers (heaven), and the bride her dressing room (earth), paralleling the parable of the virgins in the context of a gathering of elect (Matt 24, 25). [I want to thank Brainard here. His line of reasoning brought this verse to my attention, allowing me to strengthen the pre-wrath view even more.] This may even suggest that children and babies will be gathered at the rapture, as many hope and believe.

244

Then in the following verses Israel is told to repent and pray for their deliverance and restoration. When they do this God will become zealous for them and restore them. The chapter ends with the sixth seal and the promise that those who call upon the name of the Lord in that day will be saved. Thus Joel 2:16 parallels Zephaniah 1:7, which also mentions a set apart group in relation to the sixth and seventh seals, as I discussed earlier.

In Ezekiel 32:2-8 Pharaoh, the king of Egypt, is judged as a type of the Antichrist. Egypt is sometimes used as a type for the world in its sinful state. In Hebrew, the word for Egypt means stronghold or sin. Thus the king of Egypt is the man of sin. This passage speaks of the sun, moon, and stars darkened when the time comes to destroy the king of Egypt, who is a dragon in the seas (see Rev 13:1-10). It adds that all the birds will feast on the remains of Egypt, paralleling passages concerning Armageddon. Because of these, Brainard postulates that this proves the heavenly signs occur just before Armageddon.

When I look at this passage, nothing prohibits these things happening over a period of time. We see all these things from the sixth seal on as God's process of extinguishing the beast and his kingdom from the earth. Nothing in this text requires that the Day of the Lord consist only of Armageddon.

Every man's heart will melt in fear, from the slave to the mighty ruler, when the signs of the sixth seal are revealed (Revelation 6:12-17; Isaiah 13:6-7). Brainard argues:

> But this scene of terror and panic does not greet us when we observe the world's response to the judgments of the seventieth week. When the inhabitants of the earth are vouchsafed with the sight and ministry of the angels of God *late in the seventieth week,* they do not tremble with uncontrollable fear, but obstinately ignore these rare and eloquent warnings (Rev. 14:6-11). When the *fourth vial* is poured out upon the sun, scorching them with fire, they defiantly *"blaspheme the name of God"* and *"repent not to give him glory"* (Rev. 16:8-9). (page 53)

245

He continues, showing that they do not repent at the fifth bowl (Rev 16:10-11), and celebrate over the death of the two witnesses (Rev 11:7-10), and even continue to blaspheme God when the seventh bowl brings judgment of great hail from heaven (Rev 16:21). This forces him to conclude that the Day of the Lord comes at Armageddon.

Let me illustrate using an earlier case. A prisoner usually does not thank the judge, the prosecutor, and the prison guards for showing him the error of his ways or trying to correct him. You cannot repent any time you wish, but only while God is calling to you. Mankind sees the judgment of God, but has no desire to repent but rather to throw off the chains of God (Psalm 2). In the passages touted by Brainard where men are seen fleeing and hiding, nothing says they repent or bow to give God glory - including even at Armageddon. It is not until the great white throne judgment following the millennial reign that mankind is forced to bow before God and acknowledge Jesus, not at Armageddon or the advent. His argument is invalid.

Brainard next argues that the DOL is a Day of darkness with no brightness in it (Amos 5:18, 20; Zeph 1:15; et al). He notes that most of those who believe the DOL is an extended period believe this refers to spiritual darkness rather than literal darkness on earth. I do not have a problem with the heavenly lights continuing to be dimmed through the DOL wrath in relation to the sixth seal. Alternatively, the first trumpet judgment creates massive fires, burning 1/3 of the grass and trees on earth. Then the fourth, which I believe quickly follows, is a comet or meteor landing in the ocean. These would produce massive amounts of smoke, steam, and debris entering the air. Thus the darkness and gloominess would be maintained. There! Problem solved!

Also, on page 192 Brainard argues that the DOL includes the millennial kingdom, with which I agree and for the same reasons he presents. So if the DOL is *only* darkness, then he is saying the millennium is darkness, as well. There is no

246

scriptural justification for such a claim. Thus there could be periods of darkness throughout God's wrath and still fit this prophecy (sixth seal, first four trumpets, fifth bowl). Problem solved - again!

Isaiah 13 describes how the angels will destroy all the earth, making it a desolate wilderness on the DOL. It says that Day will come as destruction from the Almighty. Some expositors say the world will limp into the millennium largely intact, and that the better, cleaner works of man will pass muster and be allowed into the Kingdom. Brainard points out that Scripture is clear the whole land will be made a desolate wilderness, and that this is brought about by the heavenly hosts (pp 54-56).

He believes Joel 2:1-3 parallels this, describing angels going throughout the earth at Armageddon. On close inspection it seems this is the armies ransacking Israel at the Abomination, as I mentioned briefly above. If you look carefully at the description, it sounds a lot like modern warfare and equipment. A fire before them and flame behind, leaping over mountains, appearing quickly like the horse and chariots with which Joel was familiar sounds like military jets. Some of the rest sounds like tanks and guided missiles. The smoke, the blasting bombs shaking the earth, and clouds in the sky makes the land desolate. The darkness and gloominess which dim the heavenly lights at this time is, in fact, said to be caused by thick, dark cloudiness (Joel 2:2). In contrast, with the sixth seal the heavenly lights themselves are darkened, not obscured by cloudiness.

God sends this army upon Israel through the Antichrist, just as He sent Babylon against Judah (Joel 1). These armies come when the DOL is coming, when it is impending. The Abomination is the key sign of Christ's coming (Matt 24). God calls on Israel to repent. The trumpet is blown. 2:16 says the bridegroom comes out of his chamber and the bride out of her dressing room. Israel repents (v. 17), and the times of refreshing come upon Israel - the millennium (vv. 18-27). Beginning in Joel 2:30, God breaks down how He will bring this about. The Day of the Lord will be introduced by the sixth seal and Israel will gain victory in the valley of Jehoshaphat.

I agree that Isaiah 13 describes the destruction of the DOL on the world. But this does not harm pre-wrath. The heavenly signs and earthquake of the sixth seal will do significant damage to begin with. Then the world will be systematically destroyed by the trumpets and bowls of wrath. Brainard misses just how much destruction these bring on the earth.

Brainard focuses on Isaiah 13:9, which says God will make speedy riddance of sinners in the day of God's wrath. He contrasts this with the seventieth week, in which he sees many saved by the everlasting gospel following the rapture. This will produce the tribulation martyrs of the great multitude along with the sheep at the sheep and goat judgment. Because he places the great multitude and the heavenly signs of the sixth seal at Armageddon and this judgment, he argues that the great multitude is of the sheep.

Problem 1) 2Thessalonians 2 makes this great revival impossible.

Problem 2) The great multitude is pictured in heaven, in contrast to the 144,000 firstfruits of Israel who are on earth (Rev 7), which fits dispensational theory. The multitude is nowhere called martyrs. They are clothed in white, while no passage describes the millennial inhabitants being clothed in white. So there is nothing to tie them to either the sheep or the martyred saints except doctrinal prejudice.

Problem 3) The sheep (Matt 25) enter the millennial kingdom specifically because of their treatment of the least of Christ's brethren. They seem surprised that they are allowed entry, whereas if they had repented and trusted Christ they should expect it. The sheep are called righteous, and righteousness only comes through faith, true. But like the Old Testament saints, this faith is not directed toward Christ as Savior but toward God. The great multitude, on the other hand, stand before Jesus because they were cleansed by His blood. Nothing equates these two groups of people.

Brainard concludes this chapter summarizing all his arguments. He declares that "the death knell sounds for the Pre-Wrath Rapture, and it is hanged on Haman's gallows" (pp 58, 59). The hangman's rope snapped and the pre-wrath rapture stands strong and alive.

The DOL in the New Testament

In chapter four, Brainard turns to the Day of the Lord in the New Testament. He begins by examining the gathering of elect at the end of the age in Matthew 24. Then he cites a couple of O.T. passages which describe the gathering of Israel, and the sheep and goat judgment in Matthew 25. He begins his case:

> This means we must determine from the context whether this particular gathering is the church's blessed transport from terrestrial to celestial habitation at the rapture or the gathering of the [Tribulation] saints at the advent when the times of refreshing come down from heaven to earth. And the context, as a matter of fact, affords us invincible proof that the gathering of the elect here is that gathering associated with the advent [Armageddon coming]. (p. 66)

He first reminds us of his "proof" in the previous chapter that the heavenly signs are associated with Armageddon. I believe I thoroughly demolished that argument. Second, he says that *the end of the age* in Matthew 24 is the end of *man's age*.

> Now the phrase *"the end of the age"* naturally and readily draws the mind of the candid reader to the advent, when the world system will be destroyed, the Gentile powers ground to powder, the fashion of this world obliterated.... It naturally... leads the thoughts of the impartial to the advent when this long dark age of sin and rebellion known as *"man's day"* will be abruptly cut off,

and a new age introduced, when God's will will be done on earth as it is in heaven. How can anything less be considered the end of this evil age in which we live? (p. 67, emph. his)

But man's age continues after a fashion for the millennium. Mankind will still have a sin nature during this time. Scripture says there are three root sources of temptation - the world system, the fleshly nature, and the devil. During the millennial reign the devil will be bound in the bottomless pit and Christ will rule the earth with His faithful saints with a rod of iron (Rev 2:26). This eliminates two sources. What need is there to rule *with a rod of iron* if man perfectly keeps God's will during the millennium? Also, at the end of the 1,000 years the devil is released and mankind once again rebels. Thus man will still be mere man. It is only in the new creation we might claim the end of *man's age*.

Next, Brainard argues that the *end of the age* takes place at Armageddon. Rosenthal taught that *the end* is actually the *climax* at the rapture, but followed by more stuff happening. Brainard correctly refutes this, showing that *the end* is a termination point. I will not repeat his case.

Where Brainard fall short is failing to realize all of the events from the sixth seal advent until the completion of the 1335 days (Dan 12:12) make up the end of the age. A novel often includes a final chapter which wraps up all the loose ends or shows something of the main characters following the story. The end of this age is the last chapter of the times of the Gentiles.

Matthew 24:3-8 describes the first three seals of Revelation, and says the end of the age is not yet. The persecution of the fourth seal in relation to the Abomination is the first actual *sign* of the end of the age (24:9-15). The sixth seal advent introduces the end of this age. Scripture says when we see all these things we can know that the end is at the door. The final chapter of this book in history concludes with the sheep and goat judgment.

After demonstrating that the end *means* the end, Brainard takes us to the parables of the end of the age:

Further observe that the *"end of the age"* parables themselves (Matt. 13:24-30, 36-43, 47-50) indicate that this phrase, in the mind of God, refers to the termination of the present evil age.

First, the parable of the wheat and tares...expressly teaches that at the *"end of the age"* the ungodly are removed from the world, leaving the righteous on earth to shine forth as the sun in the kingdom of their father. And the parable of the net and fishes...teaches the very same thing. It has the wicked severed *"from among the just."* This is the exact opposite of what transpires at the rapture.... But at the advent the removal of the ungodly which we see in these two parable is fulfilled to the letter. Then the goats are removed from the world, and the sheep are left to inherit the earth. This is fatal to the pre-wrath rapture. (p. 69)

Fatal to pre-wrath, huh? Pre-wrath does not stand or fall on these parables being the rapture. If it refers to the sheep and goat judgment, it harms us not one bit. We see everything from the sixth seal to the restoration of Israel and this judgment as the advent, the end of the age. Thus these parables could concern a different aspect of that end and not affect the rapture question at all. I still believe they include the rapture, though.

** I have a question for Brainard. He says the end of the age only relates to Armageddon. John 6:39-40 says all that the Father gives to Christ will be raised up on the *last day*, just as clearly a termination point as the end of the age. If the last day is at Armageddon, then the resurrection of the saints and the rapture (1Thess 4) must be post-trib. That means all his later attempts to prove pre-trib are a waste of time. He cannot have it both ways! But if the end of the age relates to all of the events from the sixth seal rapture to the sheep and goat judgment, this problem disappears.

251

Amputated

Brainard next addresses what it means that the great tribulation is shortened (Matt 24:22). He argues that the Greek word does not necessarily mean amputation, but can also mean it is not allowed to continue beyond its allotted time. While his view is possible, he cannot prove it does not mean amputation. He even admits either way is possible. He then argues:

> Therefore the pre-wrath rapturists are left without a single reason, unless it be doctrinal prejudice, to resist the following arguments which indicate that the time of great tribulation spans the entire second half of the seventieth week.

> **First**, I would emphasize once again that the signs in the heavens which immediately follow the tribulation (Matt 24:29) also immediately precede the descent of the Lord to the Mount of Olives.... This is proof positive that the time of great tribulation is a full three and a half years long and extends to the end of the seventieth week. (p. 73)

Zechariah 14 describes Christ on the Mount of Olives, but it says nothing of heavenly signs in the context. And Matthew 24 does not say Jesus descends to the mount. Thus there is no authority for Brainard to tie them together, except *doctrinal prejudice.*

> **Secondly**, the Scriptures state, in no uncertain terms, that the antichrist wars against the saints for the full three and a half years, right up until the advent. Revelation 13:5-7 states, *"power was given unto him to continue forty and two months...And it was given unto him to make war with the saints, and to overcome them."* Daniel 7:21-22 says, *"the same horn made war with the saints, and prevailed against them, until the Ancient of days came."* And v. 25 adds, *"the saints of the most High...shall be given into his hand until a time and times and the dividing of time."* Now how can these verses possibly be reconciled with the doctrine that the great tribulation is *shortened*? (p. 73)

Easily. Revelation says Antichrist will rule on earth for 42 months, during which time he will blaspheme God, among other things. He will also make war on the saints - but it doesn't say he does this for the entire time, only that it is one of the things he is permitted to do during his reign. Then in Daniel 7:25 the word *saints* was added by the translators of the version he quotes in the last clause of the sentence. It is not there in the original. Also, he cuts out a bit which adds important information. The King James more accurately says:

> *And he shall speak great words against the most High, and shall wear out the saints of the most High, and think to change times and laws:* ***and they*** *shall be given into his hand until a time and times and the dividing of time.*

They...given relates to all three points. The war against the saints is included in the timeframe, but does not necessarily take up the whole time. Daniel 7:22 says the Antichrist will prevail against the saints until the Ancient of Days comes, which according to pre-wrath is the sixth seal.

Brainard's third point is that tribulation continues against the Jews for the full amount of time. To a point I agree, though after the Jehoshaphat Campaign the beast's effectiveness will be curtailed.

He also argues that if those days were not shortened, *no flesh* would survive, not just saints. Again, an accurate observation. But it is specifically *for the sake of the elect* that those days are shortened, not for all flesh. The rabid beast pursues Israel and the saints so passionately that it puts at risk the lives of everyone in the world. That is why God must curtail it. By removing the saints, leading the Jews to victory at Jehoshaphat, and introducing His own wrath at the sixth seal, God prevents the Antichrist from destroying all flesh.

Fourthly, the doctrine that the time of great tribulation was originally slated to be three and a half years long and later "shortened up" calls the foreknowledge of God into question.

If foreknowledge originally established the length of this hour at three and a half years, why was there need to later shorten it to less? Was the foreknowledge of God somehow defective? (page 74)

First, Matthew 24 does not say the *great tribulation* lasts 3 1/2 years. It clearly says it begins when the Abomination of Desolation is set up, and is amputated as far as the elect are concerned at the sixth seal. It is true Daniel and Revelation give the beast 3 1/2 years to do his evil deeds and lead mankind in rebellion. In fact, Daniel 12:11 says that from the Abomination there will be 1290 days - an extra thirty days on top of the 1260. But this refers to how long the Antichrist continues to rule. It does not require that the *great tribulation* war against the saints continue the entire time.

The Elect

In The Rapture Question Answered, Van Kampen gives nine reasons why he believes the elect in Matthew 24 are not Israel, but the church. Brainard next presents his case against these points.

First is the pre-wrath claim that, apart from the 144,000, neither Jew nor Gentile will be saved after the rapture of the church. Brainard appeals to the sheep and goat judgment in Matthew 25:31-46 as proof that

> in no uncertain terms... men will be converted during the seventieth week after the rapture of the church, and that none will be converted when the Lord comes in all His glory... Observe when the Son of man comes...and sits on His throne in the valley of Jehoshaphat, He does not gather all the goats of the world before His throne, there being none but goats, then convert some of them on the spot into sheep... The sheep were already sheep when they were gathered. (pp 75, 76)

In reply, *why* does Jesus call them sheep? Does He anywhere say to them, "Enter into the kingdom, for you chose to repent and believe upon me in the great tribulation?" Christ is quite specific as to why they are counted as sheep - because they had compassion on the very least of His brethren during the great tribulation (context). It nowhere says they had converted to Christ.

I'll admit most pre-wrath adherents have not noticed this point, either, and most prophecy teachers believe along the same lines as Brainard - that they get saved through faith in Christ after the rapture. But that is *not* what the passage says. They hear the proclaiming angels warn them to fear God and refuse the mark of the beast. They believe and obey those instructions, and it counts to them as righteousness, so they are allowed to enter the millennial kingdom. While some of these may believe on Christ when He appears, not all the sheep are necessarily of that number.

Second, Van Kampen asserts only bond-servants of Christ are called *elect*, thus proving these elect are Christians. Brainard argues that this is the above argument turned inside-out, starting with the assumption that nobody is converted after the rapture. He says the sheep and goat judgment once again proves it wrong. In addition to the above can be added that in the New Testament the term *elect* almost always refers to the church.

> **Thirdly**, [Van Kampen] claims that if the parousia in Matthew 24:29-31 is the advent of Christ [Armageddon], then there are two future parousias - which he thinks is ridiculous - one being the rapture and one being the advent.

But even if Van Kampen is right that there is only one parousia, yet this is no argument against the pre-tribulation rapture. A pre-tribulation rapture and an advent with seven years between them as readily suits his one parousia theory as does his pre-wrath rapture and advent with one or two years between them.

Moreover, there is not the least doubt in my mind that there are two future comings. Christ will descend from heaven for

His beloved bride, and then later descend again to destroy all the ungodly and establish His kingdom. And two separate instances of Christ's presence under earth's blue sky - each distinct in their purposes - separated by many months , are two coming of Christ, regardless of what any Greek words mean. (p.77)

The problem is that nowhere does the Bible describe two distinct parousias. Scripture says Christians should be looking for it, but there is not even a single prophetic text which describes a coming of Christ prior to the Abomination. Furthermore, we do not see these comings as *distinct in their purposes*.

Van Kampen's **fourth** point is that if the DOL in Matthew 24:29-31 concerns the gathering of Israel at Armageddon, then there must be two days of the Lord, for Paul related the rapture to it (1Thess 4:13-5:11). Brainard argues that this passage does not equate them, but contrasts them. He says the Thessalonians were basically ignorant about the rapture, but were well acquainted with the DOL and had no need for Paul to write them concerning that Day. He concludes that this fact alone would be enough to convince him that the DOL will not in any way, shape or form overtake the Christian. (p. 79)

I agree to a point. Paul is clear that Day should not overtake us as a thief, as it will the world. We are not appointed to wrath, but to salvation (deliverance). What is especially being contrasted, though, is that the DOL will overtake the world because they are in spiritual darkness of night, while we are of the day and should not be surprised. Those who sleep do so at night, but we should not be spiritually sleeping - but alert, sober-minded, and watchful (5:6). Watch for what? As Brainard so strongly stresses, the subject is the Day of the Lord, in contrast to the rapture in the previous chapter. This implies we should be watchful to see the signs of the approaching Day. This aligns with the Lord's similar teaching in relation to His sixth seal advent (Matt 24:29-31, 43-51).

1Thessalonians 5:9-11 closely ties the rapture to the DOL. It says we are not appointed to DOL wrath, but unto deliverance

256

through faith in Christ. So whether we wake or sleep (alive and remain, or dead in Christ, relates back to rapture in 1Thess 4) we will forever be with the Lord. Notice especially verse 11:

Therefore comfort each other and edify one another, just as you also are doing.

We are told to comfort each other in the rapture passage (1Thess 4:18), too. This ties the two topics firmly together. There are numerous things which clearly tie the rapture and the DOL together.

On a final note concerning 1Thessalonians 5, Brainard asserts that the DOL surprises the world like a thief, and takes place at Armageddon. This is merely seven short years after the disappearance of half a billion Christians, or more. Then there is a great revival which produces a huge multitude (Rev 7), who go about the world preaching the gospel (Matt 24:14), certainly warning of God's rapidly approaching judgment - proven by aforesaid rapture. ...And the world is surprised that Jesus shows up for Armageddon, which is the DOL! Moreover, it follows the truly terrible judgments of the trumpets and bowls, which consistent pre-millennialists insist are fulfilled literally.

Even more, the beast begins gathering together a great army from every nation to Mount Megiddo *days or weeks before* Armageddon, **specifically** to fight in that great battle - demons working signs and wonders to convince the kings to send their armies and throw off the chains of God (Ps 2)... **And the world is surprised when Christ shows up?!?** Hmmm. I would have an easier time eating a whole cow than swallowing that story.

Van Kampen's **fifth** evidence concerns those who are *alive and remain* (1Thess 4:15, 17). He explains, as I do, that the Greek word for *remain* would be better translated as *those who survive*, which implies going through a trial.

Brainard counters that this does not necessarily require survival through the times of Antichrist. Throughout history the church has often endured great trials and persecutions, even today in many parts of the world. I admit he has a good point. But immediately following this Paul discusses the arrival of the Day of the Lord, which even Brainard agrees follows the great tribulation. This at least supports the implication that they survive the Antichrist, though it does not require it.

The **sixth** reason Van Kampen believed the elect is the church is that Mark and Luke used the term, too, and were written to Gentile believers. Thus the prophetic material in Matthew must be for Gentiles, as well. Brainard points out that the reverse could be argued just as easily [and it often is by pre-tribs], because Matthew wrote from a Jewish standpoint. The truth is that either argument is a meaningless straw man. I thoroughly covered this in the chapters on Matthew 24.

In the great commission, Jesus told the disciples to teach all nations to observe all things whatsoever He has commanded them, which is instruction for the church. Van Kampen's **seventh** evidence is that this includes all of Christ's teachings, including this prophecy in the Olivet Discourse. Brainard mutters:

> But is there no distinction between prophetic teaching and the commands of Christ? ... How does one obey that which is simply and merely prophetic instruction? I can obey *"enter ye by the strait gate."* I can obey *"love your enemies."*... But how do I obey *"immediately after the tribulation of those days shall the sun be darkened...and they shall see the Son of man coming...with power and great glory. And He shall send His angels with a great sound of a trumpet, and they shall gather together His elect from the four winds?"* (p. 81)

There *are* several commands within the context. Christ warns us to be wary for there will come many deceivers. He says we will see the Abomination of Desolation, which implies a command to be watchful. He warns those who live in Judea to flee when the armies approach. He again warns against false christs and against those who claim a secret coming. Things will be so bad we will lust after the Day of Christ (Luke 17), but will not see it. Luke 21 adds that when we see these things, particularly the sixth seal, we

258

should lift our heads and look for Jesus. Several other instructions could be noted. Thus we find numerous commands for the church. Also, it could be reasonably surmised that everything the disciples wrote was to instruct the church in obedience to the great commission. His complaint is invalid.

Van Kampen, for his **eighth** evidence, challenges readers to determine for themselves whether the gathering of the elect in Matthew 24:29-31 better matches the rapture as found in 1Thessalonians 4 or Christ's coming at Armageddon in Revelation 19. He says that, without exception, every member of his prophecy classes say it is the rapture rather than Armageddon. Brainard argues:

> But this is begging the question with a false dilemma. The choice here is not between the rapture and Armageddon but between the rapture and the advent. Armageddon is but one of the events that will occur at the time of the advent. At that time the Lord will descend to earth, trample the ungodly at Armageddon, gather the godly, and settle Jacob forever in the land of promise. And the fact that Armageddon is not mentioned here is irrelevant. No advent passage mentions every one of the events that will transpire at that time, and no event of that time is mentioned in every advent passage.

I agree that not every passage contains every event. However, there is much dissimilarity between the advent at Armageddon and Matthew 24, and absolutely nothing similar except Jesus descending and perhaps the presence of angels, though the activity of the angels is completely different in the two passages. What's more, Matthew describes Him in the clouds, similar to the rapture passages, while Armageddon has Him on a white horse, being mutually exclusive.

Brainard complains that the reason we don't see any of the Armageddon description in Matthew is that not every passage mentions every one of the events. This is ironic. I have read a few pre-tribs who whine [cited in this book] that they want later views to prove that the rapture will occur after the coming of Antichrist or the fulfillment of other prophecies, using only passages they accept as relating to the rapture. In other words, they intentionally pick and choose which passages fit their predetermined rapture theory based on the silence of those passages concerning Antichrist, as if every rapture passage should talk about the beast or other events of the seventieth week.

I do not use Van Kampen's ninth point at all, and agree with Brainard it should be discarded as evidence. It is not really needed, anyway. The case is well proven.

Next, Brainard discusses 1Thessalonians 5:2-4:

> This passage associates the day of the Lord with *"sudden destruction"* which steals upon the world as the pangs of birth seize a woman big with child... The fact is, *"sudden destruction"* which none will escape perfectly and readily harmonizes with the advent, but is only with great difficulty harmonized with the rapture. For the judgments which follow the rapture of the church do not spell the *"sudden destruction"* of all the ungodly. They spell but the gradual decimation of their ranks over seven long years. Many are the wicked who will pass through the entire seventieth week without tasting death. But at the advent all the ungodly and unbelieving will perish in one fell swoop. (p. 83)

First, this is one of the few times he argues with an incorrect statement relating to the pre-wrath understanding. He says it is difficult to line up the sudden destruction with judgments which take place over seven long years after the rapture. With pre-wrath, God's wrath is likely only a year or two, perhaps even less.

Second, this passage (1Thess 5) does not say the destruction will be completed suddenly or in mere hours, but that it arrives suddenly and the world will not be able to escape it. Unbelievers will continue about their merry way, willfully oblivious to the coming judgment - until, all of a sudden, the heavenly lights are darkened in the midst of a world-spanning earthquake, producing tsunamis. Jesus appears, removes the church, leads Israel to victory at Jehoshaphat, and the trumpets of wrath begin. All these happen within about one day, and suddenly the tide is turned against the world in one fell swoop. The destruction then continues until completed.

Continuing with 1Thessalonians 5:2-4, Brainard asserts that the cry of *"peace and safety"* poses no difficulty with the Day of the Lord equating to Armageddon. First, he notes that this cry suits the rationale and mood as the world commences ridding the world of the Jewish problem, which they see as the reason for all the troubles in the world. Second, this cry is in keeping with the world's determination to throw off the chains of God (Psalm 2:2-3) and their desire to live peacefully on their own terms instead of on God's. Third, the two witnesses are slain just before Armageddon, and the world sends gifts and makes merry (Revelation 11:7-10), believing their fortunes are changing by overcoming these two prophets whom they were unable to kill before this point.

If the DOL comes with Armageddon, then this would be correct. But the first two points fit pre-wrath just as easily, and the third point is not necessary. We see the beast warring against the saints of Jesus and overcoming them, and putting Israel on the run and killing many of them (Rev 13; Dan 7). Thus they perceive that they are winning, meeting Brainard's first two points. But how can they being crying *peace and safety* until Armageddon? Consider again the trumpets and bowls which precede that Battle - at least 1/3 of mankind killed, those who took the mark tormented, drinking water turned to blood, 1/3 of the plant life burned up by a meteor shower. How is this *peace and safety*?

2Thessalonians 2

One of the cornerstone passages for later rapture views is 2Thessalonians 2:1-8. Brainard turns here, next (pp 84-88). He explains that the King James rendering is more accurate, which reads:

261

We beseech you brethren, by the coming of the Lord, and by our gathering together unto Him, that ye be not soon shaken in mind... as that the day of Christ is at hand.

Brainard explains that this is a petition. *We beseech you... that ye be not... troubled... as that the day of Christ is at hand* is the petition itself. *By our gathering together unto Him* is the reason assigned why the saints should not be trouble by the DOL. And the very nature of this petition contrasts the DOL and the rapture. It by no means equates them. We ought not be troubled about the DOL because our lot is to be gathered before it arrives on the scene.

Brainard argues that, because some translations say "*concerning the coming of the Lord*," it creates the idea that Paul is teaching about the coming of the Lord and the rapture. He states that the Greek sense would more accurately be "because of" or "by reason of", rather than "concerning." He spends two pages arguing this point, and concludes that, by his reckoning, the Greek word used here only means *concerning* once, out of about 120 times it is used in the New Testament. Thus, he argues, the correct sense of the passage is: *I beseech you, by reason of the second coming, and by reason of the rapture, that you not be troubled as though they Day of Christ is at hand.*

Brainard first argues that the two clauses, "*by the coming*" and "*by the gathering*" contrast the rapture with the advent, rather than equating them. But the word "*by*" only appears one time, not twice, so the two phrases are not contrasted but joined. There is a Greek rule of grammar, the Granville-Sharp rule, which says that two clauses joined by the word "*and*" which only have one reference such as "*by*" are tied together in meaning. An example of this would be Titus 2:13, which reads literally in the Greek that we are looking for the glorious appearing "*of the great God and Savior of us, Jesus Christ.*" The reference is "*of us*" and the passage declares that Jesus is our God and our Savior. Thus we find in our passage that Paul is beseeching "*by the parousia of the Lord and our gathering together to Him.*"

262

If Brainard is correct, then Paul is beseeching them by reason of the parousia and the rapture, to not be concerned that the DOL were at hand (impending or arrived). For that day cannot come unless first the apostasy comes and until the man of sin is revealed. While Brainard may be correct that Paul implored the Thessalonians by the coming for the rapture, it causes no problem.

Also, we must always consider the context. Brainard completely ignores 2Thessalonians 1 in his book, and this utterly negates his assertion. Here we are told God will give us rest when Jesus comes with His angels in flaming fire taking vengeance. Sure enough, the angels do not take vengeance in Revelation until the trumpets, and the first trumpet is fire falling from heaven. Even Brainard agrees this follows the actual opening of the sixth seal. Furthermore, at the fifth seal God tells the martyrs under the altar that vengeance has not yet started. Thus the entire passage (2Thess) could be summarized:

> The persecution you endure is proof that God's judgment of the world is just. You will receive rest when Jesus appears with His angels in flaming fire taking vengeance. I beseech you in behalf of the advent of Christ and the rapture, the promised rest I just mentioned, that you not be troubled as though the Day of the Lord, the day of vengeance, were at hand. Do not be deceived, for that Day cannot come until after the apostasy and after the revealing of the man of sin.

Seems clear enough to me! Either way, it teaches the same thing.

The Sixth Seal

Brainard concludes his consideration of the DOL in the New Testament by looking at the sixth seal. He agrees that this seal is obviously a DOL passage in the same vein as Isaiah 2:10-21. For chronology, he places the heavenly signs and earthquake at Armageddon. He agrees that the seals, trumpets, and bowls are

263

opened sequentially. He argues that as each one is opened it continues until its culmination at Armageddon, stating that we cannot prove they transpire back to back without overlap.

Moreover, two unanswerable points demonstrate that the visitations introduced by the seals, trumpets, and vials do overlap.

First, each of these series of judgments culminates at the advent, i.e. on the day of the Lord, when the Son of man arises to shake terribly the earth..., judge the world..., reward His saints... and establish His kingdom.

That the seals take us down to the advent is evident from the fact that under the sixth seal we find the signs in the heavens, the *"yet once more"* earthquake, the appearance in the heavens of an angry God come to judge a terrified world for their sin, and the reward of the godly souls *"which came out of great tribulation."*

The seventh seal, moreover, as it introduces and contains the seven trumpets, also takes us down to the advent. [He next shows how the kingdoms of the world become the kingdom of Christ, the saints are rewarded, etc., for the seventh trumpet. He then points out that the bowls take us to the advent, shown most clearly by the great earthquake (Revelation 16: 18-20).] (page 89-90)

He agrees with pre-wraths that the seventh seal contains the trumpets and bowls, so obviously continues to the end. He then states that

The sixth seal... in actual *chronological* order, *opens* with the sealing of the 144,000, *spans* the remaining months... and *closes*... at the advent. The order given in the text - judgments, sealing, blessing of the righteous - is the *moral* order... (pp. 90-91, emph. his).

He specifically points out that the fifth seal martyrdom and the second seal warfare all continue to the end.

264

I fully agree that the seals all continue in some measure until Armageddon. Likewise the trumpets and bowls and their effects. Where I have a problem is with his treating the sixth seal differently than every single other judgment. In *every other case* the judgments of the seal, trumpet, or bowl begin at the start. When the first seal opens either the Antichrist signs the covenant or there is an upsurge in false christs. When the second seal opens, peace is taken from the earth. When the third seal opens, famine begins. The fourth seal immediately introduces persecution over 1/4 of the earth. The fifth seal proclaims the continued martyrdom of the saints. But Brainard would have us suddenly switch gears in the sixth seal, have the 144,000 sealed to protect them from coming wrath and the martyrdom of the multitude, but have the judgment in heavenly signs and earthquake hold off until just before Christ comes at Armageddon. Then with the seventh seal the angels receive the trumpets. The trumpets sound and immediately produce their results. The bowls are poured out with immediate results.

So my question is: What makes the sixth seal different from every single other judgment? Pre-wraths see the sixth seal events happening in order when opened, just as with every judgment. Also, we do not insist that they occur back to back, with one ending and another beginning. We only insist that they happen in strict sequence.

I already addressed his change of order of the sixth seal at the beginning of this chapter. By what authority does he change it, other than preconceived doctrine? He does not defend his case by showing other places in Scripture where the order of prophetic events was changed to demonstrate some moral imperative.

To disprove pre-wrath, he chose first to address the DOL by making it start at Armageddon. In order to do that, he had to find a way to make the signs of the sixth seal appear at that time, or else **his whole system fails** - for the frequent testimony of Scripture closely relates the DOL and that seal. The only way he could do that is by changing the order of the sixth seal (Rev 6:12-7:17).

Thus this single point makes or breaks his primary case against pre-wrath - taking nearly one-third of his book... And he has to change it around to make it fit!

Brainard finishes the section with this chronology:

> These observations necessitate the following overlapping chronology. The seals are opened in order...including the last which introduces the seven trumpets. The seven trumpets are sounded in order.... And the vials, introduced before the trumpets have all sounded, are the last [and] are poured out in order. (page 92)

Regarding this, he claims that the bowl judgments are introduced before the trumpets have all sounded. He makes this claim, but fails to even attempt to prove it from Scripture. According to the seventh trumpet, after Christ is declared King of kings the heavenly temple is *opened* and the Ark of the Covenant is seen. According to the prelude to the vials, the same temple is seen *still open*, the angels come out bearing the vials, and then the temple is sealed and filled with smoke until the judgments are complete. As you can see, the bowls demonstrably follow all of the trumpets, which is in perfect keeping with the seventh seal.

He concludes that "the New Testament is a barren field for the pre-wrath rapture." Yet his every relevant argument to this point has failed the test of close scrutiny.

Revelation 3:10

Brainard next turns to Revelation 3:10, which he says provides the clearest testimony for the location of the rapture. I will not spend a lot of time on this, as I already explained and defended the pre-wrath view.

First, he briefly summarizes that this promises the church some kind of protection. He correctly notes that the word *trial* is used in Scripture for everything from the testing of a person's character to

266

the judgments of God against man. Second, he claims that this hour falls between the rapture and the coming of Christ at Armageddon. Third, he states

> The only test given here for determining whether a visitation belongs to the hour of trial is whether or not it is world-wide in scope. ... The upshot of Revelation 3:10, then, is that we need only find the first prophetic event in the book of Revelation which falls upon the whole world as a trial, ... and we can rest assured that before this trial is visited upon the world, the church will meet her Lord in the air. (p.100)

He briefly explains the pre-wrath view that this promises protection through the hour of trial for certain believers during the reign of Antichrist, which Van Kampen limited to the fifth seal martyrdom of the saints.

> And - as it is obvious that multitudes of saints are not delivered from the antichrist's clutches - they limit this promise of deliverance to a small class of Christians, which they call the overcomers, though the context of the letters to the seven churches clearly indicates that it applies to every believer. (p.101)

My first issue concerns this statement. How does he justify that this promise is to every church and every believer? Now it is true that the part of each letter making promises to overcomers is for every believer, regardless of church type. But this particular promise is not in the overcomer section, but in the portion addressed to the Philadelphia church. Each letter has warnings and promises which are for that specific church type, not to believers in general whether they are part of that church or not. If I am not engaged in idolatrous practices, or in sexual immorality, then those warnings are not directed toward me. However, the promised rewards to overcomers do apply, because they are addressed by the Spirit to the churches.

But the promise of Revelation 3:10 is not in that section. It is given to a church which has notable spiritual strength and maturity, and has no major issues the Lord needed to address. They keep Christ's Word and do not deny His name by their actions. Because they persevere, Jesus promises to protect them in the hour of trial. Brainard says this promise is to every believer, but the context clearly gives this promise to those who have been keeping Christ's command to persevere in life. After this, as with all the letters, Christ makes promises for overcomers which apply to all qualifying believers.

Over the next several pages, Brainard discusses the phrase "*keep from,*" in the Greek, "*tereo ek.*" All he succeeds in doing is demonstrating that the phrase can mean an outside position as well as an inside position using extra-biblical sources, but does not prove that it requires an outside position.

Beginning on page 115, Brainard contends that the hour of trial includes all of the seventieth week, including the seals, the rise of Antichrist, and the wrath of God in the trumpets and bowls. This does not cause the slightest problem with pre-wrath.

Revelation 3:10 promises that God will preserve the Philadelphian type church from the hour of testing which comes upon the whole earth to prove those who dwell on the earth. This parallels 2Thessalonians which says the oppression of believers by the world proves God's judgment is just, and that we will enter the rest when Christ appears to take vengeance. 1Peter 4 says concerning fiery testings that judgment begins with the house of God, and if it begins with us what end will come to the ungodly and sinner.

Therefore, I have no problem with the hour of trial encompassing the entire seven years, though I lean more toward the second half. This faithful church is given some kind of protection during the hour of testing. After the fourth seal testing the saints are raptured. The rest of the world remains under trial through the trumpets. They still have the opportunity to repent, though most do not. The heavenly temple is not sealed until the seventh trumpet, at which time their test is over and they receive the results through the bowls, Armageddon, and the sheep and goat judgment.

Brainard's final case in this chapter looks at the many promises in these letters. He notes that the tree of life, the crown of life, the hidden manna, the white stone, etc., are all given to the church at the time of her rapture and reward. He argues that the promise that the church will be kept from the hour of temptation as notice she will pass through the time of great tribulation is a sour note which does not harmonize with these blessings. What does hot-footing it to the hills or fleeing the great tribulation have in common with these promises?

As I already noted, these other promises are in the sections addressed to overcomers. Revelation 3:10 is not under that heading. Many of the letters promise them great tribulation, warn of their lamp being removed, warn to prepare for persecution, etc. This verse fits in perfectly. It is not a *sour note*, but consistent with all the other letters.

The First Five Seals

In chapter six Brainard turns to the first five seals of Revelation.

> The pre-wrath rapture advocates were forced by their sixth/seventh seal day-of-the-Lord rapture theory to deny that the first five seals are judgment. And this denial they attempted to strengthen with a host of feeble corroborating arguments. Now that their rapture theory has been thoroughly discredited, many will drop their case against the first five seals, and let these corroborating arguments fall forgotten by the wayside. (p. 127)

Most of Brainard's points here are tangential to the pre-wrath view, and are not required for it to be correct. In fact, I find myself agreeing at least partially with some of those points. Some of the issues discussed in this chapter I do not present in my study because I find Van Kampen's and Rosenthal's argumentation unconvincing, though they may be correct. As we have seen, the pre-wrath rapture is certainly not discredited up to this point, and these corroborating points are not necessary to support the position.

269

He first turns to a claim made by Van Kampen that the first five seals are judgments upon the household of faith (1Pet 4:17), designed to separate the false believers from the true. Brainard says the seals clearly fall on the world, not just the church. I agree in part. Certainly the first three seals, which bring wars, earthquakes, and famines in diverse places, are not directed at the church, though believers are also tested by them. However, like Van Kampen, I now believe that the fourth seal is the persecution of Israel and the church - along with others who refuse the mark and those who help the brethren of Christ. I could be wrong, though, and it would not harm pre-wrath. In fact, when I first started this study I tied the fourth seal to the first three as upon the world, and only changed my mind as I was writing the last couple of drafts.

Brainard correctly argues that 1Peter 4:17 is not necessarily prophetic, but an ever-present issue. Christians have suffered for their faith from the beginning, and God does test and judge believers to bring them to maturity (Jam 1; Rom 5). Trials and persecutions give us opportunity to live our faith in the world, and gives God opportunity to author greater faith in us. The church is at her strongest when enduring tribulations. In the relatively free countries much of the church is weak and tepid, though, because we have been able to practice our faith in relative safety.

Hebrew 12 says God is going to shake *everything that can be shaken,* so only that which can enter His kingdom remains. I believe this includes the household of faith through increased trials and tribulations. The first three seals shake the entire earth, including the church. The fourth seal tests believers, separates the wheat from the tares. The fifth seal is not so much a judgment as it is recognition of the persecution of the fourth seal. In the midst of these Revelation 3:10 promises that God will closely watch over certain faithful believers.

In relation to Revelation 3:10 Rosenthal claimed that there is no prophesied or known adversity through which the church must persevere prior to the seventieth week. Brainard rightly takes issue with this. The relative freedom we have had in some places to practice our faith is an anomaly and luxury which much of the church age has not known. Thus this promise, in a loose manner, promises God's keeping power in the midst of difficult times for those who persevere. Scripture says God is a very present help in times of trouble.

But nowhere does God promise to take us out of trials and troubles, but rather that he helps us go through them. Romans 8 says the church is appointed to tribulation, persecution, the sword, and hunger. In all these things we are more than conquerors through Christ who strengthens us.

I agree with several of the next points by Brainard concerning the security of the believer, the involvement of angels in judgment, and God's permissive versus His active will, so for lack of space I will not repeat them. But these are merely tangential and have no real bearing on the rapture question.

Brainard then turns to the pre-wrath observation that wrath is not mentioned until the sixth seal.

> Van Kampen claims that the first five seals cannot be judgment because the word "*wrath*" does not appear in the book of Revelation until the sixth seal. But this is an argument from silence, and worth exactly nothing. We do not find, for instance, the word "*wrath*" in Acts 12:20-23. Are we to conclude , therefore, that Herod's death from a fatal case of worms was not an instance of judgment? (p. 140)

Pre-wraths do not deny that the seals are judgments of God on earth. The church is promised deliverance away from God's wrath, but these are not condemning wrath. The seals are of a different order from the trumpets and bowls - consisting of man released to greater evil on earth. When God brought similar judgments against Israel in the O.T., whether by war, famine, pestilence, or captivity in Babylon, the righteous were just as affected as the unrighteous. What makes pre-tribs think it will be any different during the seal judgments, which are of the same nature?

271

When God manifested His wrath as at Sodom and the great flood - our specific examples - however, the righteous were removed to safety before wrath fell. Luke 21 says when we see the sixth seal to lift our heads for our deliverance is coming. Pre-tribs cannot show that the church is exempt from the kind of judgments found in the first five seals.

In the next few pages, **Brainard actually makes the same case**. He agrees the church is subject to disciplinary anger such as the Old Testament saints endured. It seems strange that he would exclude the church from the seals when they have the same characteristics. He goes on to note God's provision for the widow of Zarapheth (1Kings 17), for example, when famine was on the whole land - this was the exception rather than the rule. Aah! Thank you for the biblical example for the promise of Revelation 3:10 - this is the exception, not the rule.

He continues on page 143:

> Such promises as Romans 5:9, 1Thessalonians 1:10 and 5:9 only preserve the saints from judgments - typically supernatural - of that degree and kind manifested in the flood, in the destruction of Sodom, in the earth swallowing up the habitations of Korah, Dathan, and Abiram, in the trumpet and vial judgments of the seventieth week, in the day of the Lord, and in eternal punishment.

My point, exactly! He even acknowledges that exemption from God's wrath does not forbid the church from entering the seventieth week, which is contrary to what nearly every other pre-trib teacher I have read says. I admire Brainard's understanding and honesty about this point. He takes a different tack to keep the church out of the seals.

> The church will be removed from the earth prior to the seventieth week because her members are Christians. As Christ was in the world, so are they. They are in the world but not of the world. They have an heavenly calling, not an earthly, and pass through this life as pilgrims in a barren land.

272

They have no inheritance here on earth, but patiently wait for one in heaven. They are seated with Christ in the heavenlies and their life is hid with him in God. And this heavenliness is not merely positional. It is organic. He is the head and the church is His body. Now the fact that the church is not of this world necessitates that God remove her from the world before He pours out His judgments upon the world. For He can no more pour out judgment upon those saints seated with Christ in the heavenlies, than He can upon Christ himself. He can no more pour out the hour of testing upon the body of Christ than He can upon the head of the body. (p. 144)

He misses the point of his own analogy in its context. He admits that the church has been subject to persecution, famines, and death throughout her history. He agrees that the church undergoes testing and trial and even judgment from God, and provides many Scriptures to back that up - more than even I do. He even admits this is the basic characteristics of the first five seals, and that the church is not exempt from this kind of judgment. But he keeps us out of the status quo because this time of testing comes upon the whole earth to prove all those who dwell on the earth.

Because this testing comes upon the whole earth at the behest of God, he says, the church cannot be here for any part of it. The bubonic plague swept across the entire globe, killing multiplied millions; Was God not in control then - was this not a testing and judgment upon mankind? We have had two world wars which left very few countries out. How is this hour of trial different from the plagues and the great wars which encompassed the globe in the past?

Perhaps it is because this time of testing is prophesied rather than general in nature. But in Matthew 10 Jesus prophesied that believers would face persecution, and even be betrayed by family, but those who endure to the end will be saved. Then in Matthew 24 it describes the first four seals, and tells us the end is not yet. *"Therefore, when you see the Abomination...."* So this logic is invalid.

273

He goes on that we are ambassadors to an enemy country trying to win souls to Christ. And as such we shall be removed from our posts and summoned home before our King will storm the world with heaven's cavalry (Rev 19:11-21) (page 144). I agree. I have demonstrated that the sixth seal, which introduces the wrath of God and describes the rapture of the church, well precedes the coming of Christ with His armies. But His coming with heavenly armies happens at the end of the seventieth week, and wrath begins with the sixth seal, which does not preclude God's ambassadors from being here for any part of the seven years.

He also addresses the issue of whether or not it is even possible for the elect to be deceived (Matthew 24:24), arguing that this is impossible. He agrees believers may "experience a temporary fog or a season of uncertainty under the ministry of a false prophet" (p147), but will eventually get his bearings straight. He quotes from John 10, which states, *"My sheep hear my voice, and I know them, and they follow Me.... They know [My] voice. And a stranger will they not follow, but will flee from him..."*

Why then did Jesus warn His disciples repeatedly in Matthew 24 and other end-time prophesies to be wary. So did Paul (1 and 2 Tim, and others). They warned there were wolves that looked like sheep, deceivers and false teachers. Apparently there is possibility of at least temporary deception among those who are weak or who sit under bad teaching. Also, considering how difficult the great tribulation will be, if the pre-wrath view is correct then many who had wrong teaching may chase after rumors of a secret coming - as Jesus warned. I don't believe Jesus used hyperbole in Matthew 24:24.

Also, in Revelation Jesus dictated letters to seven churches in Asia, many of whom had false doctrines. But He still said they were churches. So this also illustrates that believers can be deceived.

I am not saying that those who truly seek to follow Christ will remain deceived, or necessarily be drawn away from faith in Christ to follow the beast. The context is deception by those who claim a

274

secret coming. They may stumble, however, and fall away temporarily even among those of understanding - to refine them and purify them and make them white, until the end, which is still for an appointed time (Dan 11:35, following the Abomination in v. 31).

On page 149 Brainard again makes a statement that supports the pre-wrath understanding:

> The rise and reign of the antichrist (the first seal) certainly belongs to *"the hour of testing, which shall come upon all the world."* It is peirasmos from God. It will try all men in every land, unbeliever and believer alike. It will try the ungodly, and prove them adamantly determined to walk in darkness. It will prove that they are not just a little mixed up, but willing to consciously worship both the antichrist and the devil. It will try the hypocrites, and find them *"wretched, and miserable, and poor, and blind, and naked."* And it will try the saints, and prove that they love the Lord their God with all their heart, soul, mind and strength. It will prove that theirs was no empty profession when they embraced the cross of Christ by which men are crucified to the world, and the world to them.
>
> And what could more meetly open *"the hour of testing"* upon this Christ rejecting world than the rise of the antichrist?

I agree. The believers he speaks of will be the current church, not some fresh set of saints after the rapture. Jesus is coming back for a church without spot, or wrinkle, or any such thing, and this time of testing will winnow out the false, and purify the true saints. Peirasmos not only proves who has faith, but it also purifies those of faith the same way fire both proves and purifies gold.

It is amusing that, in explaining his point, Brainard quotes from the last of the seven letters to the *churches* in Revelation 3 - the lukewarm, hypocritical church. Following the disappearance of the church, and with the quickly rising persecution of the new saints, I don't think there would be lukewarm new converts under those circumstances in such a short time.

Van Kampen (and I) pointed out that if the first five seals are wrath, as pre-tribs often claim, then the fifth seal would have God pouring out wrath on faithful saints. Brainard calls this libel against pre-tribs. He says that this seal is certainly not wrath poured out on saints, but is testing tracing back to the devil who comes in wrath against them. He agrees this is part of the hour of testing, but not divine wrath. He spends a few moments further defending this.

That is exactly our point! This is divine testing, not wrath. And it is not libel when most pre-tribs do proclaim the seals are manifestations of wrath - often insisting quite strongly so they can keep the church completely out of this time. The church is promised deliverance from wrath, but never from testing.

Brainard goes on to say:

> And under the fifth seal we witness ... nothing other than the particular effects this test will have on the saints of God during the last three and a half years of the seventieth week. During those awful days most of the members of the *little remnant* will, sooner or later, be brusquely dealt with, [to choose] idolatry or death. Hence it is that only in not loving "*their lives unto death*" do the faithful prove themselves to be the saints of God. Here is the faith and patience of the saints. (p..151)

Again, this is what we teach. Brainard calls these a *little remnant* that are saved after the pre-trib rapture. These are the great multitude that comes out of the great tribulation (Rev 7). Their number is so large John called it uncountable. Hardly a little remnant. This better fits the many believers over two thousand years of church history.

Brainard's concluding testimony in the main portion of his book gives a chilling example of what I warn against several times in this work.

> ...And this fixes our heart fast to the anchor of the pre-tribulation rapture. We anchor on the promise of Revelation 3:10 and rest assured that if even one moment of the seventieth

week crosses the threshold of the church's experience, *then Scripture has been broken.*

Statements like this always alarm me, and when I read this it caused me to fear for my brother, though I was somewhat reassured by another statement he makes later, in his appendices. Does this mean that if his interpretation of the rapture is wrong and he finds himself under the auspices of the beast he will reject Christ and follow Antichrist, because he considers the Bible to be invalidated? It is this very attitude I warn against when I remind you of Christ's own warning to endure to the end, that these false prophets in the seventieth week will be very convincing if we do not stand for the truth.

If I am wrong, it does no harm for I will go in the rapture if it is pre-trib, as long as I am remaining in the faith. But if those who choose to believe pre-trib are wrong and find themselves in the midst of the hour of testing, will they stand firm for Christ to the end regardless? *He who endures to the end, the same shall be saved.* I mean, I don't hold to the post-trib, Armageddon rapture; But if I am alive to enter this time and discover I am wrong, I will still follow Christ in the midst of the trumpet and bowl judgments until either I die or Christ returns. I will not declare Scripture broken, but my own understanding.

Let me again reiterate - our hope is **not** the rapture. Our anchor is not missing the seventieth week. Our hope and anchor is *the Lord Jesus Christ,* **HIMSELF, ALONE!!!** (Yes, I am shouting!) He is our resurrection and life, our sure foundation on the solid rock, not some event we have termed the rapture.

Brainard comments how easy it is to find objections to the evidence for a pre-trib rapture when the heart desires them. I would have preferred a pre-trib rapture - that would be my heart's wish. I would rather not face the time of great tribulation, and the pre-trib rapture would give many who previously did not believe in Christ another chance to be saved - perhaps including friends and family who do not know the Lord. I could think of a number of reason why I would like to be wrong. But I refuse to let my natural

277

desires and preferences interpret the Bible for me. *I will not be like the Israelites of old who rejected the doom-and-gloom, true prophets of God in exchange for the false prophets who promised deliverance from the previous beast empires of Assyria and Babylon.* I have to take God's word for what it plainly teaches, and it is clear the church will face the Antichrist.

Chapter 14: Answering Brainard, part two

Brainard's book includes extensive appendices where he addresses a number of shorter points which do not warrant an entire chapter, and where he makes his case for pre-trib.

In **Appendix A** (pp 158-159) he accuses pre-wrath advocates of starting with a theological predisposition to a post-trib rapture, which influences us to automatically reject pre-trib. As *proof*, he quotes Van Kampen, who admitted he leaned toward post-trib prior to arriving at pre-wrath because of the clear testimony of Matthew 24. Brainard insists, "And how could such prejudice possibly be convinced of the pre-tribulation rapture? It was a foregone conclusion that the church would go through the tribulation. There was no need to sift and weigh this chapter and take into account light shed by other passages to determine whether the gathering of the elect here is the gathering of the Jews at the advent or the gathering of the church at the rapture..."

He ignores the fact that Rosenthal, the other pre-wrath writer he critiques, was a stout pre-tribulationist and had taught that position for many years before turning to pre-wrath. The same is true for many who have come to believe this view, including myself.

Appendix B (pp 158-163) presents Brainard's case that dispensational theory requires a pre-trib rapture. He claims that pre-wrath adherents scoff at locating the rapture with dispensational distinctions. He admits we do distinguish between the Christian and Jewish economies, but takes issue with the way we overlap them.

It is categorically impossible for God to simultaneously require some believers to embrace Christ as *"the end of the law,"* and others to embrace and observe the law.

Now I grant that there was a period of transition between Judaism and Christianity at Christ's first coming, but this transition was not a time when God enforced both Judaism and Christianity at once, but a time when He made allowance for ignorance [until men realized they did not need to bear the yoke of the law].

He continues that while mankind slowly transitioned, in God's mind the transition took place in the instant Christ was dead.

I agree with his case to this point. The transitional period was not so much having both systems in place as it was God's continuing mercy on those under the legal system while He gave them time to put faith in Christ.

Where Brainard errs is when he insists God will restore the old system of the Law during the seventieth week - once again requiring all believers to be circumcised, etc. Galatians 5:2 says if you become circumcised for the law's sake, faith in Christ will be of no profit to you. *Period.* The saints in the great tribulation are said to be saints of Jesus, who keep the faith of Jesus. They overcome the beast *by the blood of the Lamb.* Brainard argues that the Gentile believers who get saved after the rapture must be circumcised, essentially become Jews. But Paul was adamant - You cannot be under the Law and saved through faith in Christ at the same time! It is impossible!

Brainard provides five reasons why he believes dispensational theory requires the church to be gone during the seventieth week.

First, the nature of the seventieth week demands it. Seventy weeks were determined by God upon the Jews and upon Jerusalem as their holy city (Dan. 9:24-27). During the first sixty-nine weeks the Mosaic economy was enforced of God, the temple...was honored of God, Jews were saved as Jews, God required circumcision and Sabbath observance...

He concludes that this leaves no choice, unless using a spiritual method which leaves no affinity throughout the seventy weeks, but that the Mosaic law be enforced during the final week.

This one is easy to answer. Look closely at Daniel 9:24, at the part he cuts out:

> *Seventy weeks are determined **for** your people and **for** your holy city, to finish the transgression, to make an end of sins, to make reconciliation for iniquity, to bring in everlasting righteousness, to seal up vision and prophecy, and to anoint the most holy.*

There is a whole list of things which must be completed in by the end of the week. Every single item is fulfilled by Christ or through acceptance of Him as their Messiah. Through faith in Him we bring and end to sin and are reconciled to God for our iniquity (Is 54). Christ brings in everlasting righteousness, for His name is Jehovah Tsidkenu - the Lord is our Righteousness. The second coming seals up vision and prophecy, brings it to completion. And Christ is the Most Holy, whom the Jews will finally accept and anoint as Messiah and King at the end of the seventieth week, finishing *the transgression* of rejecting Him. The purpose of the seventieth week is for Israel to accept Jesus as Messiah. Jesus began His ministry after the 69 weeks, but Israel rejected Him. Now we await the seventieth week, when the mystery of the hardening of Israel comes to an end (Rom 11).

Secondly, the temple in Jerusalem is "the temple of God" during the seventieth week (2Thess 2:4 and Rev 11:1), a designation that would be entirely out of place were the "*house of God, which is the church of the living God*" (1Tim 3:15) still on earth...

Moreover, when the antichrist desecrates the temple in the middle of the...week (Matt 24:15), this is referred to as "*the abomination of desolation.*" This fact demands that the temple be the temple of God, and its service the service of God. Were this not the case it would no more be "abomination that maketh desolation" in God's eyes for the antichrist to desecrate it than if he had desecrated the Mormon Tabernacle...

281

Many Jews desire to rebuild the temple already, and preparations have already been made to rebuild when it becomes possible to do so. They have the heart to restore temple worship but are forbidden because of treaties with the Muslims, whose own temple sits on the Temple Mount. They desire to rebuild so they can restore the old system. But Hebrews 8:13 says the old system is obsolete and vanished away, along with its ordinances (*vanishing away* in the transitional period). They wish to restore animal sacrifices, which only covers sin and cannot take it away (Heb 10:4). They cannot *make an end to sin, and bring in everlasting righteousness* (Dan 9:24). Only the Blood of Christ has that power. In the seventieth week the Jews will finally receive this (Heb 8:8-13). They have been hardened in part for the times of the Gentiles, but will finally join with Christ (Rom 11).

Thirdly, God himself upholds the sanctity of the Sabbath during the seventieth week. In Matthew 24:20... Was He so concerned about the sanctity of the Sabbath [during other times of peril]?

Even today the Jews keep the Sabbath. One of our church members spent several weeks in Israel in ministry, and told us a little about it. Everything comes to a standstill in the Jewish areas on the Sabbath. If the Antichrist were to attack on that day, getting word out to flee would be hindered. Matthew 24 tells them to *flee*, an express commandment. It does not say to flee unless it is the Sabbath.

Fourthly, The ministry of the two witnesses is at variance with the character and spirit of Christianity. These two (Rev 11:3-6) destroy their enemies with fire, and call down judgments from heaven ...as often as they wish.

He goes on to note this is not out of character under the old dispensation, but in the new such behavior is forbidden. Why, if the church is still here, would this be allowed?

First, they witness primarily to the Jews, in the spirit of Elijah to restore Israel to God. Israel is still in unbelief when they begin

282

their ministry. When Elijah called down fire from heaven, it was upon the false prophets who served the wicked rulers of Israel and worshiped Baal. These witnesses come in the same power. They bring judgment against *sheol and death*, the world system under Antichrist with whom Israel has made a covenant.

Two other facts help to reconcile this. First, the Abomination is a key sign of the end of this age and of Christ's coming. It proves we are in the transitional phase. Brainard argues that the disciple were rebuked for wanting to call down fire upon a town which did not receive them (Luke 9). He correctly notes this is not in character for the new dispensation. Yet just a few pages earlier he stressed how the transition was instant upon the death and resurrection of Christ - it was then that Law ceased and Grace began. That means Jesus rebuked them while they were still under the Old Covenant, even though such action was permitted under that Covenant. You cannot have it both ways! Either a transition period allows a gradual change (thus the disciples were rebuked), or else there is no transition and they were really justified. If the change stopped the disciples from calling down judgment, then the future change can allow it.

Additionally, the seventieth week is clearly identified in Scripture as a time of judgment upon Israel to bring them to the Truth, and upon unbelieving Gentiles because they would not come to the Truth. Therefore, it is in perfect keeping with the nature of the seventieth week for the two witnesses to call forth judgments. That does not mean the church can no longer be present.

> **Fifth,** the Old Testament Scriptures prophesied of a time when "*ten men shall take hold out of all languages of the nations, even shall take hold of the skirt of him that is a Jew, saying, We will go with you: for we have heard that God is with you*" (Zech. 8:23).

He notes that this does not fit the current state of Israel, and insists it cannot be the millennium when the whole earth will be full of the knowledge of God (Is 11:9). He concludes that it must be fulfilled during the seventieth week.

The context of Zechariah does not fit this period. First, the nations turn to the Jews at a time when Israel is spiritually and naturally fruitful (8:12), *after* the time of punishment when God does good to her (8:14-15), and *after* Israel has repented (8:16-22) and seeks the Lord in Jerusalem. Many people and strong nations will go there to seek the Lord.

This is not the characteristic of the seventieth week, which has the beast and his armies attacking Israel and violating the rebuilt Temple, killing many Jews. Verse 21 says many strong nations seek the Lord in Jerusalem, but Revelation says many strong nations join with Antichrist. They come against Israel, and later against Christ at Armageddon. In Revelation 10:7 we learn that the mystery of the hardening of Israel (Rom 11) ends in the days that the seventh trumpet is about to sound. The ministry of the two witnesses is to reconcile Israel. Their ministry is successfully completed in the same time frame, and they are killed and then resurrected.

This passage in Zechariah probably points to the beginning of the millennium. Israel will be the center of worship during Christ's reign. The Jews will no longer be outcasts in the world. It will be their task to teach the world about God, and every nation will be required to send representatives to Jerusalem for certain feasts. Then the whole world will be full of the knowledge of God.

With **Appendix C** (pp 163-166), Brainard argues:

> One of the dispensational teachings that is regularly sniffed at is the doctrine that the rapture of the church was a "*mystery*" which was not revealed to the church until somewhere around the time she was weaned from Judaism....

He explains that the disciples from the beginning were neither looking for nor expecting a rapture, having been raised on the O.T. which did not teach such a thing. Their hope was for the Messiah to restore the kingdom to Israel as an everlasting kingdom. I will grant this point. This belief is seen throughout the gospels.

> But did not the Lord... teach His disciples plainly about the rapture of the Church...? I do not believe so. The Scriptures

give us every indication that He came preaching to the Jews the very consolation and redemption they were waiting for. He came preaching *"repent: for the kingdom of heaven is at hand"* (Matt 4:17). Now our Lord did... allude to the church (Matt 16:18 ... John 14:3), but the disciples did not understand that He had in mind a distinct people....

Moreover, if our Lord had clearly taught the apostles that the rapture... was their portion, then whence arose the silly notion - at the end of His earthly ministry no less - that *"The kingdom of God would immediately appear"* (Luke 19:11)?

First, just because the disciples did not understand it so does not mean Christ did not allude to the rapture in Matthew 24. Many of the things He taught were not understood until later (John 8:27; 10:6; 12:16). But by the time of this discourse they apparently had enough understanding to know Christ would come again, while the Jews typically believed in only one coming. Thus while it may be argued the rapture was still a hidden truth, it does not follow that Christ never alluded to it. Certainly, complete understanding only came with the revelation received by Paul of the distinct portion of the church (Eph 2:15; 1Cor 15:51-52). The times of the Gentiles was alluded to in the O.T., but not understood until revealed in the New Covenant. Likewise, the rapture could be alluded to by Christ, but not understood until the mystery was revealed to Paul.

Second, when the disciples thought the kingdom would immediately appear (Luke 19) Christ was on His way to Jerusalem for Passover. They thought Christ would then declare Himself King of the Jews and restore the earthly kingdom - which was not at all His intent. So He told them a parable in which a nobleman went to a far place to receive a kingdom, leaving servants behind with money to do business and bring increase. In one version of this parable, he went away for a long time (Matt 25:19) [the church age]. Then he returned and rewarded the faithful servants. In other words, Jesus taught them about His second coming in a parable just before He entered Jerusalem to be killed.

The disciples got the message. A few days later Jesus made His pronouncement against the Temple, which spurred the disciples to ask about His second coming that night on the Mount of Olives.

Brainard also agrees the promise in John 14:3 is for the church, not Israel. In fact, this is one of the key passages for the rapture to heaven - as opposed to the rapture and immediate return to earth of post-trib. Jesus spoke this a mere two days after the Olivet Discourse. So Brainard claims Christ can allude to the church and the second coming repeatedly, both before and after Matthew 24, but cannot at this point because the disciples did not understand there would be a different economy? I think I'll move on.

Brainard's next topic is the *last trumpet* (1Cor 15:52)(**Appendix D,** pp 166-169). He first incorrectly states that Rosenthal placed the rapture with the seventh trumpet. Rosenthal and Van Kampen agree with a sixth seal rapture prior to the sounding of the trumpets. I agree the seventh trumpet cannot be the last trump of the rapture. Van Kampen taught (and I agree) that this trumpet of God (1Thess 4) sounds at the Jehoshaphat Campaign when Israel defeats the armies surrounding Jerusalem. The first time God was said to blow a trumpet is in Maccabees. I will not repeat his complete line of reasoning, but refer you to The Sign. I already explained the Jehoshaphat Campaign. This gives a first trump to go with the last.

Then Brainard makes his *guesses* for this trumpet - either of which would work with the pre-wrath rapture. Because they do not cause a problem for us, I will bypass his conjectures.

In **Appendices E and F** (169-179), Brainard discusses whether there is one coming, or two. In particular, he notes that we take up the same cry as post-trib that there is only one coming, but then we describe more than one coming just like pre-tribs. I have already explained clearly that we view all of this as part of a single advent or parousia.

In The Sign, Van Kampen analyzes 2Thessalonians 2:8, and suggests this teaches that the Antichrist will be paralyzed or rendered useless at the first stage of Christ's coming, before being destroyed at the Armageddon coming. Brainard spends a couple of pages arguing against this. But this is entirely tangential to pre-wrath, and is not required for it to be true.

Rosenthal theorized that Christ would remain present on earth the entire time of the advent. He suggests this to avoid having multiple comings. Brainard rightly complains. First, the marriage supper of the Lamb takes place in heaven between the rapture and Armageddon. Also, we must be judged by Christ so we can receive rewards at the seventh trumpet. Scripture says we are raptured to heaven, and stand before Christ there (John 14:3; Rev 7; et al). And finally, at Armageddon (Rev 19) Jesus *descends from heaven* mounted on a white horse as King of kings. I compared Christ's coming to an evangelistic revival, where as part of a single revival there may be several meetings.

Brainards final complaint here is our insistence that there is only one second coming. He rightly notes the Jews believed in one coming of Christ, and were wrong. So, pre-wraths and post-tribs could be just as wrong. But this does not prove that we *are* wrong and are repeating history, but only that we could potentially be wrong. Besides which, the single coming or multiple comings is a tangential issue to whether the rapture is at the sixth seal, or not. In other words, we could call each stage a separate coming without affecting the timing issue at all.

Also, we could turn the repeating history argument right back against pre-tribs, and with greater justification. In the O.T. we read that false prophets promised Israel and Judah would not be taken captive by Assyria and Babylon, while the true prophets warned that if they did not repent, they would. And they were. This parallels pre-trib claims that we will not face Antichrist, while pre-wraths and post-tribs insist we will.

Appendix G. Some pre-wraths have suggested something akin to the partial rapture. Basically, they claim that the martyrs of the great tribulation are not resurrected until the first day of the millennium. This is based on Revelation 20:4, which seems to say that those who were slain by Antichrist came to life and reigned with Christ at this time. Most pre-wraths today allow that some may trust Christ following the sixth seal rapture, for the truth of Christ will be made obvious at His epiphany. There will be some who are not believers who still refuse the mark of the beast and fear God to give Him glory (Rev 14). When Christ appears, some of them will apparently put faith in Him. The beast will still seek to kill believers after the rapture. Thus those who put faith in Christ and are slain are promised to have part in the first resurrection at the start of the millennium.

Appendices H and I (pp 180-184) address the meaning and significance of the word *parousia*, and the fact that it only appears in the singular in relation to the second coming.

Brainard first notes that this word does not only mean visitation, but often includes the idea of the arrival of the person or event. I agree, and even state this in my study. But the primary emphasis of the word is on the presence of the person even though it includes their arrival. The concept of pre-wrath is that there is only one parousia, one initial arrival and presence on earth, even though there is some back and forth movement. It is all part of one event, one coming.

Brainard provides two observations concerning our case that the word parousia never appears in the plural. First, he rightly notes that we argue from silence, adding:

> For example, suppose we read the following sentences in a letter which said nothing further on the subject: "Juan paid a visit to his grandmother Josie who is a Christian," and "Juan paid a visit to his grandmother Rosie who is a Jew." Would we not conclude... that Juan paid two separate and distinct visits?

Scripture hardly describes the *two* comings so concisely. There are many contextual details which must be considered. The key pre-wrath rapture passages share in many details (Matt 24; 1Thess 4; 2Thess 1&2; Rev 6&7), which contrast sharply with Armageddon (Rev 19). Also, Scripture contains a few more than two sentences about Christ's second coming. Thus the issue becomes more problematic when there are numerous accounts, most of which contain more details than Brainard's simplified explanation.

The fact that there are dozens of references to the second coming and not even once do we find a plural is a bit harder to reconcile with two distinct comings. Add to this that no text describes the rapture coming before the seventieth week or the appearance of Antichrist. Without such details, it quickly becomes untenable that there are two separate comings of Christ at the end of the age. So while it is true we argue from silence, said silence is very loud.

Of all his protests, one of Brainard's weakest has to be found in **Appendix J.** Here he addresses the extra thirty and forty-five days on top of the 1260 in Daniel 12:11-12. According to the usual pre-wrath schedule the bowls are poured out during the 30 days, concluding with Armageddon. Then the forty-five days is for the sheep and goat judgment and return of the Jews to Israel on the Highway of Holiness. Brainard says:

> The battle of Armageddon and the destruction of the antichrist cannot possibly occur on the thirtieth day after the close of the seventieth week. Surely nothing is more plainly stated in Scripture than the fact that with the closing of the seventieth week, transgression is finished, and end is made of sins, and everlasting righteousness is brought in (Dan 9:24). How then can the ungodly still be foaming out their shame, rebelling against God...
>
> Nor are we free to treat the thirty days as an extension of the seventieth week. Such a course the Scriptures expressly forbid. The second half of the seventieth week is but 1260 days. This is apparent when we compare the testimony of Revelation 12:14, the woman flees into the wilderness... with Revelation 12:6, ... *they feed her there a thousand two hundred and threescore days.*

289

Whatever transpires, then... must be consonant with a world wherein transgression and overt sin are no more, and righteousness is the order of the day... (p. 184-185, emph mine)

He goes on to suggest that, just as the feast of trumpets [a type of the gathering of Israel] was quickly followed by the day of atonement and the feast of tabernacles, so it will be followed by such things as the ceremonial cleansing of the Jews (Zech 13:1), the dedication of the millennial temple, and the mourning for past unbelief and sin (Zech 14:10-14).

First, Daniel 9:24 explicitly says *Israel and Jerusalem* finish *the* transgression in the seventieth week, not the world. And the means is by anointing Jesus as Messiah. Look at Zechariah 13, which Brainard cites for the ceremonial cleansing of Israel. A bit further into the context (13:6-9) is one of the important prophecies about the death of Christ, but given in immediate connection with the refining of Israel in the last days. Then, they will acknowledge the wounds of Christ (v.6), whom they had killed. This mirrors the coming of Christ in clouds when the earth mourns, including those who pierced Him (Rev 1:7; Matt 24:29-31). Two-thirds of Israel will be cut off during the great tribulation (Zech 13:8), while the remainder pass through the refiner's fire, and will call upon the name of the Lord. This perfectly aligns with Joel 2 and 3 which says after the sixth seal Israel calls on the name of the Lord. Thus it is confirmed that the things which must be completed in seventy weeks are completed through acceptance of Christ.

Second, all indicators show that surviving Israel repents by the seventh trumpet at the end of the week (apart from the firstfruits at the sixth seal). The woman who fled into the wilderness at the Abomination is fed there 1260 days; The two witnesses who come to reconcile Israel minister for 1260 days and are killed just before the seventh trumpet; An earthquake destroys 1/10 of the Jerusalem and the rest give glory to God at that trumpet; And Zechariah 14 says when Israel repents Jesus stands on the Mount of Olives, splitting it in two so they can flee to Azal - for which the seventh trumpet, pre-bowl location seems to fit best, witnessed by that earthquake. Everything points to this time.

Third, the dedication of the Temple under the Law takes about a year to complete, not forty-five days. Following the defilement by Antichrist it would certainly be necessary to have an extensive cleansing and re-dedication.

Brainard cited Zechariah 14:10-14 for the mourning of Israel. This says nothing of mourning, but describes the plague which dissolves the eyes and tongues of Israel's enemies at the great Battle, and the gathering of the world's riches for Israel. This indeed starts to be fulfilled with Armageddon, continuing into the forty-five days and into the millennium. Perhaps he had another passage in mind?

Finally, look closely at Daniel 12:11. *And from the time the daily sacrifice is taken away, and the abomination of desolation is set up, there shall be one thousand two hundred and ninety days.* While not required, this strongly suggests that the Antichrist will continue into the thirty days, since he is the central topic of the prophecy. It is certainly easier to fit than some uncertain, *whatever transpires* event of the restoration. Blessed are those who survive through the shattering of the people (Dan 12:7) and come to the 1335 days. This is even in line with the teaching of the early church. Hyppolytus (ca 220AD), speaking of the Antichrist, said:

> He shall be proclaimed king by them, and shall be magnified by all, and shall prove himself an abomination of desolation to the world, and shall reign for a thousand two hundred and ninety days. (On Daniel, 40)

But doesn't the Bible teach the rapture will be a secret event? According to Brainard's next **appendix, K** (pp 185-186), it does.

> Many are those who scoff at the teaching that the rapture of the church is secret. And many more are those who, though they believe in the pre-tribulation rapture, yet feel uneasy with this doctrine...

Let it once be understood that the type of the advent is the rising of the sun (Mal. 4:1-3, Ps.. 19:4-6; Isa. 40;5-8, Jas.. 1:10-11), and the type of the rapture the morning star (2Pet. 1:19; Rev. 2:28; 22:16), and the secretness of the rapture will be manifest. In stark contrast to the rising of the sun which none can fail to notice, the appearance of the morning star while it is yet night is an unobtrusive affair...

The first question that comes to mind is how the sudden disappearance of several hundred million believers around the globe could be regarded as secret and unobtrusive? I'll let you figure that one out, because I sure can't.

Let's look at his passages. Notice Psalm 19, in which he says Christ's advent (Armageddon) is compared to the *rising sun*. In context He is compared to a bridegroom coming from His chambers. The church is the bride of Christ awaiting her bridegroom. This does not fit Armageddon.

Nor does James 1:10-11 relate to the rapture or the advent. This concerns the natural end of those whose faith is in their riches - they will fade away and die just like flowers in the rising heat of the sun. 2Pet 1:19 is not Christ coming to take us home, but Christ the Morning Star rising up in our hearts. The context says if we believe the prophecies of Christ's first coming and ignore those who deny the Lord, then the morning star will arise in our hearts. Revelation 2:28 relates to the authority given to faithful believers over the nations during the millennium, not to the nature of Christ's coming. And Revelation 22:16 says one of the Lord's royal titles is the Bright and Morning Star - it does not compare His coming to the morning star. There is no support for Brainard's thesis.

He also argues from the the Greek word *harpazo* (translated *caught up*, 1Thess 4:17). He claims this word was used in the Greek mythologies for such things as the divinities stealing away a human whom they loved to ravish them, or whisking their heroes out of danger. Since such usage was well established, we can surmise God's use of this word illustrates Him removing us away from impending danger, to the Bridegroom.

292

First, the word does not mean to take secretly, but forcefully (Strong's #726). In the mythologies the idea was not that the gods quietly spirited them away, but that they snatched them away whether the one snatched was willing or not. The gods might snatch someone they loved (or often more accurately, lusted after), but sometimes it was against their will. Also, they were not always whisked away secretly, but often quite openly. The Greek gods were not romantics, but self-serving, violent, spiteful womanizers.

Second, we should see how the word is used elsewhere in Scripture to better understand how God meant it.

In Acts 8:39, Philip was caught up as soon as he had baptized the eunuch, openly. In Matthew 11:12 we are told that the *Kingdom of God is suffering violence, and the violent take (harpazo) it by force (harpazo)*. Here you see the word used twice to emphasize taking forcefully. In John 6:15 the people were about to take Christ by force and make Him king. And in Acts 23:10, Paul was forcefully removed by the guards to protect him. Thus we see that secrecy is not the root concept of harpazo, but forcefulness or suddenness. There is no evidence supporting a secret coming for the rapture.

In **Appendix L,** Brainard explains how the DOL relates to the seventieth week. I have already demonstrated the error of making that Day synonymous with Armageddon.

In **Appendices M and N**, Brainard essentially defends the view that the Millennial Kingdom is part of the Day of the Lord, that this is not only a Day of wrath but also a Day of blessing. He quotes Rosenthal, who did not include the period of blessing. However, some pre-wrath adherents do include the Millennial Kingdom, as do I, and for the same reasons he so well explains. This creates no problems for the pre-wrath view.

Brainard insists that the focus of Bible prophecy is the advent of Christ rather than the coming for the rapture (**Appendix O,** pp 193-195). He explains how common it is for the church to be lopsided in their doctrine, emphasizing one truth at the expense of another - for example, the grace of God versus the requirement of obedience, or the emphasis on Christ and the Spirit while ignoring the Father. This observation is very insightful. He then extends it to the coming of Christ:

> Similarly, for many centuries the church knew of and taught only the advent. She was altogether ignorant of the rapture of the church. But when she had once come to a clear understanding and heart-felt appreciation for the church's hope, the insidious forces of extremism bulled their way until at present the rapture has become the primary focus of many a prophetic teacher.... It must be understood that the rapture is not the primary focus of prophecy in the Bible. The advent is.

So basically, he believes that Paul did not understand his own writings. The mystery of the rapture was revealed to Paul (1Cor 15:51-52) fairly early in his ministry. Since the understanding of the rapture is based on Paul's teaching, one would think he knew what he was teaching. The Greek word for mystery means something previously hidden but now revealed, so Paul was passing on a truth that God had revealed to him. The various churches had had the benefit of Paul's personal instructions as he traveled. So, logically, we should see evidence in the writings of the early church whether the rapture is separate from the advent or not. And universally the earliest church writings did not separate them. Brainard's case is greatly weakened by this.

Moreover, a few pages earlier Brainard insisted that the rapture doctrine was not taught until the church had been weaned from its Jewish roots, at which time it was given to Paul. But now he says that the church kept hold of its Jewish roots for centuries and was ignorant of the rapture which Paul had taught. You can't have it both ways!

Brainard continues, arguing that, other than a few faint types, you will not find the rapture taught in the O.T., but only references to the advent and coming kingdom. Also, the entire church age was only alluded to briefly in a couple of passages. Christ began to reveal this age, and it was fully revealed to the apostles. In our study we saw a couple of O.T. passages which seem to allude to the rapture, in contexts which line up with the sixth or seventh seal. However, apart from the revelation of the rapture given to Paul, and the information on the end time provided by Jesus in the Olivet Discourse and Revelation, there would be no reason to associate these with the rapture. It is only with the newer prophecies of the N.T. that this meaning comes out, just as with the allusions to the church age. It has been said that the New Testament was concealed in the Old, and the Old Testament is revealed by the New. Every step of the way, Scripture teaches the same things.

Brainard likewise insists that, other than a couple of brief references, the gospels also discuss the advent rather than the rapture. But of course! The rapture is only one part of the parousia of Christ, with many other things associated with it. He says:

> I might add that I find it somewhat amusing that many of the favorite rapture verses employed by rapture preachers - e.g. *"of that day and that hour knoweth no man"* (Mark 13:32) or *"the one shall be taken, and the other shall be left"* (Luke 17:34) - are taken from the Olivet discourse or some other passage which concerns itself with the advent.

This amuses me, too. Brainard relegates these to the coming of Christ in Matthew 24:29-31 at the sixth seal, which he says is at Armageddon. So he at least considers the context, something many pre-tribs fail to do. But if this advent and the arrival of the DOL were at Armageddon, it could hardly take the world by surprise, preceded, as it were, by rapture, revival, and wrath in trumpets and bowls over seven years. It doesn't fit.

Brainard next demonstrates from Acts 1:9-11 and 3:19 that the apostles taught the advent and times of refreshing for Israel. The error is obvious: This was taught at the very beginning of the church age, years before Paul was converted and before the Gentiles began to join the church. As Brainard so clearly explained, however, the rapture was not really understood until Paul received understanding from God - years later. And it should be noted that Paul went about preaching the gospel of the Kingdom even after he became the apostle to the Gentiles and stopped going to the Jews - again according to Acts. Thus the rapture is not at odds with Christ's advent and Kingdom.

Let a man turn to the book of Revelation and apart from the promise of deliverance from the hour of temptation found in 3:10, he will find but figures and types of the rapture, as in 4:1, *"come up hither,"* or 2:28, *"I will give him the morning star."* The thrice-fold *"I come quickly"* in ch. 22, though suitable to the rapture, gives no distinct testimony to the same. It is just as applicable to the advent as to the rapture. The last book of the Bible, the closing of the canon of Scripture, is almost entirely taken up with the advent and the judgments which precede it.

Let's break this down piece by piece. First, Revelation 3:10 does not promise physical removal but God's protection by watching over them. Second, we saw there is no authority to make references to the morning star prefigure the rapture. Third, making Revelation 4:1 as a figure of the rapture is tantamount to using an allegorical method of interpretation, with no warrant to back up such a reading. Fourth, pre-wrath sees a clear reference to the rapture with the sixth seal - the great multitude from all nations who keep the faith of Christ.

Brainard insists when Christ says he is coming quickly in Revelation 22, it could as easily be the advent as the rapture. However, in context Jesus says

*I have sent My angel to testify to you these things **in the churches**... He who testifies to these things says, "Surely I am coming quickly." Even so, come, Lord Jesus!* (22:16, 20).

I agree this entire book is taken up with the advent. Christ first appears at the sixth seal, which evidence puts before the trumpets and bowls.

Also, by the time this book was written (ca 90 AD) the Gentile nature of the church age was well established and understood - the Jewish Temple was destroyed (70 AD), and Christ had not yet returned, very few Jews now received Christ, and the hardening of

Israel was taught (Rom 11). Also, Revelation is specifically addressed to the church as a testimony for believers. It seems strange that, in a book intended to instruct the church concerning the advent of Christ, a pre-trib rapture was not clearly presented, if this were correct doctrine. Even if the Olivet Discourse cannot contain such reference because the church did not yet exist, certainly we should expect it in a book written specifically to the church. Yet the most pre-tribs can muster is a single, debatable verse written to one specific type of church, and another verse taken out of its context as a type for the rapture using an allegorical method. Now that is keeping pre-trib a secret coming!

In **Appendix P** (pp 196-198), Brainard insists that the type of Noah bears no resemblance to the removal of the church before God's wrath, but better fits the survival of Israel through the seventieth week, just as Noah went through the flood.

There are three basic problems with this. First, Scripture says Israel is going to be shattered during the great tribulation - other than the woman who flees at the Abomination - killing 2/3 of the Jews. On the other hand, Noah's family was kept completely safe during the flood. Second, The examples say it was business as usual until the *day* Noah was shut up in the ark, then the flood came and destroyed them all; But Brainard says it is business as usual even in the midst of increasingly intense judgments after Israel is put in the ark of safety, until the advent at Armageddon. And third, Noah and Lot are parallel, and Lot was removed from the region - thus the key concept was removal from danger, not protection through it.

Brainard next argues that on the same day Lot left Sodom the city was completely destroyed by fire from heaven in moments, while after the rapture the earth is not immediately turned into a great, smoking heap. He then argues from pre-trib that the world continues for seven long years before meeting her doom. He adds that many godly people will be preserved and emerge safely from the DOL, whether preserved by flight, by hiding, or a thousand other means.

297

But Lot did not emerge from the wrath of God on Sodom but exited before wrath fell. Also, according to Revelation the very first judgment after the rapture happens to be.... wait for it.... fire from heaven burning up 1/3 of the earth's foliage, turning much of earth into a great, smoking heap. I grant that the DOL judgments may not be as instantly fatal as the flood or the fire on Sodom, but then Jesus did not say it would be instantly complete on His Day, either. The examples illustrate how it will be business as usual until *the Day* the Son of Man appears, then suddenly wrath comes even as the church is removed to safety.

In **Appendix Q,** (pp 198-201), Brainard turns to the one taken and the other left (Matt 24). He argues that the verse says one is taken and the other left, but those who meet the Lord in the air do not comprise half the world's population.

Where does it say this represents everyone on earth? And where is the prophecy which says that either half the world goes into the millennium, or else half of Israel. Brainard suggests Zechariah 14, which says half the city (Jerusalem) is taken into captivity, which would fill the prophecy exactly. But this relates to the Abomination of Desolation, while those taken in our text relates to the gathering of elect in Matthew 24. Furthermore, the gathering of elect is from all parts of the globe, not just Jerusalem.

Then we turn to the parable of the five wise and five foolish virgins (Matt 25:1-13). It has been long understood that this relates to the church, as Jesus is the bridegroom and the church His bride who have been espoused as virgins (2Cor 11:2). Here we see the 50/50 ratio Brainard insists upon. This parable cannot be the sheep and goat judgment, for then the goats are taken out in the judgment while the sheep are left to enter the millennium, whereas the wise virgins are taken while the foolish are left behind. It cannot be Israel, for at the end of the week all Israel is saved. That leaves only the rapture.

Strangely, Brainard totally ignores the parable of the virgins in his book, even though teachers from every rapture view have understood this as the rapture of the church.

In Luke 17:37, when the disciples asked where they were taken, the Lord answered that wherever the body is, there the eagles will be gathered. In Matthew the Greek uses the term carcass rather than body. Brainard argues:

> Now why is this answer so studiously avoided by those who would interpret *"one shall be taken"* as the rapture? They avoid it because it doesn't square with their much beloved rapture interpretation.. After all, what do corpses and carrion eating birds have to do with the raptured church in heaven? But such things do square with the Armageddon interpretation. For the Scriptures very clearly teach that God will gather the birds of the air to eat the flesh of those that fall in the battle of Armageddon...

The disciple did not ask *when*, but *where*. Yet those who place this coming of Christ at Armageddon always turn it into a *when* answer. Where do vultures gather when they first encounter a dead or dying body? In the air, overhead. So, where are those who are taken go? They gather in the air, while the dead are left on earth. At the rapture the church is gathered into the air (1Thess 4, Mark 13). I do not avoid this verse.

In **Appendix R** (pp 2010-204) Brainard questions why we quote the early church fathers when they said we would face the Antichrist. I grant that they did not explicitly teach pre-wrath, and that most of their statements could as equally fit post-trib, as Brainard agrees. However, pre-wrath certainly fits their teaching better than pre-trib, and they uniformly believed the church would face Antichrist, which was the point of the exercise. He even agrees that it is an argument against the validity of a pre-tribulation rapture.

He then supposes that the early church did not yet understand the distinction of the church from the Jewish economy, and that it is entirely possible the fathers from the close of the apostolic era could have held unsound notions on the coming of Christ for the church. To not grant this is to assign weight to a historical argument which belongs only to an exegetical issue. He notes that all of us are fallible, including the church fathers.

299

I will grant this is possible. However, when every one of the more reliable, earliest church fathers who touched on the subject were in agreement that the Antichrist comes first, his case is greatly weakened. Brainard continues:

> I must admit that I am scandalized by the manner in which certain Evangelicals in our day appeal to the early fathers - whether with reference to prophetic questions ... or [other debated doctrines] - for it seems they are attempting to establish the truth of their doctrine by patristic sanction. Let folks yammer on all they will that the early fathers are more likely to have the mind of the apostles than we are. Have they never read the early fathers for themselves. Are they oblivious to the proto-Romanistic tendencies, strange notions, hyperspirituality, unsound doctrine, foggy mysticism, and reputed visions that abound in early patristic literature? We would be much better off judging the early fathers' doctrine by the teaching of Holy Scripture [than the reverse].

First of all, pre-wraths quote only from those early fathers who are considered more reliable and sound of doctrine. Certainly they were not perfect in all their doctrine, particularly on the issues of marriage and of the forgiveness of God. These errors, however, stemmed from an overzealousness to defend the holiness of the believer in his practice - a point with which Brainard concurs in end note 58. Brainard's other examples of doctrinal problems come from Clement of Alexandria and the Epistle of Barnabas. We agree their doctrines are not sound and must be rejected - just as I stated in my introduction to the early church fathers.

Furthermore, we do not start with the early church writing, then prove it from Scripture. We start with an exposition of God's Word, thoroughly demonstrating that the church will face Antichrist. Then we point out this is in line with the early church. It is only a minor point of support, much as writers today often appeal to various theologians in support of a point. It is primarily brought up to counter the claims of some pre-tribs that they believed in an any-moment rapture. *It is patently clear they did not believe any such thing!*

In **Appendix S** (pp 204-206) Brainard essentially defends defining the entire seventieth week as the tribulation. I already clearly addressed this.

Next, Brainard addresses the danger late rapture theories perceive with the emphasis of the pre-trib rapture:

> Those who believe that the church will go through the time of great tribulation claim that the pre-tribulation rapture doctrine leaves the saints unprepared for persecution. This charge, however, is libel. It is not pre-tribulationism which leaves saints unprepared for the dungeon or for burning at the stake, but the worldly, self-indulging spirit which pervades the modern church. And embracing the doctrine that the last generation of the church will suffer persecution under the antichrist will not solve this problem...

I concur. However, the mentality of the great escape certainly makes it easier to not be ready. Those who hold to a later rapture at least acknowledge more readily the potential price they may have to pay for their faith. Also, I know a few pre-tribs who still teach that the final generation Christians will likely face some trying times even in relatively free countries before Christ raptures the church. But pre-trib, more often than not it seems, leads to a safe-escape mentality which fits easily in the modern, liberal church. It is interesting that the pre-trib theory is more popular in the free countries than those in which believers are already severely persecuted. Perhaps it is because they do not have the emotional need to avoid it, so are not blinded in reading the Bible.

Some pre-tribs, including Brainard, even blatantly state that if we find ourselves in the great tribulation we should consider Scripture broken - not our own doctrine. Myself, I say that if I am proven wrong by circumstances, whether by pre-trib or post-trib, that it would be my error, not broken Scripture. While I am 100% convinced in the pre-wrath rapture, I don't have the hubris to insist that Scripture is wrong if it does not happen as I teach! At least Brainard concludes the appendix stating:

301

...if [the church] once determined to set all her hope on the glory that will be revealed to her, then tribulation and persecution, no matter the circumstances, no matter how bitter the cup, would never - and could never - break her. It wouldn't even matter, then, if the entire church found out the hard way that the pre-tribulation rapture was but "cotton candy" and that the pre-wrath rapture was the truth of God after all.

He is correct. But I personally would rather be prepared than "find out the hard way." Likewise, I would much rather find out the easy way that I was wrong and pre-trib correct, though I cannot see it anywhere taught in Scripture.

In **Appendix U** (pp 207-209), Brainard defends that the great multitude of Revelation 7 are saved during the seventieth week. He notes we find it difficult to believe in the great revival without a scriptural basis, then provides what he thinks is such evidence; He again cites Zechariah 8:23 where Gentiles grab the hems of Jews to teach them about God. I already refuted this line of reasoning.

Brainard lists three things he believes promotes this revival. First, he claims that multitudes of those who incorrectly thought they were saved will realize their error and be roused to make their calling and election sure. So, let us look once more at the parable of wise and foolish virgins, which Brainard ignores. The wise virgins are taken to the wedding. The foolish virgins tried to enter afterward, but were *not allowed entry*. Jesus did not tell them they would enter the millennium, either. Kinda pokes a big hole in that boat, doesn't it? I'm thinking, Titanic.

Next, Brainard says that friends and families of the saved who had heard the gospel and see the Christians suddenly disappear will be shocked into taking a closer look at Christianity. (Some may even after the pre-wrath rapture, I'll allow - if they listened to the proclaiming angels). But 2Thessalonians 2 clearly states that those who refused to love the truth but rejected Christ will be deceived by God Himself into continuing in their error. They will follow the Antichrist. This certainly weakens Brainard's case, though it may not destroy it.

Thirdly, the moral vacuum created during the seventieth week by the emptiness of such things as a successful ecumenical movement, secular humanism come to a head, extreme wickedness and hedonism... will have many turning away from the things that are seen to the things that are not seen, from creation to the Creator, to find peace and satisfaction for their souls.

But, some will ask, [can] a great multitude which no man can number [be] saved in the midst of the deepest apostasy ever, which culminates in the whole world worshiping both the beast and the devil? A great multitude saved in the face of the most severe persecution the world has ever known? Yes! If there were but a very small remnant converted, say one in a thousand, and two-thirds of these souls were martyrred, we could still easily see somewhere between one and two million sheep who "*came out of the great tribulation*" standing at the right hand of the Son of man when He sits on the throne of His glory. And tell me, is there a man on earth who could count such a multitude?

First, where does it say the great multitude consists of martyrs (Rev 7:9-17)? Granted, the fifth seal tells of martyrs to come, but it is really stretching the point to say these are exclusively the ones seen before Christ's throne. Furthermore, John numbered the angels as more than a hundred million. Contrasted with the mere couple million in Brainard's hypothesis, it is hard to reconcile that they were uncountable. Third, where does he get the number of martyrs as 2/3? Zechariah 13 is the only prophecy which uses that ratio, and the context is Jews killed in the seventieth week, not Gentile believers.

Brainard titles **Appendix V** *Pre-tribulationism and Orthodoxy*. Rosenthal made an issue of the degree of emphasis some churches place on pre-trib, practically making it a badge for orthodoxy. Brainard argues that pre-trib is not placed in the same category as the fundamental doctrines of the faith, such as the virgin birth of Christ, the Trinity, the blood atonement, etc.

He adds that every doctrine which has proven itself to be the truth of God is *inviolable, irrescindable, and non-negotiable.* He then basically insists the a pre-trib rapture falls into this category.

As we have seen, pre-trib is far from proven, and is easily answered on all fronts by pre-wrath. Some churches do essentially make pre-trib a badge of orthodoxy - though not actually calling those who believe differently heretics. They sometimes bluntly state those who do not believe it are wrong, and will forbid them from teaching anything other than pre-trib to be a minister in their denomination. Some even deliberately malign the character and integrity of those who hold to a different theory. This is wrong. That was the point Rosenthal was trying to make.

Pre-wrath adherents see the church's entry into the Tribulation to be, in part, for her purification. This is the topic of **Appendix W** (pp 215-216). He points out that throughout church history have been times when the churches were not pure, and did not endure great tribulation for purification. Furthermore, it is the blood of Christ which purifies us, not our own works. I agree. But there are numerous passages which speak of our responsibility to purify ourselves and to pursue righteousness, as well. Peter said fiery testings give us opportunity to demonstrate and purify our faith, which is more precious than gold. James and Paul taught that tribulations work patience and, ultimately, proven godly character. Revelation 3:10 says that the great tribulation is a time of such testing and proving, and that the Philadelphia church will have extra protection because they are already proven.

In **Appendix X** (pp 216-218) Brainard addresses a theory of Van Kampen's that the beast will set up *living* idols around the world. I will agree that this theory is highly debatable. It is totally tangential to the rapture position, so I will not discuss it. In Brainard's final appendix, he addresses a theory proposed by Van Kampen concerning the identity of Antichrist. I also disagree with Van Kampen, and it is also tangential to the rapture question. I will bypass it.

This concludes Brainard's critique of pre-wrath. Every relevant point has been examined and answered. As we have seen, he has failed at every turn to discredit the pre-wrath rapture.

Conclusion

We have seen that when we allow prophecy to naturally fall into place using a literal method of interpretation, all evidence points to a sixth seal rapture, before God's wrath. The other theories all have numerous weak points. For every issue one pre-trib says proves their view, another comes along and admits the case is weak, at best.

Some have tried to discredit the pre-wrath view. They fail at every turn. Every point they raise that is pertinent to the rapture question is easily answered from Scripture. It is up to you to seek God and decide on the correct view. May God richly bless you. Amen.

Chart A

	Angels present	Gathering of Righteous	Clouds	Jesus Descends	Trumpet Sounds	The 4 Winds	Jesus is Visible	Heavenly Signs in Sun, Moon, &Stars	Voice of an Angel	Wrath / Vengeance	Mankind Mourns
Matt 24:29-31	X	X	X	X	X	X	X	X		C1	
Mark 13:24-27	X	X	X	X		X	X	X			
Luke 21:25-28		I	X	X			X	X		X	X
Acts 1:11			X	X			X				
1Cor 15:51-53		X			X						
1Thess 4:13-17		X	X	X	X				X	C2	
2Thess 1:6 - 2:3	X	X		I						X	
Rev 1:7			X				X				X
Rev 6:12 - 7:17		X				X	X	X		X	X
Rev 14:14-16		X	X						X		

C1 –Context Matt 24:37-44

I - Implied

C2 - Context 1Thess 5:1-12

Chart B

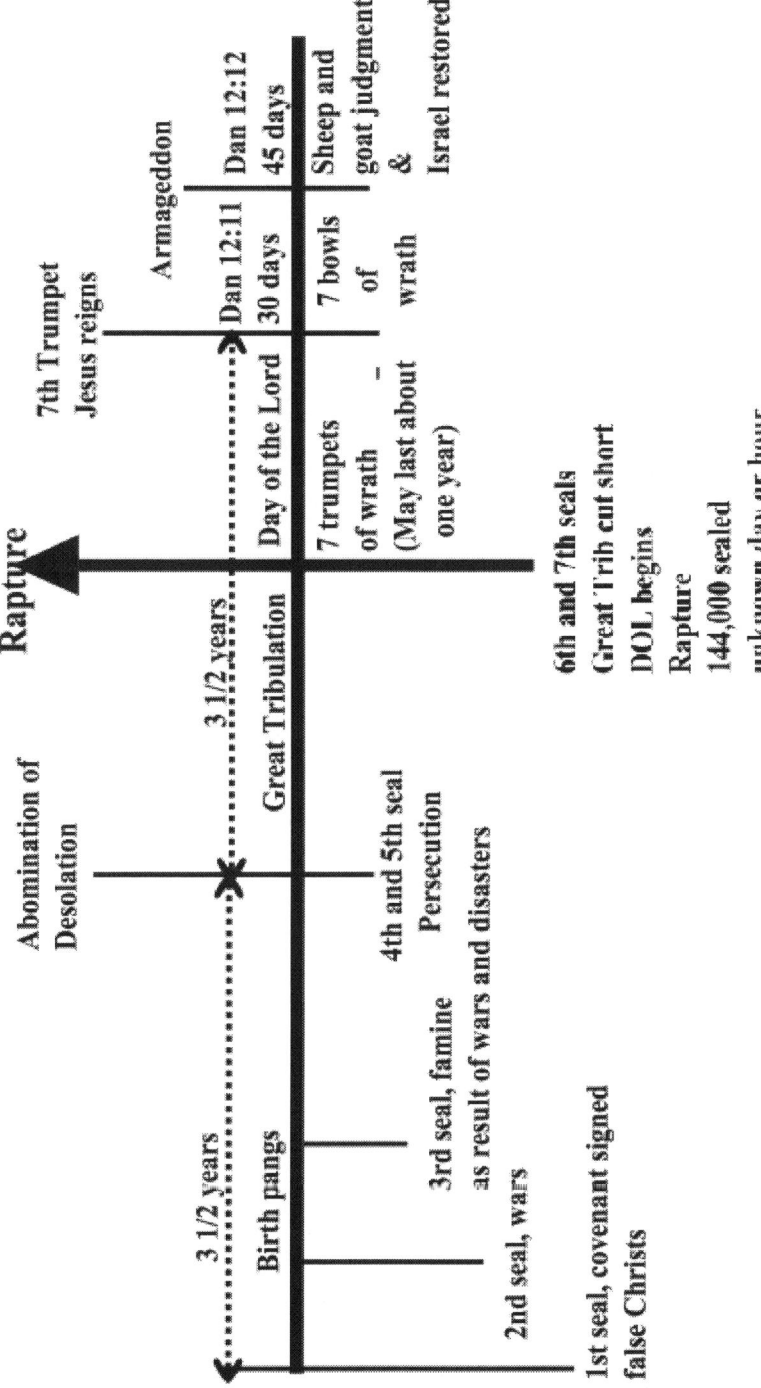

309

Bibliography

The Pre-Wrath Rapture, Marvin Rosenthal: Thomas Nelson, 1990

The Sign, Robert Van Kampen: Crossway, 1993

The Rapture Question Answered: Plain and Simple, Robert Van Kampen: Fleming H. Revell, a division of Baker Book House Company, Grand Rapids, MI, 1997

'Til Eternity: Facing the Consequences of the Second Coming, Paul Bortolazzo: Bortolazzo Publishing, LLC, 2010

When the Trumpet Sounds, Thomas Ice and Timothy Demy: Harvest House, 1995

The End Times, Herman Hoyt, Moody Press of Chicago, 1969

Christianity in Crisis, Hank Hanegraff, Harvest House Publishers, Eugene, OR, 1993

Thru the Bible with J. Vernon McGee, Thru the Bible Radio, Pasaden, CA

The Rapture: Pre-, Mid-, or Post-tribulational, Gleason L. Archer, Jr; Paul D. Feinberg; Douglas J. Moo; Richard R. Reiter: The Zondervan Corp., Grand Rapids, MI, 1984

The Coming Climax of History, James McKeever: Omega Publications, PO Box 4130, Medford, OR

The Rapture Book, James McKeever: Omega Publications

Be Victorious, Warren W. Wiersbe: Victor Books, Wheaton, IL, 1985

The Church and the Tribulation, Robert Gundry: Zondervan, 1973

Post-tribulationism Today, John Walvoord; <u>Bibliotheca Sacra</u> : Dallas Theological Seminary, Oct-Dec 1976

Matthew, H. L. Ellison; <u>The International Bible Commentary</u>, ed. F. F. Bruce: Zondervan Publishing House, Grand Rapids, MI, 1979

<u>Things To Come</u>, J. Dwight Pentecost: Dunham Publishing Company, Grand Rapids, MI, 1958

<u>The Bible Knowledge Commentary</u>, John F. Walvoord and Roy B. Zuck: S. P. Publications, Inc., Wheaton, IL, 1983

<u>The Final Chapter</u>, S. Maxwell Coder: Tyndale House Publishers, Inc., Wheaton, IL, 1984

<u>A Review of "The Pre-Wrath Rapture of the Church" by Marvin Rosenthal,</u> reviewed by Dr. Arnold G. Fruchtenbaum: Ariel Ministries, PO Box 3723, Tustin, CA 92681, nd,

<u>Dake's Annotated Reference Bible</u>, Finis Jennings Dake: Dake Bible Sales, inc. Lawrenceville, CA. 1991

<u>Welcome Back, Jesus</u>, Stanley Horton: gospel Publishing House, Springfield,MO, 1967

<u>The Expanded Vine's Expository Dictionary of New Testament Words</u>: Bethany House Publishers, 1984

<u>"I Shall Return"...Jesus</u>, Jerry Vine: First Baptist church, Jacksonville, FL, 1977 [orig published by Victor Books, Wheaton, IL]

Another Look at Rosenthal's Pre-Wrath Rapture, John A. McLean; <u>Bibliotheca Sacra</u>, Dallas Theological Seminary, Oct-Dec 1991

<u>Prophecy for Today</u>, J. Dwight Pentecost: Discovery House Publisher, Grand Rapids, MI, 1989

<u>The Second Coming of Jesus</u>, Oliver B. Greene: The gospel Hour, inc., Greenville, SC 29602, 1971

Come Lord Jesus, Mark Cambion: Zondervan Publishing House, Grand Rapids, MI, 1959

There's a New Day Coming, Herbert Vander Lugt: Radio Bible Class, 1983

The Wycliffe Bible Commentary: Moody Bible Institute of Chicago, 1962

Lectures in Systematic Theology, Henry Thiessen: Wm. B. Eerdman's Publishing Co., Grand Rapids, MI

The Archangel Michael, Marvin Rosenthal: Zion's Fire, Orlando, FL, Jan-Feb 1996

Ryrie Study Bible, Charles C. Ryrie: Moody Press, Chicago, 1978

A Grammar of the Greek New Testament in Light of Historical Research, 4th ed., A. T. Robinson: George H Doran, New Yourk, 1923

The Rapture in Reveltaion 3:10", Jeffery Townsend; The Bib Sac Reader , Dallas Theological Seminary, 1983

The Approaching Advent of Christ: An Examination of the Teachings of J. N. Darby and His Fellows, Alexander Reese: Marshall, Morgan, and Scott, London, 1937

The Revelation of Jesus Christ, John Walvoord: Moody Press, Chicago, 1966

Salem Kirban Reference Bible; "Revelation Visualized": AMG Publishers, Chattanooga, TN 37422, 1979

In Defense of Pre-tribulationism, revised ed., R.C. Sproul: BMH Books, Winona Lake, IN, 1950

Post-tribulationism Today: Part IX, John F. Walvoord; Bibliotheca Sacra : Dallas Theological Seminary, Jan-Mar 1977

Post-tribulationism Today John Walvoord; Bibliotheca Sacra, Dallas Theological Seminary, Apr-June 1976

Understanding Revelation, Gary Cohen: Christian Beacon Press., Collingswood, NJ, 1968

The Place of Israel in the Scheme of Redemption as Set Forth in Romans 9-11, Henry C. Thiessen ; Bibliotheca Sacra, Dallas Theological Seminary, Jan 1941

Look Who's Coming, Richard E. Orchard: Gospel Publishing House, Springfield, MO 65802, 1975

A Review of The Pre-Wrath Rapture of the Church, Gerald B. Stanton; Bibliotheca Sacra, Dallas Theological Seminary, Jan-Mar 1991

The Pre-Wrath Rapture View: An Examination and Critique, Renald E. Showers: Kregel Publications, a division of Kregel, Inc., PO Box 2607, Grand Rapids, MI 49501, 2001

The Pre-Wrath Rapture Answered: From the Testimony of Scripture, Lee W. Brainard: Gospel Folio Press, 304 Killaly St. West, Port Colborne, ON L3K 6A6 Canaday, 2001

23620748R00174

Printed in Great Britain
by Amazon